Life Space Crisis Intervention

Life Space Crisis Intervention

Talking with Students in Conflict

SECOND EDITION

Nicholas J. Long
Mary M. Wood
Frank A. Fecser

pro·ed
An International Publisher

8700 Shoal Creek Boulevard
Austin, Texas 78757-6897
800/897-3202 Fax 800/397-7633
www.proedinc.com

© 2001, 1991 by PRO-ED, Inc.
8700 Shoal Creek Boulevard
Austin, Texas 78757-6897
800/897-3202 Fax 800/397-7633
www.proedinc.com

Library of Congress Cataloging-in-Publication Data

Long, Nicholas James, 1929—
    Life Space Crisis Intervention : talking with students in conflict / Nicholas J. Long, Mary M.
Wood, Frank A. Fecser.—2nd ed.
        p. cm.
    Rev. ed. of: Life Space Interventions / Mary M. Wood, Nicholas J. Long. c1991.
    Inc. bibliographical references and index.
    ISBN-13: 978-089079870-6
    ISBN-10: 0-89079-870-2 (alk. paper)
    1. Educational counseling.   2. Crisis intervention (Mental health services)
3. Oral communication.   I. Wood, Mary M.   II. Fecser, Frank A.
III. Wood, Mary M. Life Space Intervention.   IV. Title.
LB1027.5.W59   2001
371.7'13—dc21

00-045873
CIP

This book is designed in Goudy, Utopia Roman, and Stanton ICG.

Printed in the United States of America

9   10   11   12   13   12   11   10   09   08

Contents

PART II
Anatomy of Life Space Crisis Intervention ◆ 77

PART III
Applying LSCI to Particular Patterns of Self-Defeating Behaviors ◆ 147

Preface

This second edition of our text on Life Space Crisis Intervention (LSCI) is about talking with children and youth who are in crisis. LSCI is a process that can be used in almost any situation or location because it requires no props or equipment, only a skilled and understanding adult. Yet obtaining the skills is not easy, and the difficulties of helping today's troubled students are enormous. Skilled verbal strategies are essential requirements for adults in helping roles. Every crisis requires talk! An adult's skills in using verbal strategies will directly influence both the immediate solution to a crisis and the long-term effect of a crisis on the student. Crisis handled well can lead to positive, long-lasting changes; crisis managed ineptly will contribute to a devastating cycle of alienation, hostility, and aggression.

Today's students come from a wider range of family structures, lifestyles, and cultures than ever before. They present the schools with social-emotional needs at a level unknown in recent history, and they demand a quality of teacher understanding and skill that was once the province of the special education teacher or mental health professional.

The decay and dysfunction of the family and the shocking social problems in communities have created a level of deviancy and disturbance never before seen by educators and other adults who work with children and youth. We are involved daily with students who come to school struggling with painful realities—problems such as alcoholism, drug use, suicide, gang warfare, rape, physical and psychological abuse, crime, parental neglect and abandonment, brutality as entertainment, and poverty. Violence at home and in the neighborhood is a common experience for many students today.

CRISES IN MENTAL HEALTH

Public mental health services are conceptualized through an illness model in which health is characterized as the absence of psychopathology or mental illness. The child-serving systems are overwhelmed and struggling, and are failing our troubled children and youth. There is growing evidence that systems are breaking down as overworked, underpaid clinicians are increasingly forced to function in a reactive mode. Professional judgment is often overruled by mavens of managed care who ration services and psychoactive drugs to silence rebellious youth. Interventions consist mainly of brief diagnostic assessments and short-term symptom management. The best practices ideal of a continuum of comprehensive intersystems services tailored to individual child and family needs has been lost.

The plight of mental health services for children and youth goes well beyond overworked staff and lack of financial support. A psychologist at a public mental health center diagnosed this problem when she said, "We have an effective psychotherapy program, except the schools and courts are referring the wrong cases to us." Her observation is painfully correct. The children and youth being referred to psychotherapists often arrive with multiple problems of developmental neglect, abuse, and rejection. They often live in hostile environments comprised of fragmented families, alienated schools, and the destructive social forces of guns, gangs, drugs, promiscuity, and poverty. Therapists are often unable to separate intrapsychic problems from ongoing ecological crises at home, in school, and in the community. Consequently, the social-emotional needs of these troubled children and youth often exceed the resources and skills of therapists. Weekly psychotherapy sessions simply are not enough to be effective, and many youths are highly resistant to traditional office-based counseling. The multiple needs of troubled children and youth demand a broader, ecologically based intervention set. Increasingly, troubled and troubling children and youth depend on a variety of adults for support, including social workers, clergy, and teachers.

CRISES IN THE SCHOOLS

The standard social constructs which defined teacher–student interaction in the past have changed. A generation ago the authority of the teacher and the school was rarely questioned. Students and parents had little to say about how teachers conducted their classrooms, and student "rights" were determined largely by teacher discretion. When conduct violations occurred, there was little interest in discovering or attempting to understand the student's point of view. The culprit was reprimanded, punished, and often marked as a misfit and a troublemaker. Students who too often clashed with the culture of the school were "removed."

Contemporary thinking, however, is inclusionary. Schools are presumed not to tolerate diversity but to welcome it, and to provide a stable learning environment amid the open expression of values and differences. Inclusion requires a shift in the way teachers think about their students. Rather than teaching homogeneous classes, teachers are now working with heterogeneous groups of individuals, both culturally and educationally. When a student is disruptive, teachers need to consider much more than what price the student will pay for his wrongdoing; teachers need to consider the motivating forces behind the behavior, whether the behavior is an isolated event or part of a predictable pattern, and whether the student is motivated to change.

Schools face these challenges at a time in which funding uncertainties abound and a shortage of teachers, especially in special education, is on the rise. At-risk and troubled students bring the social ills of society into the classroom, causing many teachers to feel overwhelmed and helpless. Interestingly, as more special education students are included in regular classes, more "alternative schools" for troubled students are also being developed. Such programs often become little more than "curriculums of control." In some areas, alternative schools are not even an option, and youth are expelled, banished to roam the streets. The legal principle of "zero reject" (all students are entitled to an appropriate education) is being overridden by the political newspeak of "zero tolerance" (students are held fully accountable, but schools abdicate responsibility for them).

Instead of providing special services, some schools are criminalizing misbehavior by transforming schoolyard conflicts into violations of the criminal code—doing whatever it takes to get rid of a particularly disruptive child. What once might have been seen as a playground fistfight becomes battery, and threats and profanity become assault. Recently, in an east coast school district, one second grader who carried a plastic butter knife from the cafeteria and another who poked a peer with a pencil were each charged with possession of a weapon. Both situations require intervention; however, we are amazed by the absurdity of placing these matters in the criminal justice system. Surely schools can address such problems more effectively and less expensively than courts.

Many seriously emotionally disturbed children are being deprived of appropriate special services with the rationalization that they don't have "real" disabilities, but are simply choosing to act in socially maladjusted ways. The key issue, however, is why a youth would decide to keep behaving in a self-defeating manner which systematically destroys the quality of life. Some school districts, perhaps in an effort to trim costs, go to great lengths to avoid identifying troubled students as handicapped in order to make behavior problems a juvenile justice issue rather than a treatment issue. In some districts, special education is off limits to students with conduct problems, oppositional-defiant behavior, or attention-deficit/hyperactivity disorder, even when these conditions interfere with the students' ability to learn. Strikingly, children with these disabilities constitute a majority of youths who end up incarcerated in the juvenile justice system (Garfinkel, 1998).

Traditional strategies for discipline fail dramatically with a significant portion of highly troubled students who do not benefit from either punishment or exclusion. Students with emotional and behavioral disorders are the most likely to be suspended and expelled, and, ultimately, to become dropouts or "pushouts" from school. These youths fail to graduate at a rate greater than that of any other group with disabilities. When behavior problems persist despite efforts at intervention, a sensible response would seem to be to discard the intervention instead of the student.

CRISES IN THE COURTS

In a typical year, three million children in the United States come into contact with the juvenile justice system. This happens to be the same number as those who come to the attention of the child welfare system because of allegations of neglect or abuse. Research by the Child Welfare League of America (Petit & Brooks, 1998) shows that these are often the same young people. Children who first encounter the child welfare system because of neglect or abuse are 67 times more likely to be delinquents before they are teens.

Whatever sympathy the public has for the young victim of child abuse quickly dissipates when the victim becomes a victimizer in the community or a terror in school. Mary Sykes Wylie, senior editor of *Family Therapy Networker*, puts it this way: "It is as if, in the public mind, a pathetic, battered little child enters a black box and emerges from the other side a strange, terrible creature . . . a vicious thug who certainly has nothing in common with the poor little tyke who went in" (Wylie, 1998, pp. 34–35).

As the mental health and education systems wash their hands of troubled children, the justice system becomes the placement of last resort. Experts in juvenile justice are calling for reforms based on positive youth development and restorative justice, which tend to build competence in offenders. However, many politicians prefer to serve out just deserts, as they continue to shift resources away from prevention and treatment, and toward warehousing. There is no scientific evidence that this punitive approach has any value. The pendulum may swing back when leaders realize they are pouring scarce resources into a black hole.

These problems with troubled children and youth will not disappear by themselves. Teachers, counselors, administrators, social workers, juvenile correction workers, and special educators are demanding more sophisticated training in crisis intervention skills to help troubled students. Daily we have witnessed the critical need for advanced skills in crisis intervention.

This book is our response. We believe in the power and effectiveness of LSCI as a crisis intervention strategy with short-term and long-term benefits in the lives of students who participate. More than 100 combined years of work with disturbed children and youth lead us to the conviction that it is important and possible to teach effective LSCI skills to others. LSCI is not easy to learn since it involves adults in the complex, often irrational, defensive, disorganized, and, at times, fantasy world of troubled students. Crisis often occurs in chaotic or destructive social settings, always involves others, and taps the emotions of the student, the group, and the adult. Once an adult learns to see a crisis through the eyes of the student, greater empathy and support, realistic problem solving, and behavioral self-control can occur. When an effective LSCI is done, a crisis situation that could otherwise end as a destructive and deprecating experience for the student instead becomes an instructional and insightful experience. This is what LSCI is all about.

The "talking" strategies we describe are based on in-depth clinical interviewing skills developed from Fritz Redl's (1959b) concept of Life Space Interviewing (LSI). Redl described the LSI process as "a mediating role between the child and what life holds for him" (1966, p. 40). The intent is to convey the adult as mediator among the stress, the student's behavior, the reactions of others, and the private world of feelings that students are sometimes unable to handle without help. This remains an accurate way to describe the expanded uses of LSCI as a mediating process. While the psychodynamic theory of LSI has been maintained, LSCI has been expanded into a multitheoretical model integrating new concepts from cognitive, behavioral, social learning, and developmental theories. For a historical description of LSI, we recommend the classic works by Redl and Wineman, *Children Who Hate* (1951) and *Controls from Within* (1952), and Redl's *When We Deal with Children* (1966). A monograph edited by Ruth Newman and Marjorie Keith (1963), *The School-Centered Life Space Interview*, offers rich reading about early applications of LSI in school settings. We include a history of the field validation of LSI in Appendix A.

William Morse (1981) describes LSI as "a living, action process" with a direct connection to a student's past experience:

> One can and should know all of the personal and situational antecedents possible. But it [LSI] has a life of its own that is not constricted by case histories. It is a slice of life action. Rather than past oriented, it is future oriented about resolutions. One begins to develop the structure of the youngster's self-concept from the current behavior—the emotional state, distortions, attributions, expectations, values, and hopes for the future. Of course, one includes that part of the past which has present currency. But one is free of the dominance that results from looking backwards. If one knows children and knows disturbance, one comes to each situation with a vast [information base] . . . and it becomes easier to associate the relevant past with the present. (p. 70)

In the first edition of this book, the term *interview* was changed to *intervention* to emphasize that crisis always evokes verbal intervention. The quality of an adult's verbal intervention is the key to success or failure in obtaining a therapeutic outcome of a crisis. When first used outside clinical settings, the term *interview* was sometimes misinterpreted to mean questioning a student to extract information about an incident and resulting behavior. To some, the term seemed to suggest interrogating students in the hope of obtaining confessions of rules violations or admissions of wrongdoing. The term also was misinterpreted to mean something done once in response to a specific problem. None of these interpretations is accurate. Such limited approaches do not produce positive, lasting behavior changes. As a result, we substituted the term *intervention* to emphasize the dynamic nature of the interactions between adults and students in a crisis. Talk is a form of intervention, and it can be therapeutic if skillfully done.

Over the last decade, thousands of teachers, childcare workers, psychologists, and others who work closely with troubled and troubling children and youth have been certified in LSCI. Their stories of how the skills have helped them work effectively in crisis situations has prompted us to add the word *crisis* to LSCI, to more accurately describe the nature of the situations in which these skills are so useful.

We hope this second edition has captured the excitement and rewards of talking with children and youth in crisis, while demonstrating that crisis presents a unique opportunity for staff to teach and for students to learn. We also want to thank our colleagues for their many contributions to the theory, teaching, and advocacy of LSCI in public schools, alternative programs, residential programs, and juvenile justice programs around the country and internationally. Specifically, we want to thank Norman A. Klotz and his production staff for their skills in filming and editing the comprehensive LSCI Video Series (1996), and the competent staff at the Positive Education Program (PEP) in Cleveland, Ohio, for their professionalism in allowing us to film them during crisis situations. We also appreciate Mary Beth Hewitt at Wayne-Finger Lakes Board of Cooperative Educational Services, New York, for her creative and successful teacher-friendly training of LSCI, and Carol Dawson, coordinator of a talented team of senior LSCI trainers at the New York City Public Schools, District 75, Alternative Program, for their success in integrating LSCI as part of their ongoing inservice training program for teachers working with students with emotional and behavioral disorders. We also want to acknowledge the important role Larry Brendtro played in promoting LSCI as a national program at the Black Hills Seminars in South Dakota, and for his creative use of LSCI in his Developmental Audit for extremely resistant youth. Finally, we appreciate our kind-spirited spouses, Jody, Norman, and Mary Ellen, for their ongoing encouragement and support during the writing of this book.

Preparing To Deal
with Stress and Crisis

1

Because you have chosen to read this book, we assume that you are working in some capacity with children and youth. We also know that to work with them in today's complex world is one of the toughest of challenges. There are plenty of problems! How to guide young people through stressful experiences, how to help them make sense out of the ineptness and meanness they see around them, how to make the most of themselves, how to help them view situations in which they have messed up—these are our concerns. Adults who can do these things have something significant to contribute. We focus on Life Space Crisis Intervention (LSCI) in this book because it is a way to accomplish these goals. We use LSCI every day in our work with troubled children and youth because we believe we have a responsibility to teach them to deal constructively with stress and crisis. This book is our dialogue with you about how we do it.

In Part I we introduce LSCI as a verbal intervention strategy designed especially to use in crisis. We describe the Conflict Cycle as a way of understanding the elements that create crisis, outline a procedure for identifying feelings and anxieties that often are expressed in students' inappropriate behavior, and discuss what you need to understand about yourself and your student as you begin every LSCI.

"I hate school!"
"I hate reading!"
"I hate Teddy!"
"I hate you!"

Crisis Is a Time for Learning

1

W hen students tell you things like the feelings expressed in the quotations listed on the previous page, the next move is yours. You are part of their daily experience, their "life space." All those who work with children and youth are confronted frequently with incidents that may require adult intervention. Sometimes incidents may seem trivial or insignificant; other times incidents are of such magnitude as to be overwhelming, with no apparent solutions. In any event, what is needed is a way to help students assume responsibility for changing their own dissocial behavior in ways that produce constructive and long-lasting results.

Students seldom assume responsibility for changing their own behavior (as opposed to relying on outside authority and control for behavioral change) until they are psychologically empowered to make choices about their behavioral alternatives and are ready to accept the consequences of these choices. But how do they acquire this empowerment to regulate their own behavior? Self-regulation emerges from *understanding* people and events in their environment, *motivation* to change unpleasant conditions, and *trust* in adults. These three essential dimensions of self-regulation are described in the following operational terms.

UNDERSTANDING AN EVENT

- Acknowledgment of the part personal behavior and feelings contribute
- Awareness of reactions of others
- Social perception about the sequence of consequences that follows
- Recognition of alternatives that can modify a chain of events

MOTIVATION TO CHANGE

- Desire to improve existing conditions
- Belief that change for the better is possible
- Sufficient self-esteem to believe that improvement is deserved
- Confidence to try something different

TRUST IN ADULTS

- Confidence in adults' respect for students' feelings
- Conviction that adults value students
- Belief that adults recognize students' attributes
- Belief that adults use authority and power wisely
- Confidence that adults can solve problems in satisfactory ways
- Willingness to accept adult guidance

Adults who work with students know that when these conditions are present, students have a working process for problem solving and regulating their own behavior. These qualities exist because of many successful interactions between students and adults, around both ordinary and extraordinary events, some pleasant and some painful. Talking together, adults and students build these conditions.

Most troubled students, however, do not have these qualities. Their perceptions of events are often shortsighted or distorted. They frequently fail to understand how their behavior upsets others. Their feelings take over and flood their rational minds. They make matters worse by behaving in impulsive, defensive, or destructive ways. Most students also are bombarded with a daily reality full of frustrations and disappointments that warrant supportive adult intervention.

Guiding children and youth in crisis is an awesome responsibility. Their reactions to stress and its by-product, crisis, are among the most difficult challenges confronting teachers, childcare providers, youth workers, and parents. The topic of this entire book is talking with students in crisis. The goal is self-regulated, value-based behavior. Here we offer a way of talking with students to achieve this goal. It is a process that teaches students to solve a crisis by understanding the behavioral reactions and feelings of those involved, including themselves. Talking creates conditions in which motivation to change develops and builds students' trust in adults sufficiently to accept guidance. The more skilled we are in talking with students, the more effective we will be in helping them learn to manage their own problems. With understanding and sensitivity to students' feelings and the circumstances surrounding incidents, we can provide the emotional support they need while we teach them to solve problems more effectively and with more satisfying results. If we are effective, students will develop beyond the need to rely on adult authority for behavior control. They will learn to manage their own behavior, control their impulses and feelings, live by rules and values, make constructive decisions, and deal with others in positive ways.

LSCI: A PROCESS FOR TALKING WITH STUDENTS IN CRISIS

Life Space Crisis Intervention is a therapeutic, verbal strategy for intervention with students in crisis. It is conducted at the time the crisis occurs or as soon after as possible.

The process uses students' reactions to stressful events to (a) change behavior, (b) enhance self-esteem, (c) reduce anxiety, and (d) expand understanding and insight into their own and others' behavior and feelings. LSCI can be used with children and youth in situations in which reaction to stress is a concern, and with students who are unable to appropriately control or manage their own behavior.

LSCI focuses on crisis that occurs when an incident escalates into conflict between a student and others. Because such crisis involves a student's immediate life experience (the "life space"), it is an optimal time for learning. Students are intensely involved in situations that hold personal significance or that have disrupted their sense of well-being. Adults who work with students in crisis need to understand the conflict from the student's point of view, while also promoting the student's active choice in and personal responsibility for behavior. Too many students in crisis defend themselves against their feelings by denying them, displacing them on others, blaming others, regressing, or rationalizing. One of the most important steps in helping troubled students become more realistic and responsible for their behavior is to help them understand the feelings that drive their behavior.

It is helpful for students to see the connections between their feelings and their behavior. Students who show emotional and social maturity can say "yes" to their feelings but "no" to improper behavior to express the feelings. This basic concept of supporting the feelings but not the behavior frequently is lost as adults struggle to guide and teach students in crisis. This is a fundamental concept of LSCI, as is a commitment to promote self-awareness and behavioral change. Unlike psychotherapy, LSCI is not an open and permissive process; yet, unlike strict behavioral programs, LSCI does not deny the power of personal feelings.

In a comprehensive behavior management program, the priority is to teach students prosocial behaviors that enable them to function successfully. This does not negate the need for adults to handle crisis skillfully. A fire department offers an analogy for LSCI as a strategy for fighting the fires of crisis. While a fire department's first priority is the prevention of fires, this priority does not prevent it from having sophisticated fire-fighting skills. Similarly, LSCI is a strategy that is used to put out emotional fires that flare up and ignite into disruptive and destructive behavior. This is the primary purpose of LSCI— crisis intervention. LSCI should be used only after "prevention" strategies such as positive talk, proximity control, bonus points, appeal to rules and values, and stated behavioral consequences have been tried. In this continuum, LSCI is compatible with behavior modification and social learning theory; it is part of a continuum of behavior management strategies.

Occasionally students may resist any attempt through LSCI to alter personal views of a problem or their behavior. In such situations the adult has a responsibility to reflect reality and situational consequences. When inappropriate behavior continues, the adult must set up a specific intervention plan based on rules and behavioral contingencies. In these situations LSCI moves from interpersonal acceptance of feelings to planned strategies for change, with clear reality consequences and no excuses accepted for making poor behavioral choices.

Originally formulated as the "Life Space Interview" more than four decades ago by Fritz Redl (1959a, 1966; Redl & Wineman, 1952), LSI was initially limited in use to those practitioners who worked in clinical settings with children and youth who had extremely serious social, emotional, or behavioral problems. As discussed in the preface, the term *interview* has been changed to more accurately convey a broader application for those who do not work in clinical settings. When first applied in more natural environments, the term *interview* was sometimes misinterpreted to mean questioning a student to extract information about the incident and resulting behavior. To others, *interview* seemed to suggest interrogating students in hopes of getting confessions of rules violations or admissions of wrongdoing. The term also was misinterpreted to mean something done once in response to a specific problem. None of these interpretations is true. Such limited approaches do not produce positive, lasting changes.

As a result, we have substituted the term *intervention* to denote "mediation for problem solving." The intent is to convey the role of adult as mediator among the stress, the student's actions, the reactions of others, and the private world of feelings that students often seem to be unable to handle without help. This idea of a mediator was used originally by Redl to describe the intent of the LSI as "a mediating role between the child and what life holds for him" (Redl, 1966, p. 40). The term crisis was added to reflect the nature of situations faced today by professionals working with troubled and troubling children and youth.

The expanded term remains an accurate way to describe the expanded uses of LSCI. The substance of the original LSI process has not been changed. For a full description of the original process in developing LSCI, we recommend Redl's classic work on the subject, *When We Deal with Children* (1966), and *Controls from Within* by Redl and Wineman (1952). We also have included a brief history of LSCI in Appendix A.

LSCI currently is used in educational programs, correctional facilities, and alternative living homes—wherever the paramount concern is to teach troubled children and youth better ways to cope with the social, emotional, and behavioral crises of life. LSCI is effective in these many different programs because it offers a way to provide emotional support on the spot. It provides a process for understanding behavior and feelings, and it outlines a procedure for adults to teach children and youth better ways to cope with stress, to change behavior, and to resolve conflict.

WHAT HAPPENS DURING LSCI

LSCI begins with an exploration of the student's understanding of the event. LSCI then expands to feelings that evoked the behaviors and the reactions of others to those behaviors. As the incident is clarified and expanded, the central issue is formed. During the process, the focus often shifts from the incident to a more serious, underlying concern not easily or directly expressed by the student. At this point the process takes a turn toward problem solving and away from problem exploration. Together adult and student explore ways to ameliorate both the immediate incident and associated long-term problems. Behavioral alternatives are selected to resolve the present crisis and to achieve better outcomes when stress occurs again.

Figure 1.1 summarizes the six stages of LSCI. Stages 1 through 3 represent the diagnostic stages, while Stages 4 through 6 represent the reclaiming stages. In the three latter stages, the adult and the student focus on outcomes, consider solutions, and form a plan of action.

This current version of LSCI is presented in detail, step by step, in Part II of this book. Here we simply summarize the purposes and content of each stage in the sequence. Keep in mind the distinct purpose and content of each stage. When linked together, these stages build a communication bridge to a fuller understanding of the student's distress, the resulting crisis, and alternative solutions that require behaviors in keeping with the student's ability to cope successfully.

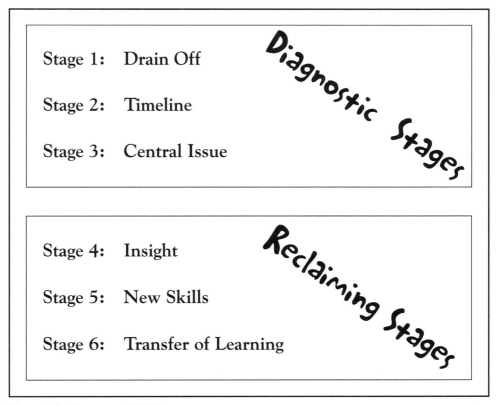

Figure 1.1. Six stages of LSCI.

For teachers and therapists using both LSCI and Developmental Therapy, the use of the term *stages* in LSCI may be somewhat confusing. The *stages* of LSCI refer to sequences of phases, or steps, in the LSCI process. The term *stages* in Developmental Therapy describes distinct clusters of social-emotional-behavioral characteristics of children and youths at each phase, or stage, of their lives. The stages of LSCI and Developmental Therapy work in concert, using sequential goals, content, and outcomes to meet students' individual needs.

Stage 1: Drain Off—De-escalate the Crisis

Purpose: To convey support and understanding of the student's stress and to start the student talking about the incident; to drain off emotional intensity in order to prepare to focus on the event.

Content: The incident itself—the event that actually brought about the need for LSCI—is identified.

Stage 2: Timeline—Students in Crisis Need To Talk

Purpose: To encourage the student to relate in sufficient detail the unique perception of the event and surrounding circumstances; to decrease emotional intensity while increasing reliance on rational words and ideas; to discover the student's unique perception of the event.

Content: A sequence of events—a timeline—is established to obtain details of the student's view of the incident, the associated stress, and personal involvement.

Stage 3: Central Issue—Select the Appropriate Reclaiming Intervention

Purpose: To explore the student's perception of the incident and associated feelings and anxieties until you have sufficient understanding to concisely state the central issue and decide which Reclaiming Intervention should be used. Specifically, to determine if the crisis represents the student's pattern of self-defeating behavior or if it is an unusual or rare reaction for this student.

Content: Determine the extent to which the student's behavior is driven by feelings and anxiety, the depth and spread of the conflict, the amount of rational control the student can exercise over these emotions, and what the long-term and short-term outcomes should be for the student as a result of the specific LSCI.

Stage 4: Insight—The Goal of the Reclaiming Intervention

Purpose: To reframe the student's perception of the event; to enable the student to gain a new insight into repetitive patterns of self-defeating behavior—to help the student recognize that change is possible. For the student to use his or her new insight into the previous pattern of behavior to develop a plan for change. If a student is not able to do this, the adult chooses a solution that establishes group values and reality consequences that will work on the student's behalf.

Content: The adult decodes the student's behavior using a range of relationship and listening skills; the Reclaiming Intervention moves toward its specific goal. The solution is selected from several alternatives, representing the student's own changing insights and beliefs about what constitutes a satisfactory solution, considering subsequent consequences. When a student denies responsibility or cannot choose a solution, the adult structures the solution for the student around group values and social norms that are within the student's capacity to use successfully.

Stage 5: New Skills—Plan for Success

Purpose: To teach prosocial skills—to consider what will happen and anticipate reactions and feelings, of self and others, when the chosen solution is put into action.

Content: Selected prosocial behaviors are specifically practiced as rehearsal for reacting and problem solving successfully when the student faces the consequences of the original incident and when a similar problem occurs in the future.

Stage 6: Transfer of Learning— Get Ready To Resume Activity

Purpose: To plan for the student's transition back into the group's ongoing activity, and to close down private topics or feelings that may have surfaced during the talk.

Content: The adult shifts the focus to help the student anticipate how to manage reentry into the peer group. If there is to be a short-term consequence associated with the original incident, the student is prepared as that goes into action. This final stage is essential also for closing down emotions and reducing the intensity of the relationship that may have occurred during the LSCI between student and adult.

PREREQUISITE SKILLS NEEDED BY STUDENTS

To know if LSCI is an appropriate strategy for a particular student, it is necessary to assess the student's readiness skills for successful participation. These skills include five general cognitive and communication processes: (a) attention span for listening and retaining what has been said, (b) minimal verbal skills to use language spontaneously and with sequential thought, (c) sufficient comprehension to understand the meanings of words, (d) mental reasoning to understand the essence of the incident and the problem it produced, and (e) trust in the adult. These basic prerequisites are detailed in Table 1.1.

Use this list to do an informal assessment of each student *before* there is a crisis. In this way, you can screen those for whom LSCI is not recommended and make a nota-

TABLE 1.1
Prerequisite Skills Needed by Students To Benefit from LSCI

- Some degree of awareness of self, events, and other people

- Ability to attend to verbal, interpersonal stimuli (the adult speaking)

- Sufficient self-regulation of body and body functions to sustain attention

- Sufficient understanding (receptive vocabulary) to comprehend the words used by the adult

- Ability to comprehend the stream of content connecting the adult's words

- Sufficient memory to recall a simple sequence of events

- Ability to produce words or signs sufficiently complex to represent the crisis event

- Sufficient trust that the adult really cares to cooperate, seek, or respond positively to the adult

- Willingness and ability to share minimal information with the adult

- Ability to describe simple characteristics of self and others

- Ability to describe personal experiences, even if in a simple form

- Ability to give simple reasons why events occur

tion in these students' individual educational or treatment plans to that effect. As skills gradually develop or improve, these students will be able to participate in a full LSCI.

OUTCOMES OF EFFECTIVE LSCIs

Both short-term and long-term gains can be expected from an effective LSCI. The specific program objectives established before the crisis should guide the problem-solving steps of LSCI. Every program has its own goals and procedures for developing individual students' objectives. Overall, long-range program goals and specific objectives for small, incremental gains reflect individual needs and circumstances. Incorporating these program objectives and goals into LSCI is essential.

In addition to specific individual program objectives and goals, every LSCI must have a responsible and satisfactory resolution of the incident. Any number of other short-term outcomes may also occur. The following are several examples:

Tommy   For Tommy, one immediate outcome of LSCI was his first attempt to use words to solve a problem instead of having a temper tantrum and using his fists to lash out at anyone standing in his way.

Short-term outcome: Tommy tells another student, "I don't like what you're doing. I want you to stop."

Joan   For Joan, LSCI created a new awareness that her verbal attacks on friends created enemies instead of the effect she wanted: to have friends admire her and seek her out.

Short-term outcome: Joan's plan of action is to find something complimentary to say to a friend: "I think she's pretty smart. I'll tell her I want to study spelling with her."

Rick   For Rick, LSCI provided enough emotional support for him to assume responsibility for his role in vandalizing school property.

Short-term outcome: Rick plans a way to work off most of the repairs: "I'm facing the music."

Gradually, over a series of effective LSCIs, long-term goals will be evident. A student should gain increased understanding of relationships among behavior, feelings, and the reactions of others. But understanding is not enough. Students also must gain more successful problem-solving behaviors for coping with stress, emotions, and crisis. As these two long-term outcomes become evident, a third outcome will become apparent: emergence of greatly improved self-esteem. The following is an example:

Tony   Tony was skilled at walking into a group and "setting someone off." He always managed to get another student in trouble within a matter of minutes. After a series of LSCIs, Tony began to understand that he got a great sense of power from doing this, but it always ended with him in trouble. He and his teacher began talking about other ways he could behave that would bring better results and still give him a sense of power and pride. Tony tried out a few of these behavioral alternatives, rather reluctantly at first. Gradually, he saw for himself that other students were beginning look to him for leadership rather than in fear. They also sought his friendship and advice, calling him "Doc, the Answer Man." This clear change in the reactions of others gradually changed Tony's view of himself from "destroyer" to "magnet."

An effective LSCI is a complex interpersonal process built on relationship and trust. It constructs bridges of understanding between a student's obvious behavior, words, and body language, and underlying feelings, concerns, and anxieties. A positive change in self-esteem is the end result in the broadest sense.

ATTRIBUTES OF THOSE WHO CONDUCT SUCCESSFUL LSCIs

LSCI is conducted by someone who is seen by the student as being in the student's natural environment—parents, teachers, principals, counselors, childcare workers, and youth workers. For adults, the LSCI process is an adventure in interpersonal relationships—a double struggle to keep themselves in control (of themselves) while conveying objectivity, control, and concern about the crisis. "Dispassionate compassion" is a term that has been used to describe what is needed from adults using LSCI. It requires adults to know and be sensitive to the emotions and the private side of the student. Adults doing LSCI are bombarded by an enormous amount of emotion (their own and the student's). It is essential that adults monitor and control their own reactions, feelings, and behavior. It is not a process in which adults lack control over their faces, body language, or feelings; nor is it a process in which adults (who have the answers?) freely give advice about how to handle problems in better ways.

Adults who do successful LSCIs seem to hold and convey some fundamental beliefs about students' needs for protection, gratification, relationship, and responsibility—basic immunizations against excessive stress and anxiety.

Protection by adults provides emotional support while enhancing a student's capacity to face stress constructively. Protection gives students confidence that they will not be exposed to embarrassment, ridicule, or failure. When adults provide protection, students are not asked to do what they cannot accomplish successfully. Protection gives assurance that adults will not violate a student's private space—that secret sore spots will not be violated. Protection also assures that adults will maintain an environment where students will not be hurt by others. Protection is a fundamental premise in every LSCI.

Gratification is a necessity of life. Somehow, every student must have hope that things will get better and that experiences will bring pleasure. Without hope and pleasure, life loses meaning and there is little, if any, energy available for learning or for emotional and social growth. A student's storehouse of memories must contain, on balance, a greater number of positive than negative emotional memories. Effective LSCI expands this memory bank and uses a student's need for gratification as a motivation for change. LSCI holds out the promise of better things to come—through change!

Relationship is connection. Adults and students "connect" for many reasons, all having to do with their unique needs. Adults have motivation to guide and teach students, seeing themselves as helpers and advocates or as nurturers and care providers. Students connect for protection and gratification, responding to the experience, power, wisdom, knowledge, and skills of adults. Students listen to adults when connections have been made. They model adult behavior and attitudes, identifying with an admired adult as someone they want to be like. Adults often see this role as a form of guidance that students seek. This may be true; but even more, an adult's effectiveness with students is in large part built on the quality of the connection-conveyed attitudes of affirmation, respect, care, enhancement, and just plain liking. Effective LSCI is built on these dimensions of relationship.

Responsibility is the basis for solving problems and coping successfully with stress. Yet few students in crisis show a sense of responsibility. Responsibility requires value-directed behavior, in which a student recognizes the need to self-regulate to assure that what happens is what the student values. A student's capacity for responsibility evolves through the development of a coherent sequence of thoughts and feelings about his or her obligations to themselves and others. This developmental sequence begins with responsibility to oneself (for basic needs), and gradually expands into values about law and order, fairness and justice, and concern (and the obligation to do something) about the needs of others. Effective management of stress and solutions to crisis by students always draw on some value. Whatever the extent of a student's sense of responsibility, it is a necessary theme to be introduced in some form into every LSCI. In its most basic form, it is the responsibility for looking after one's own interests. When adults keep in mind that ultimately a student must assume responsibility, the natural impulse to take over and tell or direct a student how to handle a problem or solve a crisis is restrained.

These four basic psychological concepts are conveyed by adults who use LSCI successfully. These messages contribute to a climate that counters the assault of excessive stress, frustrations, and disappointments experienced daily by students. These concepts are the antidotes to students' feelings of unworthiness and helplessness in controlling what happens to them. Throughout the book you will see these four concepts applied.

In the next three chapters, we review the basic background we believe to be essential for effective LSCI. In Part II, we go through each LSCI stage in detail. We describe the specific purposes and objectives for the stages, outline the dynamics of each stage in charts, discuss adults' roles and strategies, and give examples of how and when to end a stage and bridge into the next one. We also include a chapter on self-monitoring and fine-tuning your own proficiency in using LSCI. In Part III, we provide the substantive Reclaiming Interventions for those who have mastered the basic LSCI material in the first two parts of the book. We expand applications for those who have used the basic LSCI procedures and who now want to work with students with increasingly difficult emotional and behavioral problems.

EXAMPLE OF LSCI

Before going into the next chapters, study the following LSCI example, "The Math Problem Crisis." We selected this real-life LSCI as a basic illustration; the crisis is neither so complex that it might obscure the LSCI process nor so simple that it might mislead you into concluding that LSCI is a simple procedure. The crisis is typical of daily life for many students of many ages. The example takes the reader through the six LSCI stages in a straightforward sequence. We note when each new stage begins, and we also note key decision points in each stage.

As you study this LSCI example, become familiar with the basic sequence. Also learn the names of the stages. By doing this, you should find it easy to recall the general purpose of each. This structure will help you to keep even the most difficult and complex LSCI on track and moving in a constructive direction.

After you are acquainted with the sequence and purpose of each stage, read this LSCI again and look for the places where the teacher has conveyed the essential concepts of protection, gratification, relationship, and responsibility. You will find that some of the examples are explicit; others are implied in the student's body language or conveyed by the supportive remarks the teacher makes to affirm the student throughout the LSCI.

We will come back to this example several times to illustrate the background concepts presented in the next three chapters. In this way we hope to show how effective LSCI skills can be learned step by step. It is not necessary to know how to apply everything in this book before you begin using LSCI. Gradually, however, as you use LSCI, you will find yourself becoming increasingly insightful and skilled in talking with students in crisis.

"The Math Problem Crisis"

The setting is Nathaniel Hawthorne High School in a working-class neighborhood of Cleveland, Ohio. Dane is an eleventh grade student with a history of challenging behaviors. He was identified as having a behavior disorder when he was in junior high school, following a series of incidents involving lying and extorting younger students. For the past two years Dane has been assigned to a special education classroom from which he is mainstreamed as often as possible. He is well known for loud, explosive displays when things do not go his way. If Dane had a motto, it would be, "Nothing is so small that it can't be blown out of proportion." Dane's self-fulfilling prophecy centers around the belief that adults are not to be trusted and that they go out of their way to make life difficult for kids. He blames adults for his problems and accepts little responsibility himself.

Dane takes math in the special education classroom managed by Ms. Westerman, teacher, and Mr. Randall, assistant. One reason he is not mainstreamed for math is that he dislikes the subject so much that it is often a source of stress which triggers feelings of failure, frustration, and anger that he finds difficult to contain. On this day, he rushes through the assignment and turns in the paper. Ms. Westerman looks it over and realizes what has happened. She returns the paper to Dane and tells him that she will help him get through the first couple of problems, but that he will have to correct the other six before he can go to the extra gym class in the next period. Dane is not pleased with this situation, but because he values the extra gym period, he makes an effort as Ms. Westerman walks him through the first two problems. Just as the one-to-one instruction is concluding, there is a knock at the door and Ms. Westerman is summoned to the office. Dane drifts from his task and does not correct the other problems. When the bell rings, Mr. Randall says to the group, "OK, turn in your math and let's go to the gym." Dane turns in his uncorrected paper and goes to the gym with Mr. Randall and the rest of the group. When Ms. Westerman returns, she finds Dane's uncorrected paper and goes to the gym to bring Dane back to the classroom to finish the assignment. We begin the incident as Ms. Westerman (T) calls Dane (D) off the basketball court.

▶ Stage 1: Drain Off

T: Dane, would you come here please?

D: (Angrily) Talk to me later.

T: Dane, I need to see you right now. Step out in the hall, please.

D: Later!

T: Dane, I know you like the privilege of having an extra gym period. If you want to keep it, you'll come here right now.

D: (Slamming the ball on the floor and approaching Ms. Westerman with an angry scowl) What do you want?!

T: Dane, please, step into the hall so we can talk privately.

D: (Steps into the hallway, crosses his arms. and leans back against the wall)

T: Thank you for coming out here. I know that wasn't easy for you to do. And now I have to tell you something it won't be easy for you to hear. See if you can handle it. When I left the classroom I told you to correct your math sheet before going to the gym. Your math sheet is not corrected.

D: (Loudly) Mr. Randall said I didn't have to! He told me to turn in my paper and come down here!

T: Dane, what exactly did you hear Mr. Randall say?

D: He said, "Everybody, turn in your math and go to the gym!" Go ahead and ask him—ask anybody. That's what he said! You people are really messed up! Now I'm getting into trouble because I'm following the g-damned directions!

Ms. Westerman knows Dane well and understands what is probably going on. Because she had to leave the room unexpectedly, she did not communicate to Mr. Randall that Dane was to correct his math sheet before going to gym. Therefore, when he told the group to turn in their assignments and go to gym, Dane took advantage of the adults' lack of communication. Rather than accept responsibility for his expectation, Dane uses this as an example of how adults "wrong" students and blame them for their mistakes. Ms. Westerman will check out this hypothesis in the timeline.

▶ **Stage 2: Timeline**

T: Something went wrong here, and we need to figure out what. Let's start from the beginning. You turned in your math sheet with a lot of mistakes on it. That tells me you were having a hard time right from the start.

D: You know I can't do math! I hate it!

T: Math is tough for you, I know.

D: I want to go back to the gym!

T: Dane, we have to work this out. You're showing a lot of self-control and patience right now—this isn't easy, but you're handling it. Let's go on. Do you remember that I brought the paper back to you?

D: (Impatiently) Yeah, yeah, I remember.

T: Can you tell me what you thought when that happened?

D: I was thinking, I want to get out of here.

T: Sure, you wanted math to be over and you were looking forward to going to gym. What happened next?

D: You made me do the first two problems.

T: Right. And even though math is tough for you, you worked on those two until you got them right. Somehow you controlled your feelings and made the choice to work on the problems. Then what happened?

D: Somebody came to the door and you left the room.

T: True, but do you remember what I said before I left about your finishing the other problems before going to the gym?

D: Yeah, I remember.

T: What did I say?

D: You said finish them, then go to gym.

T: That's right. How did you feel just then?

D: I was sick of that stuff!

T: So you were already feeling frustrated by the assignment and one thing you did to relieve that stress was to hurry through the work and turn it in with wrong answers. You were feeling sick of math; you wanted to get it over with. Then when I brought the paper back to you, you were even more frustrated, but you managed to work through the first two problems with me. You were handling the situation pretty well at that point. What happened next?

D: Mr. Randall said for everybody—got that—EVERYBODY—to turn in the sheets and go to gym. So I followed directions like you guys always tell me to do and I went to gym and now I'm missing it because you two can't get your act together!

Dane has just dropped a clue. He knows there's been a miscommunication between the staff. Ms. Westerman will use this to move Dane toward seeing the role Dane played in the problem.

▶ Stage 3: Central Issue

T: What you're saying is important; let's see if I have it straight. You and I were correcting the first two problems, and even though you were feeling frustrated, you managed your feelings and focused on the task. Then I was interrupted and had to leave the room, but as I left, I told you to complete the corrections before going to gym. That was not good news because you were struggling trying to get through the first two.

D: Yeah, so?

T: Then when the bell rang, Mr. Randall told everyone to turn in their assignments and get ready for gym. You had not corrected your problems, but you turned in your sheet anyway and went to gym.

D: Yeah, that's right. I did as I was told.

T: Well, now I'm not sure I understand that, because it seems that if you had done as you were told you would have corrected the problems first.

D: Hey, I got another direction after that, so I followed it!

T: That's true—there was a miscommunication between Mr. Randall and me. I didn't tell him that you were supposed to finish the problems first.

D: And now, because you're not doing your job, you're giving me a hard time! What am I supposed to do when a teacher says to do something. If I don't do it, I get in trouble and if I do it I get in trouble. Don't even talk to me! You don't know how to run this classroom! You think you're helping kids but your're messing them up!

▶ Stage 4: Insight

T: Dane, listen, you're a bright guy. You're a quick study, you know people, and you're good with words. There was a miscommunication between Mr. Randall and me—no question about it. I accept responsibility for that. But clearly, there was no miscommunication between us. You and I both knew the expectation I left you with. You verified that yourself. So I have to ask you a question. When Mr. Randall said for everyone to turn in the assignments and go to gym, you knew I hadn't told him about our arrangement. What went through your mind?

D: I guess I thought, cool, they screwed up so I can go.

T: So, suddenly, there was a way out of doing the math, a way to instantly relieve your frustration. You decided to take a gamble on not getting caught and turned in the incomplete paper and went to gym.

D: You try sitting there for an hour with a bunch of boring bull! I couldn't take it any more! Don't you understand that?

T: Dane, I really appreciate your honesty. You're not telling me that you were confused or that you didn't understand. You're telling me the truth.

You're saying, look, I was feeling overwhelmed. I took a gamble—I lost. You're owning up to that. That's really impressive, Dane; that's progress. A couple of months ago, you wouldn't have been able to take that kind of responsibility, and here you are, talking about it, managing to keep your cool.

D: You don't know how much I need to get a break from that room. I hate that math mess.

T: No question about it, you've got some strong feelings about math—it's been a tough subject for you and I'm not saying those feelings are wrong. But you had a choice to make, and this time, you let your strong dislike for math get in the way of making a good choice.

▶ Stage 5: New Skills

D: So now what; what are you going to do?

T: What do you think would be a good solution?

D: I knew it! You're going to make me miss gym and go back and do that crap!

T: I asked what you thought would be a good solution—is that it?

D: (Walking toward the room) This place sucks!

T: It would be easy for you to argue and refuse, but you're making the responsible choice to finish the work. No kidding, Dane, that's really progress. I'm there if you need help.

D: All right—let's get it over with so I can get back to my game.

T: (Walking back to the classroom) You know, Dane, in a way, I'm kind of glad this happened, because I think we learned something here. We learned that even under pressure you can own responsibility for choices you make. You're just a short step from being able to independently make choices that will work out best for you, even though it's tough to do. You're getting to the point where you will no longer need adults to check up on you. That's independence, and you're on your way. Just to finish this up, can you think of some other ways to deal with your frustration about math? What other choices do you have in a situation like this?

D: I don't know, I guess I could ask to do it later, or ask for some help or something.

T: You mean you could tell Mr. Randall or me that you're having trouble and need help? That alone could relieve some of the pressure. How are you going to remember to do that?

D: I don't want to miss gym. I'll remember.

▶ **Stage 6: Get Ready To Resume Activity**

T: OK, I'll try to remind you. Now, just one more thing. What are you going to tell the other kids when they ask you where you were?

D: I'll just tell them I had to take care of something.

T: What if they pressure you or laugh or try to put you on the spot?

D: I'll just blow it off. I'll say it's personal.

T: OK—I'll back you up. Let's get that math done.

In this LSCI, in addition to supporting the student for taking personal responsibility for resolving the immediate issue, progress has been made toward long-term goals: The student has used rational control for directing behavior, shown insight into how he contributes to problems, suggested new ways to behave, and conveyed attitudes of responsibility and self-esteem. He has also seen the adult as a helper.

It may be worth noting that Ms. Westerman accepted some strong language from Dane, and some might say it bordered on disrespect. Ms. Westerman was very much aware of Dane's choice of words, and made a clear choice not to address that issue. At stake was the greater goal—for Dane to accept responsibility for his own poor choice, his failure to meet the challenge of completing the corrections. Dane was already prepared to draw the teacher into a Conflict Cycle and tried to do it by blaming the situation on poor communication between the adults. Had Ms. Westerman focused on Dane's choice of words, Dane most probably would have used that as an opportunity to divert attention from the real issue. One of the strongest features of LSCI is that it provides the adult with a road map to reach the outcome goal the adult chooses, and to avoid the "side trips" often suggested by students.

WHAT WE HOPE YOU HAVE LEARNED FROM THIS CHAPTER

- Why crisis is a good time for learning new behaviors

- Three aspects of self-regulation of behavior

- Four purposes in using LSCI when students are in crisis

- The name and purpose of each stage in the LSCI sequence
- Five general prerequisite skills needed by a student to participate in LSCI
- One overall short-term outcome of every effective LSCI
- Three overall long-term outcomes of effective LSCIs
- Four fundamental needs of students that adults can provide in LSCI to protect students from stress and anxiety

Stress arouses beliefs.
Thinking triggers feelings.
Feelings drive behavior.
Behavior incites others.
Others increase stress!

Stress, Conflict, and Crisis

2

One way of looking at crisis is to see it as the product of a student's stress, kept alive by the reactions of others. When a student's feelings are aroused by stress, the student will behave in ways that buffer the painful feelings. This behavior usually is viewed as negative by others (adults and peers), which causes them to react negatively to the student. This reaction from others causes additional stress for the student. We call this the Conflict Cycle. The Conflict Cycle is a way of looking at crisis by analyzing the interactions among a student's feelings, behavior, and the reactions of others in the environment. If this cycle, produced by these actions and reactions, is not broken it will inevitably explode into crisis.

What makes some students prone to engaging adults in Conflict Cycles? Why do some students repeatedly make choices whose outcomes make life more difficult? We propose that the pattern begins with a student's self-concept, irrational beliefs, and self-fulfilling prophecy. Early in life, infants gain a sense of security when their environments are safe and predictable. As the child grows older, he or she learns that he or she has some control over their environment and can predict and understand certain cause–effect relationships: baby cries, mother appears, comfort follows. Later, the toddler sings "Twinkle, Twinkle Little Star," and adults smile, praise, and cuddle. Still later, the preschooler throws a stuffed animal in the living room, knocking over a plant, and adults say, "That's bad!" and take away the stuffed animal. In a predictable setting, the child learns how to invite favorable reactions and how to avoid unfavorable reactions. But what if things are not stable at home? What if other responsibilities leave parents little time to teach these lessons to children, or what if children experience abandonment, neglect, or abuse? Among the ill effects of such experiences is the inner sense of unrest for the child, the sense of being unable to understand, and therefore, to have some control of events in life.

There is a need to allay this anxiety and people will go to great lengths to do so. Primitive tribes, when faced with inexplicable phenomenona like tidal waves and drought, attributed these events to the anger of the gods. By doing so, they gained the sense of having some control over their environment. They couldn't stop a tidal wave, but they might be able to avoid one by appeasing a god. Children, too, need to understand why bad things happen and to have some sense of control over their lives. Understanding comes in the form of an emerging self-concept or identity. Some children who have grown up victimized and fearful may come to the conclusion that they are "weak and worthless." They may believe that adults are fearsome and powerful, and since they depend on adults for survival, they have learned that the best way to deal with adults is to be quiet and withdrawn. Students will create data to support their beliefs through self-fulfilling prophecies. In school these children may be the quiet failures who sit at the back of the room and fade away. When a caring teacher tries to help them, these children are silent and withdrawn. They are not "fun" to have in class. In fact, they are downright frustrating because nothing the teacher does seems to reach them. These students fail, and so do their teachers. As a result, these teachers begin to withdraw from the "failing" students and turn their attention to more "rewarding" students. Masterfully, these students manipulate teachers into providing data to reinforce their belief that they are weak and worthless young people.

Other children growing up under stressful conditions may form very different perceptions about themselves and others. They may believe they are abused, neglected, or abandoned because they are, by nature, bad. Otherwise, why would they always be in so much trouble? Their experience with adults may have taught them that adults are not to be trusted, that they enjoy bringing pain and suffering to children, and that unless the child fights them, they will hurt the child. In the experience of these students, such beliefs may be founded in reality. These beliefs become irrational, however, because students are unable to distinguish among the very few adults in the world who will harm them, the vast majority of adults who are completely uninterested in them, and the very few adults who truly want to help them. These students treat all adults as if they were in the first category. They very successfully reinforce the self-fulfilling prophecy by engaging otherwise well-meaning adults in Conflict Cycles. They will find ways to anger adults through direct challenge or by exposing a vulnerability, and some adults will end up saying or doing something hurtful or punishing to these students. This is, at some level, reassuring to these students. The teacher has reinforced the young person's self-concept as a bad kid and has followed through with something painful, just as the student had predicted. The ability to predict and control life events is comforting because it overrides the dreaded feeling of helplessness.

This circular concept, developed by Long (1965), is known as the Conflict Cycle. The term represents the idea of conflict between two opposing forces: needs within the student clashing against the expectations of others. Healthy adjustment results when the conflict between these two opposing forces is minimized or resolved; maladjustment results when these two opposing forces continue to conflict.

To break the cycle, you must first be able to recognize that it is happening. Then you can analyze the ingredients and plan ways to intervene. Figure 2.1 illustrates the major elements in the Conflict Cycle, beginning with a stressful event which is fueled into a crisis. Unless this first cycle is interrupted and redirected, the Conflict Cycle spirals. The nature of the stress changes, different feelings may be unleashed, new behavioral defenses are called into play, and reactions from others expand in intensity.

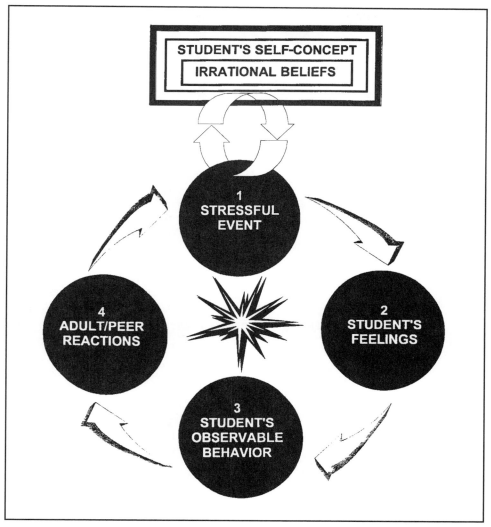

Figure 2.1. The conflict cycle.

Invariably, the result is crisis, a critical moment demanding action. Something must be done!

A crisis generally begins with a triggering event. Laden with emotion, the crisis takes on intensity and urgency for the student and others who are involved. It is not unusual for a crisis to develop from a minor incident that has spiraled. One cycle, uninterrupted, leads to another, and yet another, each expanding into increasingly complex, private depths of stored feelings, and evoking behavior increasingly driven by emotional rather than rational processes. Figure 2.2 illustrates the spiraling phenomenon. Uninterrupted, it begins with an ordinary event, expands into an incident, and then becomes a personal crisis for the student. The Conflict Cycle provides a paradigm for understanding how a student in stress creates feelings comparable to his or her own in adults, and if the adult is not trained, how the adult may mirror the student's behavior.

INGREDIENTS OF THE CONFLICT CYCLE

Every crisis can be analyzed as a series of Conflict Cycles, each of which provides four points for intervening in a crisis:

- Modifying the stress
- Alleviating the student's distressed feelings
- Changing the student's behavior
- Changing the behavior of others

We will discuss each of these four major dimensions of the Conflict Cycle. When adults understand these critical aspects of crisis, they focus their LSCI strategies with greater accuracy and effectiveness.

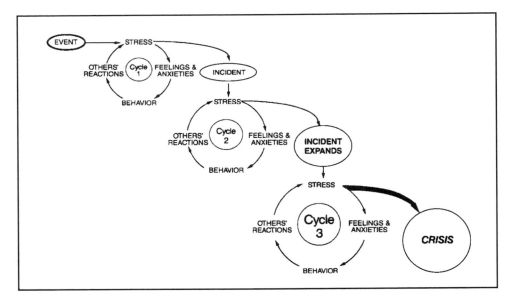

Figure 2.2. Unbroken, the conflict cycle spirals into crisis.

The First Ingredient: Thinking Patterns Trigger Stress

The sources of stress for students are enormous: reality stresses created by society, profound psychological stresses occurring in contemporary family life, and developmental stresses embedded in the normal process of growing up. As a nation we are failing to provide basic social and psychological conditions in which our young can develop in security. This situation puts children and youth at high risk for educational, personal, and social failure (Coles, 1967). Unless we expand our scope to teach students ways to cope with stress and crisis successfully, the outlook for children, youth, and society is bleak.

A national epidemic of stress is forcefully affecting our children and youth. Consider the record. Our society has one of the highest infant mortality rates among industrialized nations; the highest murder rate; and a high rate of fetal alcohol damage, fetal cocaine addiction, fetal AIDS and HIV, child abuse, child crime, adolescent suicide, child and teen pregnancy, and substance abuse among children and youth. According to *The State of America's Children Yearbook* (Children's Defense Fund, 2000), one in five children in the United States lives in poverty, and one in three will live in poverty at some time during their childhood. One in three children is born out of wedlock, one in eight is born to a teenage mother, and one in six has no health insurance. We also are failing to provide children with psychological security. Nearly twelve children every day are killed by firearms, but, perhaps surprisingly, schools are one of the safer places for children. Our anxious, adult-oriented society has unrestrainedly indulged in its own preoccupations, without attempting to protect, limit, or shield our children and youth. Society bombards children with experiences of alienation, violence, and grief—in popular music, television, advertising, news, movies, books, fashions, entertainment, pornography, and art. We are, in short, a society that seldom considers that our children and youth may not be equipped mentally or emotionally to deal with this bombardment of adult experiences (Coles, 1986), nor are we teaching children ways to successfully cope with these stresses.

These concerns are widely held by child development specialists. These professionals are in agreement that children who lack a close relationship to an important adult, who lack an awareness of being loved and protected (or who perceive themselves as unloved or unworthy) suffer intense emotional pain. The resulting anxiety is debilitating. It compounds other problems of general development. Without alleviation, this sense of abandonment can persist into adolescence and adult life, permeating self-esteem, heightening sensitivity to stress, and compounding the problems of forming and maintaining satisfying relationships with others.

A number of studies provide support for the need to be concerned about the social and emotional development of our nation's children—their behavior, the quality of their family relationships, and their future status as adults. One example is the Berkeley Guidance Study of four generations used by Elder, Liker, and Cross (1984) to study economic and psychological stresses on families. The researchers examined interrelationships among family members, generational characteristics, irritability, hostile and inconsistent patterns of parenting, and interactional patterns among parents and children. The results are not surprising: Relationships within families significantly affect children. Hostile and inconsistent patterns of parenting tend to produce negative behavior patterns in children, especially aggressive and antisocial behavior.

Similarly, the New York Longitudinal Study (Thomas & Chess, 1984) followed a group from the first year of life to age 26. The researchers found that psychopathology in adults had antecedents of disturbed behavior in early childhood. No disturbed adults were found in the study who were not disturbed as children. Thomas and Chess also found that the best single predictor of adult mental status was the presence (or absence) of parental conflict during the preschool years.

In reflecting on the impact of contemporary society on children, youth, and adults, Jerome Kagan (1986, pp. 44–45) sees two major sources of chronic stress. The first stress theme is the concern with being loved: "All members of our society feel relatively deprived." He suggests that this may be a result of the failure of status, accomplishment, and power to gratify; with the one remaining source of gratification being a close relationship with another person. Yet close relationships seem to be increasingly difficult to establish or maintain. The second stress theme is uncertainty about one's value and worth—the inability to control events that lead to the attainment of goals. Failure to achieve gratifications that provide reassurance about worthiness contributes to this "modern mood of anxiety."

The result is a generation of stressed children and youth, living in a psychologically complex, unpredictable, generally nonsupportive, anxious, adult-oriented society. This problem is so widespread that it has reached epidemic proportions. It touches every classroom and family in the United States, and affects individuals without regard to income level, race, sex, personality, and intellectual ability.

Some say schools reflect society. This is probably true, for schools today generally are failing to alleviate stress. The social and psychological conditions in schools leave considerable doubt about our national priority and capability to provide quality of life and educational excellence for all children and youth. Schools make unique demands on each student, setting expectations to conform, achieve, share, perform, produce, and bend to the wills of others. Endless scenarios exist that illustrate the stresses promoted in schools. The following are a few examples of stress-producing situations that occur daily in classrooms:

- Personal put-down
- Failure to do something correctly
- Failure with friends
- Ridicule and derision
- Scapegoating
- Being left out
- Infringement of rights

- Failure of justice
- Deprivation of a valued object or opportunity
- Confusion
- Boredom
- Confinement
- Not understanding what is expected
- Threats of harm
- Expectations beyond capacity

Sometimes the consequences of stress are obvious: embarrassment, restrictions, failure, punishment, deprivation, or denial of opportunity. But often the consequences of failing the expectations of others are subtle and psychological: estrangement, rejection, alienation, disapproval, or a judgment of being unworthy. When the expectations of others and a student's personal needs and feelings collide, the tension may become so great that stress occurs. This stress sets the Conflict Cycle in motion. An incident may seem innocuous in itself and hardly worth the conflict that results. Keep in mind, however, that the Conflict Cycle builds on itself. Seemingly minor incidents often escalate into major events, sometimes to traumatic proportions. The original stress becomes masked by the floodgate of actions and reactions among the student and others.

These stress themes must be addressed if we are to assist children and youth with the difficult process of adjustment and achievement in today's complex society. Earls (1986) suggests two major streams of effort to help children and youth survive the intense stresses they experience. First, parents, teachers, and other primary care providers must learn how to be major sources of emotional support, buffering and protecting students from excessive stress and explaining the meaning of daily events in ways that are understandable and reassuring. Second, these adults must learn how to strengthen each student's innate or learned capacity to cope successfully with adversity, stressful events, and daily pressures. LSCI is a procedure that includes both priorities, showing adults how to provide emotional support and how to teach behaviors for coping successfully. Using LSCI, adults can teach students how to manage stress more constructively, regulate their own behavior, and break the Conflict Cycle.

Understanding cognitive interpretation of events—how a student thinks—is important in understanding how thought can relieve or fuel stress. Adults work with many children and adolescents who never seem to be at peace with themselves. They seem always to be a hair's breadth away from a violent outburst, and the victim could be anyone who happens to say or do something that triggers an irrational belief. Their struggle for competence and their desire to be recognized by peers as "worthy," "equal," or "included," brings these youngsters face to face with the unbearable possibility that they are incompetent, inadequate, and unworthy. Past experiences of failure and rejection, and memories of the pain that comes with them, make all the more desperate their attempts to find acceptance, and all the more tender the wounds of ineptitude. This raging internal struggle results in the irrational belief that every life event is a test in which they must prove themselves, or fail. If every day is a walk through a mine field, then one must be very, very sensitive to anything that bears even the remotest resemblance to a trap.

To the student in this heightened state of sensitivity, a laugh from a corner of a room, a glance of a teacher, or a bump in a crowded hallway all can be perceived as menacing. These random events, in the mind of a young person, can take on inflated significance and set off a volley of irrational beliefs: "They're laughing at me because they think I'm stupid-looking; Mr. Smith is looking at me—I must have flunked the test; John's trying to muscle me in the hallway in front of Sue!" These irrational beliefs trigger a cascade of feelings: embarrassment, dread, and fear, which may be expressed through many of the behaviors of children and youth that adults find puzzling—withdrawal, giving up, aggression. Redl advised that adults must be able to understand the psychological perspective of the young in order to comprehend their stress.

The Second Ingredient: Stress Triggers Feelings and Anxieties

A public event has players and witnesses and occurs in a common psychological and physical space. It is a public reality. While everyone may not agree on what happened or why, they have a common event on which to focus. This observable aspect of an event provides the point at which LSCI can be used.

A public event also has a private reality for each individual involved. This reality is the emotional memory bank where thoughts, feelings, and anxieties are stored. This private perspective, the drive behind public words and behavior, is seldom expressed in an open or direct way. Private realities are among the most powerful forces that drive behavior, forming a large part of individual personality and specific behavioral responses. In this personal storehouse of thoughts, feelings, and anxieties, the memories of previous experiences are filed away with emotional notations. These memories lie in wait to be expressed and can be triggered by stress from even the smallest, most seemingly insignificant event. This is no minor force! Understanding this private dimension of a student is central to an effective LSCI.

The Conflict Cycle builds on the stress created by these public and private realities. At the beginning of this chapter, we mentioned the many stresses permeating contemporary life. Students are caught up in lifestyles that are hurried, unpredictable, and bombarded with stress. No age group is exempt. Relationships and personal emotional needs often seem to be ignored in the push for things, action, and performance. Then, when clashes between private, unmet emotional needs and expectations set by others occur and are unresolved, stress develops that demands relief.

Some of the feelings and anxieties stored in a student's emotional memory bank result from daily frustrations and disappointments. Other emotional memories are of painful or assaultive individual life experiences. These are the psychosocial stressors discussed previously—memories of unhappy and hurtful experiences. Protecting oneself from reexperiencing such feelings is a major motivation: People will go to great lengths to avoid these feelings.

Other feelings and anxieties occur in response to the demands made on students in the course of normal development. Called "developmental stressors," these are the standard demands for performance made on children and youth at various ages. The following is a basic illustration. Expectations for performance from infants are uncomplicated. We expect them to smile back at us, cease crying when we comfort them, and swallow their food when fed. If they fail to respond, we react—with concern, frustration, disgust, anger, or a sense of ineptness or helplessness. The reaction is cycled back to the infant in the form of "doing something." If the situation is ameliorated and the infant gives us the desired response, the rewards for both the infant and adult are significant. Feelings of well-being permeate the emotional memory banks of both. In contrast, if the infant does not give back the desired behavior, the result is stress for both, and the emotional memory banks are crowded with feelings of unhappiness and discomfort.

Project that same interaction further, as development continues. Expectations for the toddler's performance have increased enormously. Bowel and bladder control are important; talking is essential, as is obedience to simple commands and self-feeding. The first preschool experience requires additional sitting and sharing behaviors. The primary grades demand learning reading, writing, and arithmetic. Upper elementary school demands appropriate group behavior governed by rules and concepts of fairness. In high school, students face complex demands for employment, vocation, and intellectual expansion. At the same time, they are expected to stay out of trouble while being thrown into a sea of adult social ills.

Such age-related expectations for performance are stressors experienced in some form by all children and youth during the normal stages of social and emotional development. If the expected performance is not forthcoming, adults react. When adults' reactions are supportive and oriented toward helping students achieve success in overcoming these developmental problems, crises may be averted. When students achieve developmental expectations, we say they are "well adjusted." If students fail to perform as others expect, we talk about "problem students" and "poor adjustment." For these students, developmental stressors, like reality stressors, have produced painful feelings and defensive behaviors. These memories seldom disappear. They are simply stored in emotional memory banks, where they are protected by defensive behaviors. Because feelings and anxieties play a central role as antecedents for crisis and because they are essential elements in breaking the Conflict Cycle with LSCI, we discuss this topic in greater depth in the next chapter.

The Third Ingredient: Feelings Drive Behavior

In a Conflict Cycle, an event always triggers feelings that, in turn, result in observable defensive behavior. We call these behaviors defensive because they are attempts by students to protect or insulate themselves from the feelings and anxieties evoked by the stress of an event. Almost all behavior problems are defensive maneuvers by students to cope with developmental stresses or the stresses of contemporary life.

Clinicians refer to the idea of psychological defenses when they use the term *defense mechanisms*. By identifying a student's behavior as a particular type of defense, you will know (a) that the student is sufficiently anxious about the event to need psychological protection (defense against painful feelings and anxieties), and (b) the general defense strategies the student is using.

At every age defensive behaviors enable students to cope with stress. They go to great lengths to protect themselves from the emotional pain of unmitigated stress, whether it arises from normal developmental stressors or from assaultive life experiences. When successful, defensive behaviors enable a student to cope comfortably. But if defensive behaviors fail to produce the needed relief, new behaviors will be substituted. If these new behaviors also fail to produce relief, a student's behavior becomes increasingly dominated by excessively defensive maneuvers; the student's perceptions are distorted, and his or her functioning is impaired. Chronic defensiveness can permeate a student's personality development, influence the way the student learns (or fails to learn), and affect the way he or she responds to adults, peers, and daily events in the classroom.

Defensive behaviors can be loosely grouped into three categories: denial, escape, and substitution. Table 2.1 defines each of the major defensive behaviors.

Denial. Behaviors in the first group are those in which the student actively denies ownership of the problem:

"Nothing happened." (denial)

"I never got angry." (repression)

"I thought the test was tomorrow, so I made a dentist appointment for today." (rationalization)

"I'm trying to play by the rules, and he (someone else) keeps breaking them." (projection)

Escape. In the second group of defensive behaviors, the student tries to escape facing a problem by mentally or physically withdrawing:

The student spends much class time staring out the window or drawing doodles around the edge of his or her papers. (daydreaming/fantasy)

The student simply gets up and walks out of class when things don't go the way he or she wants them to go. (withdrawal)

Whenever the student cannot get his or her way, he or she has a temper tantrum. (regression)

TABLE 2.1
Definitions of Major Defensive Behaviors

Denial

1. *Denial*—A defense mechanism in which the individual protects himself or herself from unpleasant aspects of reality by ignoring or refusing to perceive them, remaining unaware of facts that could create one side of a conflict.

2. *Repression*—A defense mechanism in which the individual's painful or dangerous thoughts and desires are excluded from consciousness without awareness of what is happening.

3. *Rationalization*—A defense mechanism in which logical, socially approved reasons to justify past, present, or proposed behavior are used. It helps the individual to justify actions and beliefs, and it aids in softening disappointment connected with unattainable goals.

4. *Projection*—A defense mechanism in which the individual transfers blame for shortcomings, mistakes, and misdeeds to others or attributes to others his or her own unacceptable impulses, thoughts, and desires.

Escape

5. *Defense through the opposite (reaction formation)*—A defense mechanism in which dangerous desires and impulses are prevented from entering consciousness or from being carried out in action by the fostering of opposed types of behavior and attitudes.

6. *Withdrawal*—A defense mechanism involving emotional, intellectual, or physical retreat from a situation.

7. *Intellectualization*—A defense mechanism in which the affective charge in a hurtful situation is cut off, or incompatible attitudes are separated into logic-tight compartments.

8. *Regression*—A defense mechanism in which the individual retreats to an earlier developmental level involving less mature responses and a lower level of aspiration.

Substitution

9. *Displacement*—A defense mechanism in which there is a shift of emotion, symbolic meaning, or fantasy from a person or object toward which it was originally directed to another person or object.

10. *Compensation*—A defense mechanism in which the individual covers up a weakness or feeling of inadequacy by emphasizing a desirable trait or makes up for frustration in one area by overgratification in another.

11. *Sublimation*—A defense mechanism that involves the acceptance of a socially approved substitute goal for a drive whose normal channel of expression or normal goal is blocked.

12. *Identification*—A defense mechanism in which the individual identifies with some person or institution, usually of an illustrious nature.

Substitution. In the third group of defensive behaviors, the problem is modified or distorted by the student, so that it is somehow transformed into something more manageable by substituting a more acceptable behavior that still provides control of painful or dangerous feelings:

> A science student is angry at the teacher, so he takes apart his 6-week project, "It's no good, and it won't work!" (displacement)

> A student who is without friends and generally ignored by other students carries snacks in her purse. (compensation)

> An adolescent handles his aggressive impulses by playing the drums in the high school band. (sublimation)

> Just before final exams, a student becomes sick and has to leave school. (psychosomatic reaction)

> A student imitates the mannerisms, expressions, and style of a current television star. (identification)

The Fourth Ingredient: Inappropriate Behavior Incites Others' Reactions

In the Conflict Cycle, a student's defensive, negative behaviors typically evoke hostile or defensive reactions and widespread alienation from peers and adults. These reactions produce greater stress for the student, and the Conflict Cycle goes into a second round, again tapping into feelings and anxieties that require more defensive behaviors, and producing more negative reactions from others. Unless it is interrupted, the cycle will continue to expand in intensity and scope.

This situation is pivotal for an adult involved in a Conflict Cycle. The student's behavior encourages adult counterbehaviors. Student comments such as "No!" "Make me!" or "So what?" beg for aggressive responses. These students, who defy authority or refuse to participate, are detrimental to constructive group activity. What complicates the adult position is that it seems justified and natural to react in a negative way and put such students in their place. After all, adults are responsible for the maintenance of law and order!

An amazing aspect of the Conflict Cycle is how students under stress can create their own feelings of anger, frustration, helplessness, and insecurity in adults, to the point that adults will behave in counteraggressive, impulsive, or rejecting ways. Defensive adult reactions create new stress for the student. The student now has to deal with the adult's rejection or anger in addition to the original stress. For an adult to respond with any counteraggressive behavior is self-defeating. If you act out the feelings you have and "do what comes naturally," your behavior will perpetuate the cycle by mirroring the student's own aggression or inability to control behavior. As a result, the statement "aggression elicits aggression" becomes true, and the student becomes the one determining the adult behavior. The more involved you become in struggling with a student, the more likely it is that you will be the one who ends up in crisis. Even if the student loses the battle, by succeeding in getting you to escalate counteraggression by expressing open dislike, hostility, or rejection, the student wins the emotional war by demonstrating the self-fulfilling prophecy that adults are hostile and cannot be trusted.

What must adults do to stop this destructive cycle? They must understand the dynamics of conflict as represented in the Conflict Cycle, see clearly how they can be seduced by their own feelings and reactions, and not fall into the trap! An experienced adult sees the potential for student aggression to evoke counteraggression from the adult. Understanding and self-control is required to disconnect from the struggle, putting aside personal emotions that arise in reaction to a student's behavior. Again, the expression "dispassionate compassion" is a useful way to think about emotional reactions during the Conflict Cycle. Reject the natural instinct to win out over the student; it is not necessary.

Through careful self-monitoring, you can stop your own potentially destructive involvement in the Conflict Cycle. By recognizing the existence of your own counteraggressive feelings, you can exercise choice and control over your own behavior, and not allow yourself to be drawn into the Conflict Cycle. In Part II we describe the changing role of the adult during each stage of LSCI. This should help you to stay focused on the task, conveying to students that you are a responsible, dependable adult who understands what they are feeling, respects them, and offers ways to bring about solutions to their problems.

SUMMARY OF THE CONFLICT CYCLE

Students seldom learn successful behaviors for handling stress on their own. Adults must carefully and methodically set about breaking the Conflict Cycle by teaching students to regulate their behavior in ways that bring more satisfying results. Without changing their behavioral responses to stress and the underlying feelings and anxieties, students will continue to behave in a less than satisfactory manner to protect themselves.

Students' negative behaviors can evoke hostile or defensive reactions and widespread alienation from peers and adults. Such feelings spiral into further alienation, with more inept attempts to handle problems. Conflict can become contagious to the group, causing further breakdowns in students' emotional and social competence. In such an environment learning can be brought to a standstill. But crisis also represents a potential turning point and opportunity for new learning. A crisis can be one of the best times to teach students how to handle stress constructively, and LSCI provides the process for doing this.

EXAMPLE OF THE CONFLICT CYCLE

It is useful to develop the habit of analyzing each incident as a component of the Conflict Cycle: stress, thoughts, feelings and anxieties, behavior, and reactions of others. Doing this as you work through the first three stages of LSCI with a student helps keep the central points clear. From time to time you may find yourself digressing from the real issue, or a student may unload a lot of feelings or thoughts that cloud the issue. This should not be a problem if you have the components clearly sorted out in your own mind.

To illustrate how to use the Conflict Cycle to analyze an incident, go back to "The Math Problem Crisis" described earlier. You may recall that the special education teacher is using LSCI with a student who has tested limits by taking advantage of a miscommunication between the teacher and the classroom assistant. The original stress spirals into three Conflict Cycles before the cycles are broken by the teacher using LSCI. By stripping away all but the essential information about the events that led to the LSCI, the analysis reveals major differences between adults and students in perceptions of events.

The original stress that started Cycle 1 was the student's frustration with a math worksheet. His past failures with math have established a mind-set: "I hate math; I'm a failure." This mind-set triggers feelings of impatience, frustration, and anger which are expressed in the student's behavior: He doesn't make an attempt to arrive at the correct answers, but turns in the paper anyway. The teacher responds to this action by requiring the student to correct the paper before going to gym.

Cycle 2 begins when the classroom assistant, unaware that the student has been given special directions by the teacher, announces that everyone should turn in papers and go to gym. The student recognizes this as an opportunity to default on his understanding with the teacher. He feels a sense of relief at this serendipitous opportunity. He goes to gym knowing he is violating a trust, but hoping it will go unnoticed.

Cycle 3 begins when the teacher discovers the situation and calls him from the gym. The student is now on the spot and filled with "righteous indignation" that he should be held accountable for a communication error between the staff. He expresses his angry feelings to the teacher verbally, but the teacher's response is disarming. She stops the Conflict Cycle by recognizing and acknowledging the student's stress. She reviews the sequence of events with the student and demonstrates understanding about why the student chose this course of action to relieve his extreme stress. Because she has a relationship with the student, she takes him to the next step of insight. She leads the student to see that, even though accepting responsibility is difficult, the rewards for doing so are great. Throughout the interview the teacher acknowledges the student's fledgling attempts to own his role in the problem.

As the teacher goes through this intervention, she touches the themes of LSCI in every stage. Sometimes she addresses the themes by reflecting what she sees in the student's responses or body language. Other times she defuses the intensity by countering it with affirmations and praise of the student's maturity and the sense of responsibility he shows in handling the crisis. At no time is there an intimation that the teacher blames the student. (Whether or not the student is to blame is moot.) What is important is that the teacher can see the crisis as a sequence of stress, thoughts, feelings, behavior, and reactions of others within the context of the student's personal history.

WHAT WE HOPE YOU HAVE LEARNED FROM THIS CHAPTER

- The two opposing needs that produce the Conflict Cycle
- How an event can spiral into an incident and then into a crisis
- How the idea of a Conflict Cycle is used in LSCI
- Points at which to intervene to break the Conflict Cycle
- Two general sources of stress for students that can set off a Conflict Cycle
- Examples of ordinary, stress-producing situations in classrooms
- Examples of typical developmental stresses for each age group
- Why students use defensive behaviors
- Three categories of defensive behaviors
- An example of each of the major defensive behaviors
- Why understanding the Conflict Cycle is basic to doing effective LSCI

"You think you know
    what I said.
But what you don't
    know is,
what I said is not
    what I meant."

From Behavior to Feelings   3

Students in crisis seldom see connections among what they feel, how they behave, and how others respond. Their responses to stress tend to be behaviors fueled by feelings, perpetuating conflict and crisis. Not only are most students unable to recognize feelings, they are also not able to talk about them. But unless a student is able to do these two things, it is difficult, if not impossible, for the student to make a lasting change from behavior driven by feelings to behavior regulated by rational processes.

Some adults are equally inept at this process. An adult can be of little help to a student until the adult recognizes behavior that is expressing feelings and knows how to convey this understanding to the student. An adult cannot teach a student something that the adult does not understand. Learning to recognize this behavior is a major part of learning to use LSCI effectively. First, learn to recognize feelings and anxieties expressed in students' behavior. Next, learn to convey understanding of the feelings and anxieties to the student. In LSCI, the adult must be the first to make connections between behavior and feelings when students cannot do so themselves. Finally, during the LCSI the skilled adult teaches students to recognize the part feelings play in their own behavior and that of others.

In this chapter we focus on the foundation adults need for teaching students to recognize feelings conveyed through their own behavior and that of others. First, we outline a framework for identifying students' developmental anxieties that are a natural part of personality development for all children and youth. This material provides a framework for identifying general types of deep concerns of students of all ages. Second, we describe a process for decoding behavior, used directly with students to translate their behavior into genuine statements about specific feelings. Decoding is a process of responding to students in ways that build bridges between students' private, developmental anxieties and their public behavior. When students recognize feelings and connect them to their own behavior and that of others, the Conflict Cycle can be broken. This is necessary to accomplish the goals of LSCI.

DEVELOPMENTAL ANXIETIES

Anxiety is a private, chronic reaction to unmet emotional needs and stress. Anxiety results from experiencing life as a series of unpleasant events. For some students, growing up will inevitably produce debilitating developmental anxieties. These are the students we call "at risk." They live with insecurity, unpredictability, alienation, helplessness, or failure. The developmental stressors these students experience are usually similar to those of other students of the same approximate age, but there is a difference: Students who are already stressed by negative psychosocial forces seldom are able to successfully navigate through the normal crisis of each developmental stage.

As noted in the previous chapter, developmental stressors contribute to a characteristic crisis at each general stage of social and emotional development. The age-related stresses compound the scope of anxiety, contribute to an increasingly complex set of unmet emotional needs, and, if left unresolved, result in social, emotional, and behavioral failures.

There are five general types of developmental anxieties, encompassing complex interpersonal and intrapersonal processes from birth through adolescence: abandonment, inadequacy, guilt, conflict, and identity (Wood, 1996). Figure 3.1 illustrates the dynamic interactions between personal needs and expectations of others that produce these developmental anxieties. By identifying the developmental anxieties in your students, you will have a framework for decoding their behavioral responses to stress. This information also will give you direction for individualizing a student's program and selecting specific intervention strategies to break the Conflict Cycle. We summarize the salient points of each developmental anxiety in this chapter. In Part II we describe how to put this information to work during LSCI.

Abandonment

"No one cares!"

Abandonment is the fundamental anxiety, arising from fears of physical or psychological deprivation, abuse, or annihilation of the self. It occurs as a normal developmental crisis in infants and children under age two. The need for basic physical and psychological nurturing predominates behavior. If it is unresolved, anxiety about abandonment permeates personality development and all subsequent relationships. In older children, adolescents, and adults, this anxiety is expressed in attempts to satisfy primitive needs at any cost: by eating, hoarding, stealing, and pursuing sexual gratification and superficial emotional attachments.

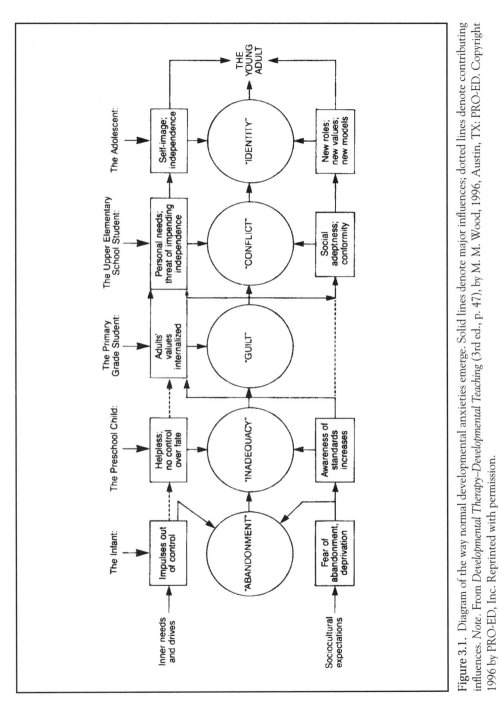

Figure 3.1. Diagram of the way normal developmental anxieties emerge. Solid lines denote major influences; dotted lines denote contributing influences. *Note.* From *Developmental Therapy–Developmental Teaching* (3rd ed., p. 47), by M. M. Wood, 1996, Austin, TX: PRO-ED. Copyright 1996 by PRO-ED, Inc. Reprinted with permission.

Developmental anxiety about abandonment can be resolved with consistent care; expressed, unconditional affection; and an environment that provides consistency, pleasure, comfort, care, and security.

Inadequacy

"I can't do anything right."
"You won't like it."

In normal development, the anxiety of inadequacy typically becomes the emotional crisis of preschool children as they become increasingly aware of the expectations of the important people around them. The dynamics of this anxiety include self-doubt and fear of the unknown, the need to avoid failure by denying association, and the avoidance of experiences with uncertain outcomes. Imagination runs rampant, and students see most events as clashes between right and wrong, good and bad. Punishment is always imminent from powerful adults and other external sources (magical forces, nature, rules, authority). There is no control or escape. When anxiety about inadequacy continues in school-age students, they seek to avoid blame, criticism, punishment, and failure at any cost. The driving motivation is to cover up mistakes (by blaming others, denying responsibility, lying, or by avoiding failure or being put in a position of looking "bad").

Anxiety about inadequacy can be overcome as students learn skills to become successful, build self-confidence, and receive adult approval as individuals who can accomplish things. They learn that problems have solutions (not just punishments), and they begin to see themselves as having some power to control events around them.

Guilt

"I'm no good. I'm a loser."

Guilt is a more complex form of inadequacy, in which the source of judgment about a student's unworthiness changes from others to self. Typically this is a normal developmental crisis for students during their first 3 years in school (about age 6 to 9). Guilt signals the presence of a basic value system. The expectations and rules of others are accepted as one's own. The student then serves as judge and jury to the self, determining that personal inadequacy (failure) deserves punishment.

If it is unresolved, guilt arrests a student at a developmental level where self-denigration predominates. Failure to meet the standards of others is absorbed as excruciating evidence of unworthiness. Older students with this anxiety often allow themselves to become scapegoats, exploited by adults and peers. Their behavior may be outrageous. They perform unacceptable acts to prove their unworthiness and to be punished as atonement. Or they may violate rules so clumsily that it is evident that they want to be caught.

Another defensive strategy seen in students with guilt is the massive cover-up. Clinicians sometimes call this passive aggression. These students are so aware of expected standards of behavior and so in need of approval from others that they cannot afford to put themselves in the position of being rejected. Yet they are so troubled by their personal failings and so angry at others for their miserable situation that they express their anger in devious ways to avoid blame. Every adult has worked with such students, and often call them manipulators.

Developmental guilt normally resolves as the student emotionally expands successfully in independent experiences with friends and adults. Adult sanction of this new independence is essential. Students gradually develop alternative standards to judge their own unworthiness. The potency of a single performance standard diminishes, and students' views of right and wrong expand. They begin to see that there is more than one point of view, and that there are other ways to judge a person's worth. This insight frees students to explore alternative ways to achieve recognition, relieving their sense of guilt.

The Independence–Dependence Conflict

"I want to, but they won't let me."
"Try and make me!"

This developmental anxiety first emerges as an independence–dependence tension between a student's need for independence and a continuing need for adult approval (dependence) during the upper elementary school years (age 9 to 12). In some students it may be evident even earlier. It is usually triggered when a student begins to identify and conform to new peer group values. As a strong, independent self expands with social experiences and increasing self-confidence, anxiety takes the forms of willfulness, aggression, defiance, independence, and resistance to authority.

Typically the developmentally based anxiety over this conflict is resolved when a student has learned that conformity brings its own rewards and can be traded off for new personal freedoms and recognition. The old saying, "With freedom comes responsibility, "is the understanding that resolves this developmental anxiety and fortifies the student for approaching adolescence.

In contrast, if this clash between the need to be an independent person and the requirement to submit to authority (in order to be affirmed by adults) is unresolved, a student is ill-equipped to take on the next developmental stresses in adolescence. Such students continue to resist authority and fight the system. They manipulate, act out, aggress, and transgress, continually seeking to meet their intense dual needs to control and to receive affirmation and admiration. These students are inevitably caught in the Conflict Cycle because their behaviors always evoke negative reactions from others. Instead of obtaining the recognition they crave, they often find themselves with reputations as "bad kids."

Identity

"Who am I?"
"Am I a person who can handle this?"

The question of psychological identity is the classic anxiety of the adolescent years. It takes form as students begin to experiment with new self-images as distinctly individual persons. Students are acutely aware of new psychological and physical freedoms which also bring crisis, with new demands to perform successfully and be responsible. The dynamics of this developmental anxiety are an extension of the previous one—the clash between a need for successful independence and lingering dependency needs. The pervasive concern in adolescence is about how teens appear to others in relation to how they appear to themselves. Self-doubt and self-confidence interplay as students alternately believe, and then doubt, their ability to handle challenges.

If it is unresolved, developmental anxiety about self-worth and self-identity dominates attitudes, values, and behavior. Adolescents who are not able to resolve anxiety about self-worth and their place in society express their vacillations with all of the defensive behaviors described in the previous section. They try every means they can to obtain gratification, assuage their feelings of uselessness, and express their anger at being in such a state. For them, the Conflict Cycle may become a way of life.

Resolution of this identity crisis normally takes a number of years for most adolescents. It is such a major part of personality formation that it often continues into adult life, as careers and interpersonal relationships are forged. This developmental anxiety is resolved as students receive clear evidence of their success in new situations in which they can use new skills, try out new attitudes and values, and begin to see themselves recognized by others as independently successful.

Summary of Developmental Anxieties

Central to every LSCI is the need to recognize which developmental stresses a student is struggling with and which developmental anxiety predominates. With LSCI there are abundant opportunities to teach new behaviors which can alleviate developmental anxieties. Adults can teach students to recognize connections among their own feelings, behaviors, and reactions of others. Adults make these connections for students by decoding their behavior during crisis.

Developmental stresses produce five general types of developmental anxieties that occur in a predictable sequence in all children and youth: abandonment, inadequacy, guilt, independence–dependence conflict, and identity. Every stage of development has its own characteristic stresses and anxieties making demands on a developing child or youth. As each developmental anxiety is successfully resolved, a student acquires increasingly mature, age-appropriate behaviors. Equipped with these new behaviors, a student is prepared to face the new stresses produced by the next stage of development.

If unresolved, a developmental anxiety at one stage contributes to the stresses of the next stage of development, compounding the student's problems and having a negative impact on the student's capacity to develop further.

DECODING BEHAVIOR

Decoding means connecting what students are doing and saying to what they are feeling. Decoding has three purposes: (a) to teach students to recognize specific feelings that drive their inappropriate behaviors, (b) to build students' confidence that they do not have to be victims of their own bad feelings because there are alternative behaviors that bring better feelings, and (c) to convey that talking about feelings and anxieties may not be as awful as anticipated. Unless decoding is done, feelings continue to fester, finding outlets in all sorts of unacceptable behaviors.

Decoding begins with objective observation of students' behavior and careful listening to what they say. Accurate decoding also requires sensitivity to body language and to what is implied and left unsaid. From this information, connections are made for the student between specific behaviors and associated feelings. To fail to decode is to ignore the most potent force driving the behavior of the students you work with.

To decode you must have some understanding of a student's concerns. We suggest using the general framework of developmental anxieties we have described to guide you in identifying these concerns. Sometimes, as you begin LSCI, you may find a student's concerns elusive, or your understanding of a student's anxieties incomplete. As you talk, question, reflect, and think about the student's responses, construct hypotheses about the nature of the student's concerns. Form an initial hypothesis from the framework of developmental anxieties, beginning with the anxiety that is naturally associated with the same age group as the student. You can expect that particular anxiety to be present as a normal part of the life experience of most students of the same age, even without stress or crisis. Then, refine your ideas about the student's concerns by observing and listening carefully to what the student says and does during the first three stages of the LSCI. You may see behaviors and hear remarks that lead you to consider the presence of other developmental anxieties. Also, gather information about feelings and behaviors that are specific to the student and the incident under discussion.

The accuracy of your decoding will be evident in the student's responses. Typically a student will react when you decode accurately. The reaction may be vigorous denial or passive quietness. In either case, the decoded message has touched the student's concerns. When decoding misses its mark, students generally do not change their level of affect. They may continue the same behavior, appear to be genuinely disinterested, or simply go on to another subject without an emotional change.

As students learn that talking about feelings and connecting them to behavior is not invasive, they learn to do this themselves. They begin to decode for you, explaining what they did and the feelings that were part of their behavior. It is essential to keep in mind that when you decode, or when students learn to decode their own behavior and that of others, it is not the end of the LSCI. Students must also learn to change their behavior in ways that bring about better feelings and more satisfying results. For this reason we use different types of decoding during the first three stages of LSCI, while exploring the problem, the issues, and the feelings involved. Then, during the last three LSCI stages, as we work with students to plan and implement solutions, we prefer to use less decoding and to focus instead on new, more appropriate behaviors and the more pleasant results (better feelings) a student can expect from a change.

The First Level of Decoding: Acknowledging

We begin decoding by simply acknowledging that feelings are embedded in a student's words and behavior. Sometimes this strategy is called reflection (reflecting back a student's behavior or expressed feelings). This basic level of decoding does not attempt to interpret complex responses or characterize feelings in any particular way. It requires no particular understanding about the type of developmental anxiety involved or other deep concerns. It is particularly useful when you are just beginning a series of LSCIs with a student, when you know very little about a student or an incident, or when you need to convey acceptance and support while disapproving of behavior.

The intent in acknowledging feelings is to communicate your awareness that a student is feeling unhappy (awful, miserable, terrible, sad, etc.). When acknowledging feelings, you are not asking the student to describe feelings or motivations. Neither are you condoning the inappropriate behavior the student used to express the feelings. You are not making interpretations about why or how. You are not even asking the student to talk about the feelings. The feelings exist; you recognize how unpleasant or painful they are for the student. That is enough at the beginning. By simply acknowledging the presence of feelings, you are not intruding too rapidly into a student's private space. This respect for a student's feelings can help establish your credibility and lead to trust. It is essential to acknowledge feelings during LSCI, especially during Stage 1.

The following are examples of how we use this type of decoding to acknowledge feelings in ways that need no response on the student's part:

Sally   When asked to put away her game, Sally blurts out, "Go away!"

         Teacher decodes: "It's frustrating for you to stop a good game before it's finished. You can come back to it at the next break."

Calvin   Calvin goes to his desk and buries his face in his arms after backing down from a challenge to fight on the playground.

         Teacher decodes: "Being challenged to a fight by a big guy can make anybody feel scared and confused."

Jeff   Jeff is pulled away from a student he has been pounding on the playground.

               Teacher decodes: "Adults have to control you until you can control yourself."

Decoding behavior by simply acknowledging feelings before an incident occurs often will defuse or diminish the intensity of feelings brought to school as "excess baggage." The following are observations made by two teachers that illustrate the potential for crisis from nonspecific sources:

"He came to school today with a chip on his shoulder." [Student is angry about something and will use any opportunity to unload the anger.]

"She's an emotional basket case." [Student is so emotionally overloaded that feelings spill over into anything she does.]

Each student is conveying emotionally driven behavior. Unless there is some intervention, you can predict accurately that there will be a crisis. Even the most innocuous event can cause behavior to spiral out of control. The incident may not be an issue, but may merely be used by the student as an outlet for feelings. Decoding these feelings by simply acknowledging them can avoid misconnecting them to events that are not really issues.

The Second Level of Decoding: Surface Interpretation

Connecting freely expressed, undisguised feelings to specific behavior is the next level of complexity in decoding. This strategy, called surface interpretation, is explaining the emotional meaning expressed in the behavior. For this type of decoding, the behavior is so obviously related to feelings that decoding can be done in a straightforward way. It is easy to recognize the expressed feelings and respond to them. For example, there is a fairly direct connection between the action of a student throwing a book across the room and associated feelings. To accurately decode that behavior for the student, you need to have information about the sequence of antecedent events and know enough about the student's history, developmental anxieties, or self-image to understand how the event could be stressful. Depending on such information, the teacher might decode the book-throwing behavior in one of several ways:

"You thought the work was too difficult, but throwing the book won't make the problem go away."

"It made you angry when they didn't wait for you to finish, and the book was handy."

"Throwing the book is one way to say you don't want to do the work, but there are better ways to get the message across."

The following are several other examples of decoding that carry clearly conveyed messages explaining feelings communicated by students' behavior:

Tom   Tom is not chosen to play on his friends' team, so he walks off the playground without saying anything to anyone.

Teacher decodes: "When your buddies make you feel down you just want to get away from them."

Ann   Ann loses control and flies into a rage because her friend will not share paints.

Teacher decodes: "You do things for friends and then when they don't do things for you, you feel betrayed. It makes you angry."

Kathy   Kathy refuses to go with the group to the library: "Nobody tells me what to do. I'll damn well do as I please!"

Teacher decodes: "It seems like people are always telling you what to do, and it can make you angry when you have to do things you don't want to do."

Sometimes adults are afraid to make such statements because they fear that students will interpret the decoded message as tacit approval of inappropriate behavior. This may be true, unless the adult continues to emphasize how feelings cause behavior that results in reactions from others that are not always in the student's best interest. During the first three stages of LSCI, decoding with such follow-up discussions occurs frequently. The adult guides (and sometimes leads) a student from acknowledgment of feelings, through interpretation of surface feelings associated with the behavior, to the unpleasant reactions of others. Such discussions are essential before you and a student converge on a solution during the last three stages of the LSCI to break the Conflict Cycle.

The Third Level of Decoding: Secondary Interpretation

Vigorous denial by a student in reaction to decoding usually requires a third, difficult, type of decoding we call secondary interpretation. It is difficult because it requires shifting focus from the student's original behavior to the student's denial. It also requires decoding a second time, connecting feelings to the denial. Second decodings of denials are reformulations of the original decoding, put in ways that are more palatable and supportive but just as accurate. As in the first type of decoding, a student is not asked to describe or verify the feelings involved. It is the adult who acknowledges the presence of feelings in the observed behavior. To decode a student's denial, you need a solid understanding of which anxiety is at the root of the behavior and the types of defensive behaviors the student is using.

When students are first exposed to decoding, it is not unusual for them to react with strong denial of what you say. It often is uncomfortable and hard for them to believe that you can understand and talk about the feelings behind their behavior. They usually will deny the accuracy of the decoded message. Vigorous denial may indicate several things:

1. The student does not trust you (or adults in general) sufficiently to let you into the private domain of personal feelings.

2. The student may be asking for greater psychological "space" (distance) because the message is about feelings that have been avoided because they are too painful to face.

3. You may have the wrong explanation of the feelings and concerns behind the behavior.

The first two situations call for some form of secondary interpretation. The student's reactions indicate that you have struck an accurate (and sensitive) chord. They also tell you that the student does not want to hear the message, even if it is true. In these situations, secondary decoding often reiterates the original message in a less threatening and more supportive way. Here are examples of decoding with a second interpretation that focuses on the denial:

Carla   Carla stalks suddenly into the room: "I ain't doin' nothin' today."

        Teacher decodes: "You've got other things on your mind today?"

        Carla: "What do you know about it?!"

        Teacher decodes: "When you're under a lot of pressure, it's hard to think about school work."

Mark   Mark throws his pencil on the floor: "I'm not doin' this stupid work!"

        Teacher decodes: "This is a tough assignment; would you like some help?"

        Mark: "I don't need no help and I don't care!"

        Teacher decodes: "This work is so hard it seems like you'll never get through it. That can frustrate anybody."

Tony   After a fight in the bathroom, Tony shouts at the teacher, "You're picking on the wrong person!"

Teacher decodes: "It's hard to face up to a problem when you have hurt someone."

Tony: "No! You've got it all wrong! That's not what happened. I was just standing there."

Teacher decodes again: "I'm interested in hearing how you explain it."

You have probably noticed that this type of decoding requires no specific answer from the student. The intent is to get the message out in the open, to be built upon as the student can tolerate the insights. When a student responds to this second decoding with less emotion, less denial, no further response, or changes the subject, you know that the message has connected.

Summary of Decoding

In doing effective LSCI, it is essential to have an understanding of the feelings associated with the inappropriate behavior a student has used in response to stress. Without this understanding, it is not possible to teach a student to self-regulate behavior and the emotions that drive the behavior. We find out about feelings by objective observation of behavior and body language, questioning for information about the sequence of events, assessing the level of emotional intensity in the student's behavior, and careful listening to what the student says (and avoids saying). We put this information into the framework of five sequential anxieties which occur as a natural part of social and emotional development: abandonment, inadequacy, guilt, conflict, or identity. When you understand which anxiety a student is protecting, the student's inappropriate behavior can be understood as a defensive strategy for protection from further psychological pain.

This understanding is communicated to a student in a process called decoding. Used extensively during the first three stages of LSCI, decoding is the means of making connections for the student between behavior and feelings. Depending upon the student's behavior, there are three types of decoding. The least complicated form of decoding requires only acknowledgment that feelings are present. More complicated forms of decoding involve interpretation of surface feelings conveyed through behavior, and secondary interpretation when a student denies the first decoding. The most difficult type of decoding requires interpretation of feelings that are masked by a student's opposite behavior.

Through decoding, an adult conveys support and understanding of what a student is feeling during crisis. Decoding that is accurate and supportive enhances the trust between student and adult. The student sees the adult as understanding and as a reliable source for assistance in a difficult time. The student also begins to learn about the connections between behavior and reactions from others. And by changing behavior, the student learns that outcomes can be changed for the better.

WHAT WE HOPE YOU HAVE LEARNED FROM THIS CHAPTER

- Why it is important to recognize students' feelings when using LSCI

- A general definition of developmental anxieties

- Five types of developmental anxiety and the general causes of each

- The typical age range when each developmental anxiety emerges as part of normal personality development

- Characteristic behavior of students with each of the developmental anxieties

- How adults can combat each developmental anxiety

- A general definition of decoding behavior

- Why decoding is essential for effective LSCI

- How you can tell if you are decoding accurately

- Three levels of decoding and the purpose of each

- The LSCI stages in which decoding is most frequently used

- How observations of defensive behavior, understanding of developmental anxieties, and decoding are used together in effective LSCIs

"Who's in charge here?"
"Who's going to handle
this problem?"
"How do I know it's
going to be all right
for me?"

Questions To Answer
Before You Begin LSCI

4

To your students, you are the representative adult and authority, their surrogate for adults in general. As such, you will be the "stand-in" and recipient of a student's behavior, feelings, and attitudes toward other adults. Students bring a history of experience with other adults into every classroom and crisis. Your own behavior and intentions may be the best, your relationship with students amiable, but there is no avoiding the student's history with other adults as you and the student interact. The student has learned to respond to adults in certain ways from past experience; this behavior is what you will receive from a student in crisis. Three questions from this history arise repeatedly during LSCI: Who is the authority? Whose responsibility is it to come up with a solution to the crisis? What assurance does the student have that personal needs will be considered?

These are the concerns of every student in crisis: worries about emotional security and what adults will do. The first question reflects the need of all students to be reassured that a higher authority (adult power) will not let events get out of control. All children and youth want to believe that anarchy will not reign and that life can be experienced with a minimum of distress. They view adults as the ultimate authority for this reassurance. The second question conveys students' uncertainty about the extent to which they can rely on adults to handle problems. The third question conveys the doubts students have that their own needs will be considered as a crisis is resolved. This concern triggers students' tendencies to rely on established, defensive behaviors to protect themselves and meet their own needs. Tapping into such needs provides motivation for independent action, but independent action can produce unacceptable rather than constructive behavior.

During LSCI, such pervasive concerns are always present. If they are unresolved, they preoccupy a student and dominate the LSCI. The specific crisis will be eclipsed and crisis resolution will not occur. To use LSCI effectively, an adult must recognize the specific form these concerns are taking and deal with them. It is essential to recognize that the student's behavior is probably not directed against you as an individual but against you as the representative adult. It also is essential to understand a student's emotional attitudes and history of relationships with adults. We suggest that you actually try to answer each question for yourself at the beginning of every LSCI. Then you must be able to convey answers to the student that will be most beneficial to the student's progress. Because the meanings and feelings behind these questions are complex, we use this entire chapter to provide a background. In Parts II and III you will find these ideas put into practice through LSCI. Let's take the questions one by one.

"WHO'S IN CHARGE HERE?" (AUTHORITY, ADULT ROLES, AND INFLUENCE)

Authority is a term with many meanings, referring variously to those in command, the source of support for a statement or defense for an action, power to influence thought or behavior, independence or freedom granted, and expertise. We use the term here to include all of these meanings because the adult using LSCI effectively must be able to convey all these forms of authority, as needed. What we *do not* mean in using the term is blind obedience, which defines a different approach—the authoritarian approach.

Adult authority stands as one of the most dynamic forces in the lives of all students. Whether they accept adults or reject them, students generally acknowledge the authority and power of adults. They also have strong social and emotional needs for adults, even if they reject adults. Students recognize that adults possess special knowledge and skills, and have power to order others around, make rules, decide what is right and wrong, judge, and reward or punish. Adults also solve problems, dispense care, and affirm students. Adults are the source of approval and disapproval. Students tend to see themselves in the mirror of the views adults hold about them.

At every age students are influenced by their needs for certain behaviors from significant adults. The way adults have responded in the past to those needs contributes to forming the behavior students use with adults in the present. Students' histories are a series of fulfilled and unfulfilled expectations. When students' expectations about adults have been met, they are left with feelings of well-being; adults can be counted on to handle problems, encourage and praise, provide, and do what is needed (right, just, kind, helpful, caring, bountiful). Unmet expectations leave students with a range of unsettled feelings and confusion about adults.

Changing Roles of Adults

Specific types of behaviors from adults toward students convey different types of authority. In the normal process of development, the type of adult authority needed by children and youth changes as they mature. These changing roles of adults in the nominal developmental process are well known. When used deliberately with students at particular stages of development, specific adult roles can promote students' social and emotional development. Table 4.1 contains a synopsis, highlighting typical adult roles based on normal social and emotional development of students in various age groups. By determining where a student is in this developmental progression, you can select the general type of adult authority and role needed to facilitate a student's particular stage of development. It is not too difficult to keep a particular role in mind as you begin LSCI with a student. When you do this, you will find the gap narrowing between adult expectations and student needs. This seems to reduce stress, and the tendency diminishes for a student to displace anger onto you as a stand-in for other adults who have failed to fulfill expectations in the past.

TABLE 4.1
The Changing Role of Adults

Adult Role	Approximate Student Age	Typical Social–Emotional Needs
Satisfier of needs	Birth to age 2	Babies need a particular type of adult behavior—nurture and care. To be effective, adults must provide security and a sense of comfort, conveying that the world is a pleasant place to be.
Teacher of standards, provider of approval, motivator	Ages 2 to 6	Preschool children need success and mastery in their first steps toward independence.
Upholder of authority, director of behavior	Ages 6 to 9	Primary grade students need new learning to expand mental and physical achievement and group skills.
Group facilitator, advocate of individuals, social role model	Ages 10 to 12	Upper elementary students need guidance as they shift from external to internal regulation of behavior and form new attachments to peers.
Counselor, advocate, confidant	Adolescence	Youths need models for values and new roles for independence, identity, new relationships, and responsibilities.

Note. Adapted from "Vibes, Values, and Virtues," by M. M. Wood, 1996, *Reclaiming Children and Youth, 5,* pp. 174–179. Copyright 1996 by PRO-ED, Inc. Adapted with permission.

Adult Strategies That Influence Student Behavior

Once you have determined the type of adult authority and role you should convey in a particular LSCI, you have a range of intervention strategies you can choose from to convey a particular role effectively. Because there are so many strategies to choose among, we find it helpful to group strategies according to style of influence and fit them to an individual student's view of adults. Adult styles of influence, when used selectively, cause students to do spontaneously what they might not ordinarily do on their own. When an adult is able to assist students in spontaneously changing behavior, a major gain has been made toward independent regulation of behavior.

The most frequently used strategies for adult influence can be grouped into four general forms: motivation, relationship, shared skills, and consequences. The following is a brief summary of each of these styles of influence.

Motivation

Motivation is the preferred form of influence, in which the adult is able to influence a student's behavior while not directly controlling it. This style of influence emphasizes the student as the central player, and works through motivation to foster spontaneous behavior control and participation. The emphasis is on using indirect, motivating strategies that enable students to participate spontaneously and self-direct in acceptable ways. Indirect strategies and highly motivating materials provide intrinsic feedback for success, catching students' interest and leading them to successful outcomes without the appearance of adult influence. Peer pressure, mobilized by an adult, is an example of influence through motivation. When students participate in an activity spontaneously, or without resistance, they have been motivated by some intrinsic aspect of the activity that seldom is overtly associated with adult control.

Strategies that influence through motivation are highly effective with students who are struggling with the developmental anxiety of conflict between the need to be independent and the need to be cared for by adults. Students who think they need to be independent of adult control often relax their defenses when they begin to experience success on their own with materials and activities, and then receive recognition from adults and peers for the accomplishment. Strategies that motivate also are effective with students who distrust adults intensely and those who have developed passive-aggressive strategies. Passive-aggressive students have highly developed skills in manipulating without confronting peers or adults directly. They are experts in manipulating for social power. When you counter with effective motivation, these students are allowed to participate and experience success in an endeavor without the problem of confrontation. At some point, however, adults working with such students will need to switch from this indirect form of influence, as the student becomes less defensive and a deeper relationship between adult and student develops. Direct verbal confrontation usually is necessary at some point with these students so that they will directly face the impact of their unacceptable behavior.

Relationship

Relationship is a form of adult influence built from intervention strategies that rely on the adult's personal characteristics and connection with the student to influence the student's behavior. The goal in using strategies that influence students through relationship and personal characteristics is to convey your recognition and approval of students' positive qualities, thereby strengthening confidence in themselves as valued people with qualities admired by you, other adults, and other students. It is a form of influence that promotes qualities like helpfulness, fairness, kindness, leadership, and honesty in students.

Students respond to adults who have characteristics that they admire and like. Examples of these adult characteristics are warmth, humor, enthusiasm, relaxed friendliness, fairness, helpfulness, and approval. Students also are influenced by mannerisms of admired role models. Because many students imitate these appealing adult characteristics, it is essential that adults provide such models of behavior if they want to influence these students.

Praise and affirmation are other major strategies for this form of influence. Varying voice tone can be used to effectively convey genuine interest, support, caring, surprise, or to pique motivation for an activity. Such strategies are highly effective with students who identify with adults as role models and seek adult relationship.

Adults are using relationship as a way of influencing students when they say:

"Please do this for me."
"I really like it when you do that."
"That is really good work!"
"I think that's the best you've ever done."
"I'm proud of you."

The effectiveness of this form of influence is evident when you hear students say:

"Miss Barkley, how do you like this?"
"I knew you wouldn't like what they did."
"I made this for you."
"I did what you wanted me to do."

You also can see the results in nonverbal behavior: students looking toward adults at a time when others are misbehaving, listening quietly and intently to what an adult is saying, directing the bulk of their social communication toward adults, spontaneously recalling what an adult has said to them on previous occasions, and volunteering bits and pieces of their most private thoughts and feelings.

Strategies involving friendship and the adult's personal characteristics are most effective when they are used in combination with other forms of influence. Friendship strategies and those that rely heavily on the adult's characteristics provide positive social role models and a personal, caring dimension to adult–student relationships. But when they are used by an adult as the primary source for influence, such strategies may promote personal dependency that restricts a student's development toward independence. Such student–adult relationships tend to turn into person-to-person bonding when the adult does not exercise necessary authority and the student fails to assume independent responsibility. Separation from such a relationship is very difficult for both student and adult. Appropriate boundaries are important in the teacher–student relationship.

Shared Skills

Shared skills is a category of strategies that conveys the adult's ability to help a student solve a problem that the student cannot handle alone. The goal in using strategies of this type is to teach new skills for social problem solving by providing models in the adult's own behavior, and sharing skills and insight about the problem. The adult uses strategies that support a student through the waves of self-doubt, recrimination, panic, and anger brought on during crisis. The adult affirms the student's strengths, reviews social interactions, and interprets the behavior of others for the student. Then together they come up with a plan for the use of new ways to behave to avoid such distress in the future.

A high level of trust develops between a student and an adult who shares expertise to help the student understand events and solve a crisis. Students also recognize an adult as an expert when a crisis is managed successfully and calmly by the adult. Students respond to the expertise of the adult who decodes their behavior and that of others. Their responses to an adult's expertise may be reluctant at first, but when they begin to observe, listen, and think, then the decoding is accurate.

Sharing skills and expertise is misinterpreted by some adults who present themselves to students as skilled superiors, or who display their own particular accomplishments for the students to admire (and emulate?). Remember, the purpose is to help the student solve a crisis that the student cannot solve alone!

An adult is using strategies to share skills and expertise with students when the adult makes statements like the following:

"You don't need to worry, staff are in charge here."

"I've had other students with this problem, and this is how we handled it."

"I've been watching how you were doing in that difficult situation; you figured it out correctly."

"Your behavior tells me that something else is really bothering you."

When adults are effective in helping students solve problems, the result is trust, admiration, and a positive relationship with the adult. An adult who shares skills with a student in crisis also creates a climate of security in which the student has a new sense of freedom to learn because energy is not misdirected into defensive behaviors.

Consequences

Fear of consequences underlies a category of strategies that influences students' behavior. Often students respond to a reality consequence as if it were a personality issue between student and teacher. Consequences should be seen as results of the student's behavior. Some forms of discipline, "contract" programs, and reward/reinforcement systems modify behavior through sophisticated versions of this type of influence. The underlying fear is that deprivation or punishment will result if the student fails to meet behavioral expectations. Examples of adult strategies that influence through reality consequences include privileges denied, withholding adult approval, time-out, authoritative or physical proximity (standing over a student), hostile verbal confrontation, restriction, suspension, and exclusion.

When adults continually use strategies that are threatening, as opposed to giving students choices with reality consequences, students are left in a powerless position. Powerless, students either give up, which arrests further development, or begin to acquire negative attitudes, defensive behaviors, and resistance to adults. When this happens, anger often is subverted to passive aggression or explodes in violent or cruel acts.

With a few exceptions, these strategies seldom contribute to creating an environment conducive to successful LSCI. We only use such strategies with students who are so entrenched in their own unacceptable behaviors and alibi systems that they have great difficulty accepting the idea that change in behavior is needed. Students who have been in environments where adults have extensively used coercion and fear against them often rely on these types of behaviors themselves. With such students, you may need to begin as a powerful authority, using fear of consequences to maintain discipline. This may be the only type of authority they understand initially. All students must know that an adult (authority) is in control and that they are physically and psychologically safe. When you find it necessary to use such strategies to influence students' behavior, keep the encounter short and look for ways to change to strategies based on other forms of influence. You will find the climate changing rapidly in a positive direction when you switch strategies.

Summary of Adult Roles

The answer to the first question raised in this chapter, "Who's in charge here?" is simple: It must be the adult! But this answer does not imply authoritarian control. Rather, it requires an adult to convey the type of adult role that will produce the greatest possible social and emotional development for the student.

Some students need clearly visible adult action that cares for, controls, and directs the student. Other students need a less central, less visible adult so that their independence and personal responsibility will develop. Using the chart presented in Table 4.1, you can identify the general type of adult role that each of your students needs for optimal development.

The effectiveness of your influence with students will be the degree to which they do what you expect them to do. Most strategies for influencing student behavior can be grouped into one of these categories: motivation, relationship, shared skills, or consequences. Adults exercise these forms of influence over students almost continually, sometimes intentionally, other times unknowingly. The extent to which an adult is effective depends on an accurate fit between the strategies the adult uses and the student's present attitudes and past experiences with adults. An effective adult must be able to understand what type of influence is needed for a particular student in a specific crisis and use the strategies that convey it, as the need arises.

Study the strategies you typically use to influence students. If you find that you are relying on only one adult role and using only one or two types of strategies to influence your students, broaden your repertoire. To be effective in LSCI, you should be able to use strategies from all four types of influences to convey the adult role needed by your individual students.

"WHO'S GOING TO HANDLE THIS PROBLEM?" (THE EXISTENTIAL CRISIS)

The previous discussion focused on adult authority and the absolute need for adults to influence the psychological and interpersonal climate in positive ways during crisis. An adult must always have control of the environment during crisis. But this does not imply that the adult is responsible for the solution to every crisis. In this section, we consider the second major question raised in this chapter: Who resolves the crisis? Is it the adult's or the student's responsibility?

Few students are capable of managing crisis resolution independently when LSCI is needed. Yet in LSCI students must begin to learn how to assume responsibility for their behavior and its consequences. The long-term goal of LSCI is to teach students to regulate their own behavior and meet their own emotional needs in appropriate ways without dependence on adults. We view this gradual transfer of authority and responsibility for problem solving from adult to student as occurring in three phases centering around a major developmental event in the lives of all children and youth. We call this developmental event the Existential Crisis.

The Existential Crisis is a phase in social-emotional development when a student's belief in the absolute, omnipotent authority of adults begins to falter (Wood, 1996). It is called existential because it deals with new awareness about the limitations of adults for taking care of life events in satisfactory ways. This uncertainty about adults leads a student to question authority and to look for other sources of security. It is called a crisis because it raises concerns about alternatives to adults taking care of problems, with the possibility that the student must be responsible. Most students doubt their own ability. Yet they must change, learn new behaviors, and take on new consequences. The challenge is nearly overwhelming to some students.

As we begin each LSCI, we have found it helpful to determine if the student is in the preexistential phase, going through the Existential Crisis, or in the postexistential phase. If the student is preexistential, the LSCI will need to be directed and controlled by the adult. If the student is going through the Existential Crisis, the LSCI must provide abundant adult support and direction but also must begin to shift responsibility for crisis resolution to the student. For students in the postexistential phase, the LSCI focus is on assisting them to handle crisis with independence and a focus on personal responsibility. To help you recognize which of these general phases each of your students are in, we briefly review the dynamics involved and the management strategies that are appropriate for each phase.

The Preexistential Phase

In the preexistential phase, a student's emotional need is for an expert and all-powerful adult who directs behavior, makes rules, judges violators, punishes the guilty, handles all problems, provides protection, and provides what is needed for satisfaction. When students conform, adults like them and therefore will reward them.

To preexistential students, adult authority is all-powerful. Every first grade teacher knows about preexistential students:

"Teacher! Teacher! . . ."
"He's not playing by the rules."
"Make her give it to me."
"He's bothering me."
"I'm going to tell my mother."

Notice how each remark is directed to the adult, even though the issue involves peers. Such responses are normal for students under age nine. Adults are seen as benevolent authority, dictating and enforcing standards of behavior. In the view of preexistential students, adults are responsible. These students look to them for protection, problem solving, and maintenance of law and order.

Adults use many behavior management strategies that suit this stage of development and that are useful during the problem-solving stages of LSCI with preexistential students. The following are several examples:

- Token systems

- Fixed classroom procedures

- Contingencies for adult approval
- Systems of concrete rewards (smiling faces, grades, treats, privileges, selection by teacher as "leader," checks)
- Rules and prescribed punishments
- Adults as behavioral role models

When you are using LSCI with older students who are still preexistential in their development, these management strategies can provide only short-term solutions to crisis. These students expect to be controlled by outside force. However, if you continue to rely only on these approaches, the students will remain preexistential; that is, they will continue to look to you as the enforcer, the one responsible for finding solutions to their problems. At some point you will have to take these students through the Existential Crisis and into the postexistential period. The management issue here is one of gradually shifting the source of authority and responsibility from external controls to controls from within. It will not happen if you continue to maintain external control at all times; students will simply continue to rely on you to set standards and then will test and defy you as they experiment with independence.

During LSCI, there are many opportunities for learning self-regulation. Much self-regulation comes through the opportunity to explore alternatives and make choices. Throughout LSCI there are opportunities for individual input, exploration of "what happens when . . . ," alternative rules to live by, and alternative behaviors to choose. Every successful choice moves responsible, independent development one step closer to self-governance and responsibility. Every failed choice halts the progress and leaves authority, responsibility, and control with the adult.

The Existential Crisis

Normally, this period starts about the time children begin school and continues for several years until the student has completed the shift from relying on adults as the sole source of authority and behavior control (preexistential) to a view of authority as coming from more than one source, including oneself, and assuming responsibility for control of one's own behavior.

During the Existential Crisis, students have doubts and uncertainty about adults. This leads to testing adult authority and credibility, defying directions, ignoring rules, denying responsibility, and shifting blame to others. During this phase, students vacillate unpredictably, one minute trying to conform to adults' expectations and then defying these same standards, losing control, regressing, or assaulting others.

Examples of strategies that are useful during LSCI with students who are in the Existential Crisis phase include the following:

- Positive feedback and praise from adults
- Verbal reflection of words, actions, and feelings

- Interpretation of meanings behind behavior (decoding)
- Adult responsibility for rule maintenance and consequences

The volatility and lack of stability in student–adult relationships make this period particularly difficult for many adults. It requires us to use preexistential strategies (adult authority and control) at one time and then switch to postexistential strategies (adult guidance but not control) when a student begins to show control and responsibility for self-management. By recognizing and understanding the dynamics of the Existential Crisis, you can prepare to provide changes in your own strategies, loosening and tightening control as needed.

Should we be concerned about younger students who go through the Existential Crisis too soon because of life experiences that have thrown them out on their own at an early age? What about older students who have failed to resolve the Existential Crisis satisfactorily—will such deviations in the normal sequence of development affect their behavior and the way they are managed in the classroom? The answer is clearly, "Yes!" These will be controlling, testing, untrusting, manipulative students who do not take adult direction, yet avoid responsibility for their own behavior. They cannot accept authority and cannot allow adults to direct them. They seek reassurance and nurturing while lashing out at the adults from whom they seek approval and support.

The Postexistential Phase

As students turn increasingly to peers for behavioral models and affirmations of themselves, there is gradual detachment from psychological dependency on adults. Adults now become mirrors for students to see themselves as others see them and to encourage students in independent, self-regulated behavior. As this course to independence is charted, adults are needed as backstops when challenges become overwhelming and behavioral skills are insufficient for successful navigation through crisis.

Effective teachers in upper elementary school and high school know about postexistential students and have teaching styles that allow independence while providing sufficient direction for students to achieve success in independent personal and educational endeavors. These adults serve as role models for effective interpersonal relationships and independence in problem solving. Postexistential students know they have responsibility for self-regulation and generally exercise some degree of responsibility for crisis resolution. In LSCIs with postexistential students, you will see them making an effort to resolve the crisis, making suggestions that show a sense of responsibility for the crisis and the resolution.

Summary of Who Is Responsible

In summary, the answer to the second question in this chapter, "Who's going to handle this problem?" is that it must be the student, with adult support to the extent that the student needs an adult in order to have a satisfactory resolution. To determine this need, we use the existential crisis as the reference point, using the three-phase guide summarized in this section. Begin every LSCI with a quick review of how your student views adults. Some students will have the preexistential view that adults must solve problems and are responsible for crisis resolution because they are in charge. Other students will be experiencing the Existential Crisis, in which they will swing between attempts to solve a crisis on their own and retreat to a preexistential position, defer to adult authority, and deny responsibility. Postexistential students will make attempts to resolve a crisis, even if their skills and judgment are seriously lacking. From this information, you will be able to balance the extent to which you assist and direct a student during each LSCI or leave the selection of a solution and implementation plan to the student.

"HOW DO I KNOW IT'S GOING TO BE ALL RIGHT FOR ME?" (MOTIVATION TO BE RESPONSIBLE)

The previous discussions focused on adult authority and the absolute need for adults to influence the psychological and interpersonal climate of LSCI. We also described the changes students go through during the Existential Crisis as they begin to doubt the absolute nature of adult authority and learn that problems must be faced by themselves (with adult support). The question we raise in this section considers a student's motivation to be responsible for personal behavior and crisis resolution.

While we are concerned with making the transfer from adult authority to student responsibility, the student is concerned that personal needs will be met. Students behave in ways that produce results they value. They also try to avoid causing results they do not value. Values are the internal rules students (and adults) live by. They are the fixed points of reference for daily behavior—the glue that holds together the structure we know as personality and character. What students care about is what they value. Their values shape their choice of activities, influence their reactions to stress, and regulate their behavior.

What the student cares about the most during crisis is to avoid the unpleasant feelings of stress. This is the fundamental value. The Conflict Cycle presented in Chapter 2 is fueled by this motivation for self-protection. Any attempt to break the cycle must guarantee that emotional stress will not continue. Satisfactory resolution of crisis must be constructed from this fundamental value. Unless emotional protection is provided, students will not be able to change established patterns of defensive and unacceptable behavior. Students must believe that, in the end, they will be all right. When they believe this, they will participate in crisis resolution. If they doubt that their own interests are being considered, they will raise their defenses.

But assurance of emotional protection is only the first element in successful crisis resolution. Central to every goal in LSCI is the idea of learning independent responsibility for behavior. This gradual transition from guaranteed protection to independent, self-regulated behavior is not an easy task. To exchange dependence on others for independent responsibility requires a powerful motivation.

How do we provide this motivation for behavior change? Think of providing motivation as building solutions to crisis based on (a) a gradual change in a student's values, and (b) a gradual shift away from emotional dependency on adults toward emotional independence. The following is a review of these ideas in a framework that should be helpful in identifying your students' values and levels of emotional dependency. From such information, you will be able to build motivations during LSCI for them to change their behavior.

Identifying Students' Values

Students' values develop in a natural sequence that can be summarized in five general stages: personal needs, adult approval, fairness, responsibility for self, and responsibility for others (Wood, 1996, pp. 88–90). The basic value begins with the premise that one's own needs are paramount. Any behavior that meets personal needs is satisfactory.

Gradually, students move from that orientation to a belief that adults' standards are the ones that bring personal benefits; therefore, their behavior should conform to please adults and avoid punishment. As students develop further, their views broaden to include justice and fairness as valuable guidelines for regulating their own behavior. When fairness first emerges as a value for regulating behavior, students are concerned that they receive fair treatment from others. Gradually, their view of fairness expands to include fairness for others. Finally, students embrace society's values of responsibility for self-regulation, justice, and care of others. Empathy and altruism also are added as values that regulate behavior.

Figure 4.1 summarizes this sequence of values and provides examples of solutions to crisis that would be considered satisfactory to students holding these particular values. (We refer to this sequence again in Part II, Stage 4 of LSCI.) In this illustration the band of dotted lines indicates the approximate place in the developmental sequence when the Existential Crisis occurs. The two concepts tie together students' changing values and their changing views of authority. Concern about personal needs begins to blend into the notion that satisfactory interactions with others bring satisfactory results for oneself. With this development, a student's sense of responsibility begins to broaden to include the possibility of giving up something in order to get something in return.

The arrows in Figure 4.1 indicate ways to challenge students to consider solutions at the next stage in the sequence of values. As you bring LSCI to the solution stages, you have two basic choices: (a) encourage students to choose solutions at their present stage of values, or (b) challenge students to consider solutions at a higher stage. Sometimes

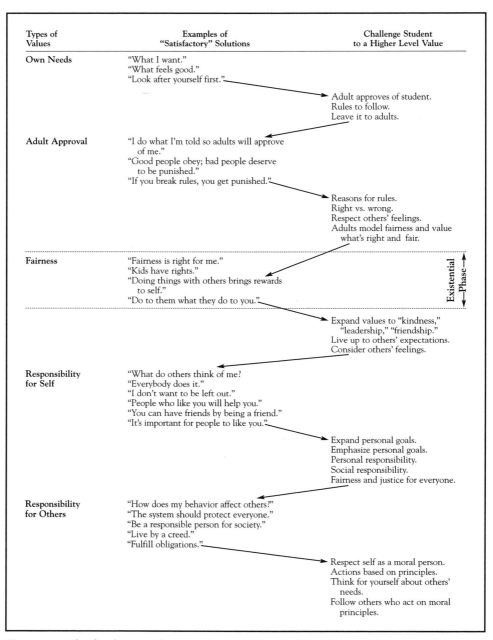

Types of Values	Examples of "Satisfactory" Solutions	Challenge Student to a Higher Level Value
Own Needs	"What I want." "What feels good." "Look after yourself first."	
		Adult approves of student. Rules to follow. Leave it to adults.
Adult Approval	"I do what I'm told so adults will approve of me." "Good people obey; bad people deserve to be punished." "If you break rules, you get punished."	
		Reasons for rules. Right vs. wrong. Respect others' feelings. Adults model fairness and value what's right and fair.
Fairness	"Fairness is right for me." "Kids have rights." "Doing things with others brings rewards to self." "Do to them what they do to you."	*Existential Phase*
		Expand values to "kindness," "leadership," "friendship." Live up to others' expectations. Consider others' feelings.
Responsibility for Self	"What do others think of me? "Everybody does it." "I don't want to be left out." "People who like you will help you." "You can have friends by being a friend." "It's important for people to like you."	
		Expand personal goals. Emphasize personal goals. Personal responsibility. Social responsibility. Fairness and justice for everyone.
Responsibility for Others	"How does my behavior affect others?" "The system should protect everyone." "Be a responsible person for society." "Live by a creed." "Fulfill obligations."	
		Respect self as a moral person. Actions based on principles. Think for yourself about others' needs. Follow others who act on moral principles.

Figure 4.1. The developmental sequence of values used to determine "satisfactory" results.

it is necessary to guide students to choose solutions to crisis that are a part of their current value system. These solutions may include results that will bring specific benefits or better feelings, concrete incentives, adults providing rules and highlighting consequences, or adult affirmation and approval for "the right choice." These are preexistential solutions, necessary because the student may have tenuous confidence in making choices or doubts about your reliability as an adult authority. Such students will resist making choices, leaving it up to adults instead. However, if you continue to fill the adult-as-authority role too long, you may restrict the student's development, and responsible independence will not develop. When you notice themes of fairness in a student's remarks, you can be confident that the student is moving beyond the Existential Crisis and may be ready for some self-responsibility. Then it is time to challenge the student to consider solutions at the next stage. You probably will find the student receptive to new ideas for solutions with themes of friendship, leadership, consideration, responsibility, and kindness.

One caution about challenges: Sometimes adults tend to foster solutions to crisis that are beyond a student's current ability to handle successfully. If a planned solution has no value to the student or the expectation requires too great a leap forward for the student to accomplish, the desired behavior will not be forthcoming and the plan will fail.

Identifying Students' Emotional Dependence

A goal of most intervention programs, like the goal for LSCI, is learning independent control of behavior. When a student exits a program, the expectation is that the learning will generalize (independently) into other settings. It is enormously frustrating to most adults when students fail to achieve this goal. This failure may indicate chronic emotional dependence. Emotional dependence sustains the preexistential values held by some students about adults (described previously in this chapter). Students who are emotionally dependent still fear that their own needs may not be met by significant adults. As long as a student clings to this view, the student will not be able to assume independent regulation of personal behavior. The student will be preoccupied with meeting emotional needs and protecting feelings.

Another form of emotional dependency results when a student lacks or has failed to form primary attachments to an adult or has been deprived of emotional care and support. Attachment is a concept that describes the essential human need to be connected and cared for. This fundamental need for emotional attachment may supersede all other behavioral motivators. It provides children and youth with confidence that they are valued by others. Normally an infant's caregiver is the first source of emotional significance. When students' basic need for emotional attachment has been satisfied, they do not have to struggle to attain it. They use it as a base of confidence to venture beyond the attachment to pursue new relationships and independence.

If attachments fail or never develop, emotional dependence results. A student has to put major effort into seeking and holding on to substitutes. Failed attachment is a major part of the first developmental anxiety, abandonment (discussed in Chapter 3). If this anxiety is left unresolved, the student may seek substitute forms of gratification (e.g., work, hoarding, overeating, addiction, etc.) that erode interpersonal relationships and can severely modify the course of an individual's personality development. Such students often lack empathy and sensitivity to the feelings of others. They bend rules to gratify their own needs, operating from a "look out for number one" basis.

The developmental counterforce to attachment is separation, a drive for independence. Students show a willingness to forgo primary attachments as they mature, seeking independence. The success of the separation process depends on the previous success during the attachment phase of emotional development. Successful separation centers around the balance adults achieve between providing security and comfort (dependency needs) and simultaneously allowing freedom (independence needs). This is the daily challenge for children, youth, and adults.

If the separation process is experienced without success, psychological independence may not be achieved. Fear of failure, fear of inadequacy, and fear of not measuring up to the expectations of others spiral into a restricted personality. Such students fail to take initiative, resist change and new experiences, pander to others, and follow those who will control and direct them (the developmental anxiety, inadequacy, described in Chapter 3). These students also may be selected as scapegoats or isolates by their peers.

Whenever the attachment process or the separation process fails, anger is a major by-product. A student feels anger toward family members who have failed to nurture and protect, and anger at those who have ridiculed and criticized the student's attempts at independence. These failed relationships from home and community permeate the student's view of adults at school. They bring this emotional baggage with them. And their teachers become the substitute adults, the recipients of the anger these students hold toward adults outside of school.

In contrast, resolution of the conflict between attachment and separation produces emotional independence. It is clearly observable in most students in upper elementary school. These students believe that the important adults really care and will provide emotional protection when it is needed, while permitting the students freedom to be successfully independent. Such students have no need to be preoccupied with protecting themselves emotionally. Keep in mind, however, that all students continue to experience stress, and they never will be totally independent of their need for emotional support and relationships with adults they admire. Emotional independence increases in direct correspondence to the extent to which dependency needs (attachment) are met and independent experiences are successful.

The following is a simple example of failure to maintain this delicate balance between the dependence and independence needs of a middle school student. This brief exchange was overheard at an office telephone.

JACK: Mom, when are you coming home?

MOM: You'll know when I walk through the door.

In this simple exchange is a depth of implicit emotional need. These two lines are not sufficient to tell us exactly what the need is, but it is there. Consider the many possible needs. Jack needs to connect to his important adult. This may be an exchange that fosters independent behavior, or it may erode it. There may be connections and reassurance between mother and son, or it may be an expression of Jack's insecurity or Mom's insensitivity. Could it simply be a call made when things are boring at home? Permission to leave? For transportation elsewhere? To be relieved of babysitting a younger child? To talk about something important that has happened? For reassurance that Mom is all right? To reassure Mom that he is all right? (Does she want to know?) For the hope of protection against real or imagined terror at home?

And what about Mom's response? We do not know if this is her "style" or if she is conveying some of her genuine feelings about Jack. Could it be a simple put-off because she thinks Jack should not bother her at work? Maybe she thinks Jack should learn to be on his own and not cling to her. She may resent Jack for reminding her of her burdens at home. Could there be remnants of her own conflict between emotional attachment and independence in her response?

Jack's reaction to Mom's abrupt remark will also be drawn from the same attachment-independence needs. He will interpret and respond to Mom from either need, whichever is paramount for Jack. Does he hear it as a put-down? Rejection? Dislike? Criticism? Could he resent the restriction of staying home? Perhaps he resents adult control? Or perhaps this is such a standard exchange that neither Jack nor Mom thinks anything about it. If this exchange is typical between Jack and his mother, it is a legacy that he will carry with him—adults are indifferent to his needs and so, for emotional insulation, he will be indifferent to them. This behavioral defense may come to school with Jack. The following is a teacher–student interaction that mimics the indifference in the parent-child exchange:

TEACHER: Jack, you must hurry along to finish your assignment before the end of this period.

JACK: I'll do it when I feel like it. And maybe I won't do it at all.

Jack's behavior comes from his history with adults: the models they have presented, the feelings they have aroused, and the developmental anxiety that has become a part of his personality as he struggles to resolve the conflict between his growing independence and his latent need to be cared for by others. The strength of his feelings about adults will play out in LSCI between Jack and his teacher.

Summary of Students' Motivations To Be Responsible

In summary, the answer to the third question in this chapter, "How do I know it's going to be all right for me?" is that students must believe that their emotional needs will be met. Until they are secure in this belief, they will not move toward appropriate, independently regulated behavior. Students will take ownership of a solution to crisis when they can see it to be of value to themselves. These values are the internal regulators of students' behaviors. To have an effective outcome of LSCI, a resolution to the crisis must be framed within the context of current values held by the student. The belief that something beneficial will occur in exchange for using a new behavior is a fundamental motivation for change.

During LSCI it is essential to determine what a student really values. This information then can guide you as the LSCI shifts focus to solutions. A solution to crisis that takes into account a student's values will be accepted as satisfactory. When a student believes that a solution is possible and desirable, the student will take ownership of it. To produce lasting change from LSCI, solutions must be owned by the student, not the adult.

The gradual transfer of responsibility from external control to appropriate, independent, self-regulated behavior also depends upon successful transition through the Existential Crisis, from emotional dependence to emotional independence. Emotional dependency is a major roadblock toward independent responsibility. Students must experience freedom from concern about protecting their feelings and meeting their own emotional needs, if they are to achieve emotional independence. When you use LSCI, awareness of a student's level of emotional dependency is essential. It is a major force in the eventual progress made toward accomplishing LSCI goals.

SUMMARY OF AUTHORITY, RESPONSIBILITY, AND MOTIVATION

The topics covered in this chapter are sometimes difficult to apply at first reading. Although we included a summary at the end of each topical section, it may be helpful to integrate the information by considering the following application. The concepts we are dealing with are adults' roles, influence of adults, students' existential phases as they change from outer- to inner-directed behavior, personal values that regulate students' behavior, and the extent of students' emotional dependency. The example of Harry illustrates how you can use this material. We have identified Harry's shifting values, using Figure 4.1; the three-phase guidelines for Harry's position in relation to the Existential Crisis; the various adult roles and influence, using Figure 4.1; and the extent of Harry's emotional dependence, using observations of Harry's behavior and remarks.

It is not surprising to find that age does not necessarily determine views about authority or the values students use. We see numbers of older students responding to crisis with simple, self-protective values. We also see students who attempt to use more complex values. When they are not successful in their independent attempts to solve a crisis with these values, they tend to slip back to more primitive values. Unfortunately, it often is an adult, using inappropriate values and ineffective forms of influence, who provides the inappropriate model. The following is a brief example of such a student and the adults who are involved in his crisis.

Harry

A fight breaks out on the middle school bus. Harry is a known instigator and has a history of fights and suspensions. His view is that he is being picked on by the others and is simply defending himself. The scenario unfolds in a typical way. The angry bus driver reports Harry to the assistant principal. Harry cools his heels in the outer office for an hour or so until the assistant principal returns for a talk. The result is a call to Harry's mother and another suspension. Harry (H) explains all of this to the coach (C) as he prepares to leave school.

H: I got busted again.

C: The bus?

H: It wasn't my fault! Leon had some bleach in a spray bottle, and he threatened to spray me with it.

▶ **VALUE:** Modeling adult standards of right versus wrong.

EXISTENTIAL PHASE: Postexistential. Student tries to handle the problem independently.

C: What did you do?

H: (Defensively.) I told him to put it away or I'd kick his ass! It's my right to protect myself!

▶ **VALUE:** Rights for self.

EXISTENTIAL PHASE: Postexistential.

C: You thought Leon might really be serious?

H: You can't ever tell about Leon!

C: So, what happened next?

H: He didn't put it away so I told the driver that Leon had some bleach.

▶ **VALUE:** Adults are powerful and should protect students.

EXISTENTIAL PHASE: Crisis. Independence was not working, so adult authority was needed.

C: What did she do?

H: She told us to get off the bus or settle down. Then she turned us both in.

C: Now you're suspended! What will happen when you get home?

H: I guess my mother will get mad about them throwing me out of school when it wasn't my fault. So she'll come down here and straighten out that principal. She won't let them pick on me!

▶ **VALUE:** Adults are powerful.

EXISTENTIAL PHASE: Preexistential.

C: Will she punish you?

H: Nah, she'll wait for my dad.

C: What will he do?

H: He's always telling me to stick up for myself. He says there's only one way to settle some scores. He'll tell me, "Next time, Harry, just beat the shit out of Leon, so he'll know not to pick on you again!"

▶ **VALUE:** Adult authorizes punishment for bad kids.

EXISTENTIAL PHASE: Preexistential.

Harry tries to solve this problem on his own, at a fairly advanced value level. Without success from his first attempts to handle the problem himself (postexistential), Harry gradually regresses to a preexistential attitude that it is someone else's problem (his mother's) and he will follow the authority of the powerful adult in his life (his dad).

Track back through this scenario again to identify the vacillations in the adult roles and types of influence conveyed to Harry:

Bus driver [Sent Harry to office for punishment]

Role: Upholder of law and order

Influence: Fear of consequences

Assistant principal   [Sent Harry home for punishment]

                        Role: Upholder of law and order

                        Influence: Fear of consequences

Coach   [No shared skills; perhaps friendship?]

                        Role: Counselor, friend

                        Influence: Not clear

Mother   [Wait for father]

                        Role: Advocate

                        Influence: Shared skills [taking care of basic need for protection] and fear of consequences

Father   *Role:* Teacher of behavior

                        Influence: Fear of consequences

Harry's attempts at emotional and behavioral independence crumble under pressure. We can be fairly confident that Harry is still emotionally dependent on the approval, power, and authority of adults.

Compare this analysis with Figure 4.1, which outlines the general sequence of adult roles needed by students to develop social and emotional maturity. It is clear that each adult is responding to Harry from a personal "style," with no thought of Harry's potential for social problem solving and what he needs in order to learn to regulate his own behavior and resolve the crisis independently. The coach was a key. He could have used this crisis to reinforce Harry's emerging attempts to solve problems in appropriate ways. It was a time for LSCI!

If you had been the coach and carried the LSCI forward, what role would you have taken? What type of strategies would have been helpful in influencing Harry to change his behavior? What existential phase should you emphasize? What value level should be used as you and Harry approach the resolution phase of LSCI? These are the same questions to be answered as you begin every LSCI.

EXAMPLE OF ADULT ROLES
AND STUDENT VALUES

By now you should be quite comfortable with the LSCI between student and teacher in "The Math Problem Crisis" at the end of Chapter 1. Let's go back to that example to see how the concepts from this chapter are applied in a full LSCI with Dane.

Dane's Values: He has not yet learned to care about being recognized for personal initiative, for being responsible, and for people to see him as mature. He needed the adult to encourage him to approach the next value stage for adolescents: being a responsible citizen and contributing to the group well-being.

His View Of Adults: Existential. Dane acts on his own impulses, but expects adults to correct him and set the limits. The LSCI reinforces his emerging level of responsibility while expanding Dane's understanding of competing values (his own and that of authorities).

Adult	Role of Adult	Influence Strategies
Teacher	Upholder of law and order; also advocate	Motivation (encouragement to be responsible)
Assistant	Upholder of law and order	None, in this situation

In contrast to Harry, Dane, who is struggling with his math assignment versus his desire to go to gym, gives many indications of emotional dependence. He shows that he still relies on adults to keep him on the right track. What is clearly evident is that Dane needs affirmation for his fledgling attempts at acknowledging his poor choice, and support from adults to grow toward becoming independent and responsible. He needs support as he learns that self-directed behavior must be restrained when results may work against him. He is clearly ready for this insight, and the LSCI with Dane in Chapter 1 is on target.

WHAT WE HOPE YOU HAVE LEARNED FROM THIS CHAPTER

- The five general types of adult roles, and the social and emotional support these roles provide to students

- A definition of an adult's social influence from a student's viewpoint

- Four general types of influence used by adults in their daily work with students

- The adult role and type of influence you typically use, as you work with students in crisis

- The three-phase guideline for identifying a student's attitude about who should solve problems

- Examples of intervention strategies to be used with students in the preexistential, post-existential, and Existential Crisis phases in their relationships with adults

- The sequence of five general types of values that can influence a student's ownership of a solution to a crisis

- How emotional dependence can keep a student from learning self-regulated behavior

Anatomy of Life Space Crisis Intervention

II

In Part II, we describe each stage of LSCI with an introduction to the purpose and content of the stage, a description of what happens in each stage, a synopsis of what the adult should do and say, and suggestions about how to end a stage and bridge into the next one. By outlining the six stages of LSCI, we hope we have given you enough detail to learn a basic structure for using LSCI in crisis situations with almost any student.

As you read this book, you are building a mental model of LSCI. In order to help you form a construct for what LSCI is, we have presented the skills in a "paint-by-number" format. Our goal is to help you to forge a gestalt, or whole picture, of LSCI. The stages are clearly outlined and sequenced. In actual practice, however, you will find the LSCI stages blending together. Often you will cycle back to repeat a stage as new information or insight is brought out. To continue the metaphor, real-life application of LSCI is not a paint-by-number experience; it is more like watercolor painting, in which stages and insights blend together. Gradually, as the stages become familiar, you will see many more ways to use LSCI than we are able to describe in a single book.

The last chapter in this section contains our perspective on the entire helping process. We believe it is important to view every LSCI in this framework—as a helping process. We include a checklist of skills adults need for using LSCI effectively. To illustrate how small errors in strategy can cause adults to lose the helping perspective, we also include a review of potential pitfalls.

We hope that you will find LSCI such an effective strategy for helping students through a crisis that it will become one of your most frequently used interventions. Throughout your LSCI experiences, keep focused on the end results you can obtain with this process: positive change in a student's view of self, ownership of solutions to resolve crisis, responsibility for changing behavior, and greater understanding of others' reactions. Gradually, over a series of LSCIs, there should be a reduction in a student's emotional memory bank of negative thoughts and feelings. The student's changing insights, behavior, and underlying feelings begin to build self-esteem because of greater insight, more impulse control, more positive feelings about self and others, and more positive self-regulated behavior.

"Talking about my past is like trying to put Humpty Dumpty back together again."

A Guide to LSCI Basics

5

When you work closely with children and youth in crisis, their personality characteristics and patterns of behavior for maintaining an emotional comfort level become apparent. Some students become aggressive and willful, blaming others for their misfortunes. Others put gratification of needs first and feel little guilt. Still others become confused and disoriented under stress, while others withdraw from involvement, develop debilitating anxieties, experience profound guilt, or spend their energies defending against real or imagined inadequacies in themselves or others. Most of these students are unaware of their ways of dealing with stress and crisis. Unless they learn to recognize these behaviors and feelings in themselves, and change their responses to stress, the Conflict Cycle (see Chapter 2) will continue unabated. For many students, it is safer to believe that the world picks on them than to feel that they are "no good," "a misfit," or "stupid."

Students often are in crisis because they have failed to recognize the meaning of events that have led to the crisis. Their perceptions and insights about an event are distorted by their defenses and the intensity of their emotional reactions to stress. They fail to anticipate the reactions of others and seldom see how their own behavior contributed to the crisis.

Crisis is the result of students' unsuccessful attempts to cope with stress at a specific moment. Usually, their reactions to stress are emotional and defensive rather than rational. The incident touches their vulnerable private storehouse of thoughts and feelings; and they react with more feelings, words that upset others, and counterproductive behaviors. The result is the Conflict Cycle we describe in Chapter 2: Reaction to stress evokes negative reactions from others, which, in turn, cause more uncomfortable feelings in the student, more unacceptable behavior, and more negative reactions from others. From this cycle, a crisis is born.

LSCI is a verbal strategy for providing active intervention in students' lives in times of crisis. It assists students to understand and cope with the specific crisis that they could not handle on their own. It is conducted by someone who is part of their natural environment and takes place as soon as possible after the incident occurs. The time shortly after crisis is a productive time for students to learn new social skills and gain new insights into their own feelings and behavior and that of others. Because current behaviors have failed them and emotional distress has intensified, students are more receptive to change immediately following crisis than at any other time. By using LSCI, the adult conveys to a student that (a) problems can be solved, (b) the student has an advocate in the adult, (c) the adult sees the good qualities in the student, (d) the student has the skills to solve the crisis, and (e) even though the student must exercise restraint, he or she is still a valued individual.

USING LSCI WITH A GROUP

The focus of this chapter is on the basic LSCI stages used with an individual student, but the application for use with a small group of students is similar. We use this LSCI process frequently with two students, or a group, when they have been party to the crisis. Group LSCI sometimes follows an individual LSCI, when one student has played a central role in a crisis but the group has been involved. Bringing the issue back to the group emphasizes group responsibility and individual responsibility to maintain a satisfactory group. Sometimes we begin with group LSCI, when a crisis is clouded by the involvement of everyone. As we go through the LSCI stages with the group, several central issues begin to emerge. Usually, this is followed by one or more individual LSCIs, as particular perpetrators, instigators, and victims are identified.

When using LSCI with a group, the adult must take the central role and maintain control. Relationships in a group are usually tentative, volatile, and can be destructive to individuals if care is not exercised to provide psychological protection for everyone participating. Face-saving and posturing for peers is a major element that you will find in most group LSCI. Individuals under stress must be supported when emotionally charged discussions begin. Individual group members also must learn how to participate in group discussions constructively and be respectful of each other's space.

Morgan (1981) summarizes the group LSCI process vividly in his illustrations of its use in therapeutic camp settings. He describes five applications for group LSCI: organizing group functions, solving group problems, reinforcing group values and expectations, reinforcing a healthy group perspective, and creating awareness of group progress. Morgan also emphasizes the skills needed by an adult using LSCI with a group: "The teacher must be aware of the prevailing group code, roles, and the power structure as basic conditions of leading a group LSCI" (p. 37).

Similarly, for teachers and therapists using Developmental Therapy, the group LSCI is a major intervention strategy with students learning to invest in group processes (Developmental Therapy Institute, 1992; Wood, 1996). There are important developmental milestones to achieve that goal that can be taught with group LSCI. The following is a summary of such milestones:

- Participating in group discussion appropriately
- Interacting with peers in socially acceptable ways

- Expressing pride in group achievement
- Asserting oneself in a group
- Responding appropriately to the group's leadership choices
- Participating in group problem solving
- Expressing feeling appropriately in the group
- Responding to group suggestions
- Respecting others' opinions
- Identifying others' differing values
- Drawing social inferences from group situations

Just as individual students must learn how to discuss feelings and actions, students in groups must learn these group communication and social skills if they are to deal with crisis more successfully in the future. Following the basic steps we describe in this chapter, you can teach these group skills as you also teach your individual students more successful ways to respond to crisis.

ESSENTIAL STRATEGIES

Redl (1959a), Fagen (1981), Heuchert and Long (1981), and Long and Fecser (1996) describe several essential processes to consider while using LSCI. Throughout this chapter we expand on these ideas, as summarized in the following list:

- Discovering the personal "vital interest," central to the crisis, which the student is defending

- Drawing the student into a dialogue which helps simplify, clarify, and organize aspects of the issue which lead to a new perception and understanding of the issue (insight)

- Conveying an adult role compatible with the student's view of authority and the therapeutic needs of the student

- Relying upon sound, predictable management strategies in a specific crisis when LSCI may have to be cut short because emotions or fatigue interferes

- Timing LSCI to follow as soon after crisis as a student can participate without being so upset that talk would be useless, and allowing sufficient time to complete the process without interruption from other mandatory activities, such as the bus leaving or recess

- Selecting conditions under which an LSCI can be conducted such that privacy and freedom to talk are provided

Some crises are so specifically related to events that you can track the sequence, during the first two stages of LSCI, in a straightforward timeline from antecedents to the crisis. From that point on, the problem-solving stages of LSCI address the incident that provoked the crisis. Resolution of the crisis becomes the primary outcome. A complete LSCI is not needed.

However, many crises have little or no significance in themselves. They explode as ways to express thoughts and feelings in disguised forms. A student who walks into class with "emotional baggage" or as "a crisis about to happen" is a student dominated by anxiety and full of defensive behaviors. When a crisis results, there is an agenda behind the incident that may not be easily spotted. The student perceives events through a filter of private thoughts and intense emotions, using the incident as a vehicle to discharge greater concerns. In such situations, the incident may not be the real issue, so the LSCI focus shifts from the incident to the underlying issue.

Determining the central issue for a particular LSCI may be the hardest thing to learn. Your role as a significant adult in the student's life is put to the test as you become the mediator among the student, the feelings behind the student's behavior, and the central issue embedded in the crisis. Your purpose in using LSCI is to expand the student's insight about the central issue and how feelings and behavior of the student and others played into producing the crisis. With changes in insight, students can change behavior for more satisfying results.

Lasting change seldom occurs with a single LSCI. Think of LSCI as a series of interactions between you and the student. Because trust, acceptance, and developing relationship are all necessary ingredients for effective LSCI, it is important that consistency be maintained in dealing with each student. A student cannot be shifted from adult to adult for LSCIs and then be expected to achieve the same amount of progress that would be achieved through a consistent relationship with one adult over a series of LSCIs. Chapter 1 contains a discussion about short-term and long-term outcomes of LSCI. The end results can be summarized as positive changes in students' views of themselves, ownership of solutions to resolve crisis, responsibility for changing behavior, and greater understanding of others' reactions to themselves. Gradually over a series of LSCIs, a reduction should occur in a student's emotional memory bank of negative thoughts and feelings. The student's words, behavior, and underlying feelings begin to change because of greater insight, better feelings, more impulse control, more positive feelings about self and others, and more positive self-regulated behavior.

THE SIX LSCI STAGES

As you may recall from Chapter 1, the six stages of LSCI can be divided into "three and three"—the first three stages focus on the skills to diagnose the type of crisis and the central issue, while the last three stages address the specific Reclaiming Intervention. In the remainder of this chapter, we describe the basics of each stage in detail. For each stage we present a synopsis of major points to summarize the purpose of the stage, students' characteristic responses, the adult's major task, and the way to tell when a particular stage should end and bridge into the next stage. See Figure 5.1 for a map of the six stages of LSCI.

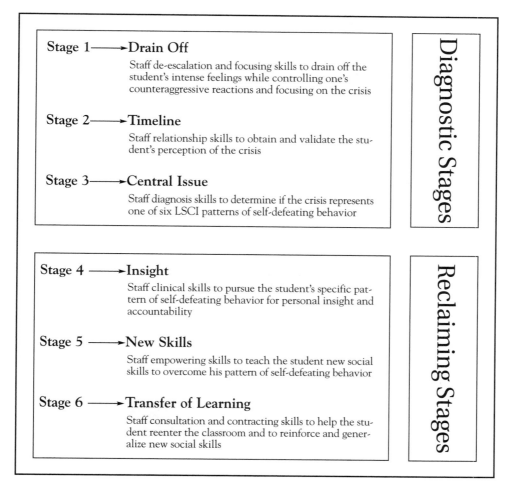

Figure 5.1. Map of the six stages of the LSCI process.

Throughout the stages, we recommend abundant use of affirmations. With some students, you may need to begin LSCI with an affirmation, conveying a positive view of the student and reflecting on some positive quality to defuse intense defensiveness, emotional flooding, or resistance. When you begin to decode, connecting behavior to feelings, you also will need to provide affirmations. Affirmations offer support for students, communicating understanding of what they feel without demeaning or disapproving. Perhaps the most important results from abundant use of affirmations are changes in a student's attitude toward the adult who affirms the student. Messages are communicated that the adult likes the student, believes that there is a better side of the student, and is an ally for bringing out better qualities. Almost all students are hungry for this mirror of a positive image. It is their only hope to be better than they have been before!

Stage 1: Drain Off (De-escalate the Crisis)

> **SYNOPSIS OF STAGE 1**
>
> Since many students are not eager to talk immediately after a crisis, the first stage in LSCI is used to convey support and understanding of the student's stress and to drain off emotions to the point where the student can begin to talk about the incident in a rational way. Intensely angry feelings, "shock" words, and inappropriate actions are almost always present as you intervene in crisis and begin LSCI. This is the point at which inexperienced or untrained staff fall into the Conflict Cycle trap with students. Rather than acting as a thermostat to regulate the emotional intensity, they unwittingly act as a thermometer, reflecting the student's intensity. This is when we must remember to act on what is best for the student instead of acting on our own feelings and counteraggressive impulses. When a student believes that someone will help and when the student can begin to use words instead of being dominated by emotions, LSCI can start and therapeutic gains can be made.
>
> Hopefully, Stage 1 is brief. Sometimes it takes only a sentence or two. With other LSCIs, it may take as much as half an hour to diminish emotional flooding so that a student can begin to talk. If emotional intensity does not diminish to a point where the student can use words, do not go further into LSCI. Instead, try Emotional First Aid, which we describe in Chapter 6 as part of the helping process.
>
> Table 5.1 illustrates the dynamics and process in Step 1. A student is ready for the next stage when (a) the student begins to use words to talk to you, and (b) the reason for the talk has been brought out in the simplest words possible.

What Happens in Stage 1?

When a crisis occurs, emotions are near the surface or already welling over. When a student is so overwhelmed by emotional flooding that speech is not possible, wait! Nothing can be gained by beginning the LSCI when a student is not able to use words.

Support the Student. While waiting, convey calm support. Communicate that you hear and see that the student is upset but that the situation is not beyond solution, and that you are not emotional about it. Sometimes these messages can be communicated non-verbally through your body language and facial expressions; sometimes by holding (dis-

TABLE 5.1
Stage 1: Drain Off

Student	Staff Goals	Staff Skills
Crises	**De-escalation**	**De-escalation and Focus Skills**
I'm upset and out of control!	What I need to do to drain off the student's intense feelings and control his inappropriate behavior	Understanding the dynamics of the Conflict Cycle and Counteraggression
		Crisis De-escalation skills
		Affirming skills

passionate restraint); and sometimes by a few simple words, sounds, or statements such as the following:

"You are really stirred up today."
"Walk with me; you don't need to have any more problems."
"In a few minutes we're going to figure out why you're so mad today."
"Sounds like you need some extra support."
"When you calm down, we can work on this problem."
"I can tell you're almost ready to talk. You've stopped most of the yelling."
"It's understandable that you're upset if you believe you have been cheated."

When the student begins to give some verbal response, it usually means that a shift is taking place from an emotional mode to a rational mode for dealing with the problem. Now you have a way to begin the LSCI process. By converting difficult feelings and destructive behaviors into words, you and the student have the tools for problem solving.

As Talk Begins. When a student starts to talk about the incident, you probably will not know exactly what your therapeutic goal will be, what type LSCI will be needed, what you will say, or what the outcome will be. You will build the LSCI around the specific incident, shaping the direction from the responses given by the student. The following are some examples of inducements that may help get LSCI started:

"I really want to hear what happened from your point of view."

"It seems you are ready to tell me what happened."

"Why are we here?"

"Let's see if we can make sense of what happened to you."

"Tell me where the trouble began."

"Who was there?"

"When you are upset it is difficult to remember what happened, but let's give it a try."

"Let's talk. It's important for me to understand what caused you to become so (mad, scared, frightened, angry)."

If a student is eager to talk, you have moved automatically into the next LSCI stage. But if words are slow in coming, it may require considerable effort to begin (see Your Role in Stage 1, which follows). The important point is to *begin* a dialogue about the incident. It is not important to confront lies or straighten out distortions in perceptions during this first stage, nor is it necessary for you to get your own position on the matter out in the open.

If a student continues to be dominated by emotions or has not begun to focus on the incident, don't go further into the LSCI. Continue to focus on the incident, on your ability to help, and on the student's potential to talk about it. (Chapter 6 contains a discussion about emotional flooding, and how to respond to severely resistant students who will not talk.)

Your Role in Stage 1

Begin Stage 1 by being a representative of fairness for all—an accepting, impartial adult who shows concern for the student's situation (the crisis, feelings, or dilemma). You are setting the tone for the relationship that will follow throughout the six LSCI stages. Questions and statements like the following help to convey the idea that adults can listen, understand, and be objective and fair:

"This is a difficult situation, but we can work on it together."

"Sometimes things seem terrible, but there are always different ways of looking at them."

"When you lose control, everything seems to go wrong."

"This is a serious situation. It calls for some serious thinking about what will be helpful to you."

The student must have confidence and trust in you. Provide support and a sense of optimism that the problem can be handled. Convey your belief in the importance of being fair. Communicate your confidence in the student. Let the student know that you understand and respect the student's feelings even though you cannot accept the behavior. Focus on the student's positive attributes that can be used in solving the crisis. With practice, you will develop increasing verbal skills for even the most difficult problem. In time you will find few, if any, students failing to respond to your strategies for getting the LSCI rolling in Stage 1.

As You Transition to Stage 2

You are ready to phase into Stage 2 when the student responds to you with words (or in some instances, positive gestures or grunts) that acknowledge willingness to go along with you on the topic. The following are examples of ways to transition to Stage 2, affirming your confidence in the student, your support, and your confidence in a good outcome:

> "When you talk about a problem like this, it begins to make sense out of confusion." [affirmation of the student's ability]

> "This is a difficult situation, but we're not going to give up until we understand why you . . ." [affirmation of your support for the student]

> "Even the worst problem can be understood." [affirmation of hope]

> "I can see this is hard for you to talk about, but you're managing to work through it." [affirmation of the student's self-control]

Stage 2: Timeline (Students in Crisis Need To Talk)

> ## SYNOPSIS OF STAGE 2
>
> This is an intensely interactive stage: The student talks and the adult questions, clarifies, and decodes. The exchange between adult and student during this stage has two objectives. For the student there must be a decrease in emotion and an increase in rational words and ideas, organized around the sequence of events—a timeline. If these do not occur, the student cannot benefit from the problem-solving phases later in the LSCI. For the adult the objectives are to expand and clarify details about the student's perception of the incident, begin to decode behavior, and begin to construct an answer to the question, "Is the incident the issue, or is some underlying anxiety the real issue?" The answer will shape the rest of the LSCI.
>
> As Table 5.2 shows, our goal is to encourage the student to tell a personal story and to feel understood. The decoding process is used along with questions to clarify the student's perceptions about the "when," "where," and "who" of the incident, and the events leading up to it. Stage 2 phases into Stage 3 when the talk has produced a review of the time, place, and people involved in the incident. The adult then has a sufficient understanding of the student's reactions and point of view to begin to focus the following stage on the central issue—the incident or the underlying anxiety.

TABLE 5.2
Stage 2: Timeline

Student	Staff Goals	Staff Skills
Timeline	Relationship	Interviewing Skills
This is what happened to me as I remember it!	What I need to do to encourage the student to tell hisstory and to feelunderstood	Empathy skills
		Attending skills
		Verbal listening skills
		Nonverbal observing skills
		Responding skills
		Level One Decoding skills
		Probing skills

What Happens in Stage 2?

Stage 2 is a student's chance to "tell it like it is" or, at least, to tell how the student views the incident. For the student Stage 2 is an exercise in using rational words to deal with a problem. This is not easy for most troubled students. Typical reactions to an incident are anger, denial, evasion, distortion, or verbal counterattack. For the staff Stage 2 is an exercise in attempting to view the situation from the student's unique perspective. We want the student to replay for us a mental videotape of the incident. This is not usually as easy as it might seem, as the student's perceptions are distorted by anxiety, personal history, and the intensity of the moment. The adult will have to help the student organize the sequence of events and put it into proper relationship with surrounding circumstances. Because an incident taps a student's private storehouse of intense feelings, it has infringed on personal space. So talking about the incident also should provide an opportunity to bring out deeper or different issues and concerns that may be preoccupying a student's thoughts and energy.

Student Talks About the Incident. When the incident is first identified during Stage 1, a student's reaction usually is loaded with defensiveness and intense denial of concern or responsibility. An emotional intensity exists that obscures objectivity. The student tries to justify what has happened by blaming you or others, insisting that the incident occurred in a specific way, or initiating talk that is off the topic.

As the student talks about the incident in Stage 2, you will notice a change in the tone of the exchange between you from a predominance of emotion to a more rational tone. When this happens, don't be misled into thinking that LSCI is nearing an end because the student is using rational behavior. Cooling down and talking rationally are *not* the only objectives in this stage. Until you make a preliminary choice about whether or not the incident is really the issue, the LSCI should not move to the next stage.

As students become more comfortable with you and more spontaneous in their talk, they occasionally drop small comments or make side remarks that seem to have little bearing on the incident or the discussion. We call these "signal flares." Unless you are actively listening and looking for them, you may let them pass as unrelated comments or as attempts by the student to get off the subject. It is difficult to discern a student's intent when the discussion wanders from the subject. Signal flares often represent the first attempt by a student to let you know that there is another, real issue that goes beyond the incident. A signal flare is a representation of the private reality we discussed in the introduction to this section. When you spot a signal flare, it may or may not be the right time to respond to it. If you choose to respond, a simple verbal reflection of the student's words is usually enough to highlight the fact that you hear it and recognize it as important. This response usually is enough to get the topic under way. If the student does not respond verbally but body language says there is an interest in further talk about the topic, try a follow-up question. If students are not ready to talk about a private issue, they usually initiate a shift in the conversation or show such agitation that it is apparent the topic is too uncomfortable to pursue for the moment. In this case, let it go but remember it for later use. (You will find an expanded discussion and examples of signal flares in Chapter 6.)

Adult Questions To Expand and Clarify the Incident. For the adult, Stage 2 is used to expand the student's awareness of the complexities of the incident. This is the stage for teaching the student to look at the incident as a sequence in time. Since LSCI usually takes place because of a situation that the student could not handle, the first focus is on the "here and now." We are not asking *why* a problem occurred, but rather *where*, *when*, *who*, and *what* with regard to the problem. The following are some examples of questions to ask about the problem:

"When did this happen?"
"What happened before that?"
"What happened next?"
"Did this happen before or after you got up to get your supplies?"

After confirming the timeline, explore the setting through questions such as the following:

"Where did this happen?"
"Where were you when he said that to you?"
"Did this happen at the . . . ?"
"Has this happened at that same place before?"
"What was going on?"

These types of questions easily flow into questions about the people involved, and who said what to whom, when, such as the following:

"Who made the first move?"
"Who was there?"
"Who else was there?"
"What did they say (do)?"
"Then what did you say?"
"What did they do after you said that?"
"Could you repeat what you just said?"
"I'm not sure I understand what happened. Please tell me again."
"Let me summarize what I heard, and you correct anything I didn't get right."

It sometimes helps to use words that evoke specific visual images about the incident. Such graphic imagery aids many students in making the shift from raw emotion to using words in thinking and talking about the incident. The following are some examples of ways to spice your questions with imagery:

"Was he wearing a red shirt?"
"Was he that great big guy that looks like a wrestler?"
"Did she scream at you?"
"Where did they run after that?"
"Were you sitting in the front of the bus?"
"Can you hear that noise when it's dark?"

As Stage 2 gets under way, use the discussion to separate the various issues embedded in the incident. From each remark the student makes and each accompanying behavior, you must choose whether or not to respond. Respond to those remarks that seem to hold promise for greater understanding and insight. Also respond to remarks that seem to hold significance for the student, even if they do not for you. By this selective process, you expand and clarify the incident. You also increase the student's investment in the process. It is a balancing act that requires considerable mental agility.

Your Role in Stage 2

Your role during Stage 2 is to convey a sincere interest in hearing the student's perceptions about what happened and obtaining more facts about the incident. The more information you have from the student, the more opportunities you have for decoding and understanding. To do this we find these strategies useful: questioning, listening, observing, reflecting, and interpreting (decoding).

Questioning. Questions are the most direct way to expand the information you have about the incident and the extent to which the student has invested emotionally in it. (How much of the private reality is embedded in the incident?)

Generally, the first questions ask for facts about the incident and explore the sequence of events—the timeline. Examples of these basic questions appear in the previous section. Use more complex questions when you begin to explore the extent to which the student can view the incident from the perspectives of others. You want to know if the student can associate personal behavior with resulting reactions from others. Questions also can reveal the extent to which a student is relying on adults to provide external control, and what kinds of issues the student sees as important in the incident. The following are examples of questions that expand the information base:

"How would he describe what just happened?" [perspective of others]
"Could there have been something that set him off?" [cause and effect]
"Is this a problem for kids to handle by themselves?" [source of authority]
"Is fairness (kindness, leadership, friendship) an issue here?" [values]

Active Listening and Active Remembering. Listen carefully to what a student says. Key words and ideas are the cues you use to form your own responses. The student's view is the starting point, giving you a base from which to structure the remaining LSCI stages. It also is important to remember what the student says. In later phases of an interview, or in subsequent interviews, you should be able to recall and reuse important or vivid points made by the student during these earlier stages. When students act out and trigger counter-aggressive impulses in adults, we have a tendency to be quick to speak and slow to listen. In LSCI, we must reverse that and learn to be quick to listen and slow to speak.

Observing. Active observing is an important part of active listening. The body language a student uses to accompany a statement often tells more than words. A student's behavior also tells a lot about the impact you are making.

You can be confident that the talk has validity if a student participates, responds with vigorous denial, or shows a pronounced increase in body movement, even if these reactions are negative. Occasionally, a student will be very still, making no remarks and showing no behavioral response. This particular reaction almost always indicates interest in hearing an elaboration of the idea you just brought up.

If the talk is not on track, a student will show boredom or disinterest, and may bring up another topic. This strategy also may be used by some students when content is too close to private reality. You can usually tell the difference by the amount of agitation or emotion accompanying the response.

Reflecting. Words that mirror an idea or an observed behavior back to a student convey that the student's idea or behavior is worthy of note (or in the case of a negative point, that it has not escaped your notice). Reflections require no responses from students because they are statements of fact. A reflection does not intrude into a student's space and is not judgmental. It is among the best strategies for minimizing defensiveness and keeping a sensitive topic going. It also is useful with students who have problems with authority because it does not require a defensive response. Typically a student will respond to a reflection by elaborating the details and expanding the content spontaneously; if not, go back to questions again—more facts and observation are needed.

If you have not used reflections before, you may feel a bit awkward simply turning an observation or a remark back to a student without adding your own ideas. The following are examples of simple reflections, where the student has made the first statement and the teacher has simply rephrased it:

> "It didn't sound fair to you."
> "You were sitting there minding your own business."
> "You didn't mean to make her mad."
> "You think he is the one I should talk with."
> "You were feeling good about what you had done until he made that remark."

Did you notice that these examples are not stated as questions although they could be? Reflecting involves no questions, so responses are not necessary. These examples do not reflect negative feelings or negative behavior. Also they are nonjudgmental, without innuendo that the student somehow really might need to reconsider. This technique is very effective during the first stages of LSCI when you want to encourage students to freely express their views and feelings about the incident.

Interpreting (Decoding). When you make a statement that connects meaning or feeling to a student's surface behavior or words, you are interpreting, which is a form of decoding (see Chapter 3). Interpretation expands a student's awareness of connections between behavior and private thoughts and feelings. Construct your first interpretations from reflections about the student's behavior and words. Reflections provide credibility to the interpretation, because they give observed evidence. This is a neutral way to link what is publicly observed to what may be private. The following are examples of the way reflections and interpretations are used together in decoding behavior:

> "When a student puts his hands over his ears [reflection of behavior], he is telling me that this topic is uncomfortable for him to hear." [interpretation of feeling]

> "I've noticed that each time you get around him, you end up in trouble. [reflection] Maybe he enjoys seeing you out of control." [interpretation]

In the first example, the third person pronoun is used to provide psychological space for the student. Because the interpretation does not directly address the student, there is enough distance for the student to hear the message without having to be defensive. The student is not forced into a position of having to respond. The reflection and interpretation are simply matter-of-fact.

When a student's response suggests that decoding has been accepted, follow it with a question. This helps the student begin to deal with the new material. Usually a yes or no question is the easiest to answer, particularly if the interpretation is heavily laden with private concerns.

With sophisticated students and those who have had previous LSCIs, you can begin to shift responsibility for decoding and making interpretations to the student, using statements and questions like the following:

"That comment must have hurt your feelings."

"What went through your mind when she said that?"

"What is your idea about why that remark set her off?"

"Do you think your comment had anything to do with the way you were treated by them last week?"

"Some people really know how to make other people feel bad."

While you or a student are decoding, you are seeking answers to the question, "What is the real issue here?" Decoding is the simultaneous mental process used to translate interpretations of behavior into broader networks of meaning, connecting the obvious to the not so obvious. Decoding should shape the direction of your LSCI, moving it toward a focus on the surface incident or toward a more private, underlying issue. (If you are still hesitant about decoding, review Chapter 3. Decoding is a skill that must be used for effective LSCI.)

As You Transition to Stage 3

Stage 2 begins to merge into the next stage when the student has reviewed the incident and you have used interpretations, decoding, and affirmations of the student to forge links of confidence between you and the student. Inaccurate interpretations, failure to decode, or a shortage of strong affirmations will dilute confidence the student may have in you: "This adult is like all the others and doesn't really understand (or care)!" Through accurate interpretations and sensitivity to the student's private space, however, the student begins to believe, "This adult really does understand!" When this happens, the student will be ready to go with you into the next LSCI stage. The following are examples of ways to bridge into Stage 3:

"This is what I hear you saying . . ."

"You've described the situation clearly. Let's review what you have said."

"It's interesting how something that you meant to be nice backfired and led to all this trouble."

"It seems like the problem that got you in here to talk isn't the real problem after all."

Stage 3: Central Issue (Select a Goal)

SYNOPSIS OF STAGE 3

Stage 3 builds a conceptual structure about what is really significant in the incident. At the moment of the incident the student's life space includes both public and private realities. It is the adult's job in Stage 3 to sort it all out and make decisions about which reality predominates and what is needed. Stage 3 is the decision-making point for selecting a therapeutic goal.

The key processes in Stage 3 are to explore the student's view of the incident and underlying anxieties until you have sufficient understanding to (a) concisely state the central issue; (b) assess the student's perceptions, insights, and motivation to change behavior; and (c) decide what the goal should be for this particular intervention.

Table 5.3 illustrates the dynamics of Stage 3. In this stage a logical outcome will begin to take shape and the information is used to structure the remainder of the LSCI. In Stage 3 you are preparing the student to consider another perspective of the situation, one that requires the student to accept some responsibility for a part in creating the crisis. What is difficult at this point is that we have the insight; we know the student's patterns of perceiving, thinking, feeling, and behaving, and how he or she most likely contributed to the crisis. We need to fight our impulse to bring this insight into the bright light of day. The goal of the LSCI is to plant a seed of insight which we hope will take root over time and eventually grow into a new realization of repetitive patterns of self-defeating behavior. The art of Stage 3 is "preparing the soil" to accept the seed of insight which we hope to plant in Stage 4. Stage 3 gives way to Stage 4 when the issue has been stated concisely by the adult or student and the adult has chosen a Reclaiming Intervention. (The first six chapters in Part III provide in-depth discussions of how to conduct each Reclaiming Intervention.)

What Happens in Stage 3?

Preliminary information needed to identify the central issue is obtained in the previous stages by decoding the student's words and behavior. As Stage 3 begins you have an ini-

TABLE 5.3
Stage 3: Central Issue

Student	Staff Goals	Staff Skills
Central Issue	Diagnosis	Diagnostic Skills
So this is the central focus of my crisis!	What I need to do to determine: [A] If this crisis is characteristic of how this student perceives, thinks, feels, and behaves during a crisis [B] If this crisis is best managed by short-term intervention in order to get the student back into the program [C] If this crisis is best managed by using one of the six Reclaiming LSCIs	Understanding and using the student's history and current life stressors Knowing the six Reclaiming LSCIs and selecting the right one Stating the central issue behaviorally with age-appropriate language

tial idea about whether the incident itself or an underlying anxiety is the central issue. During Stage 3 this idea is tested and expanded by obtaining information in greater depth, looping back for more verbal exchanges, and performing more decoding. At Stage 3 we are assessing the situation for potential insight gain. Will the student best benefit from short-term intervention to quickly return to the ongoing program, or is this event so characteristic of the student's repetitive patterns of perceiving, thinking, feeling, and behaving that we will use the LSCI to maximize the insight potential?

Find the Central Issue and Form a Concise Statement. The first decision in Stage 3 is whether to focus on the incident or to put your effort into unfolding some of the underlying anxieties associated with the incident. A focus on the incident assumes that relevant antecedents (the chain of events that triggered the incident) are observable and are major ingredients of the incident.

A focus on underlying, developmental anxieties assumes that the incident is not actually the issue but serves only as a means to express a hidden concern. Such issues often are obscured by behavior or words used by students for protection against invasion of their psychological space or from being overwhelmed by private thoughts or feelings that cannot be expressed or recognized openly.

To focus on underlying anxiety is difficult and complicated. Yet unless this is done, a student's private reality remains untouched and unresolved. Emotional volatility builds up as a student attempts to function while avoiding a private burden. If the underlying anxiety can be brought out and dealt with in a satisfactory way, emotional tension is reduced. Then rational problem solving becomes the bridge for management of these private feelings and thoughts.

With increasing information comes greater clarity about the incident and underlying anxiety. This information must be distilled into a single statement that represents the central issue. The central issue should be clearly stated in one or two simple sentences before continuing further into the solution stages.

In some interviews the adult summarizes the central issue; in others the student will be able to blurt out some version of the central issue. The following are examples of statements about central issues. These examples state the incident as the central issue:

"It seems that messing with others leads to problems. And here you are, having the problem."

"So, you are the one who is always picked on. He called you a name and then you hit him. . . . And here you are."

"You tried to follow the rules, but it's really hard to do right when everyone else is breaking the rules."

"You think he deserves cussing because he cussed you."

"She thinks she knows everything and that gets to you."

"You really didn't mean to hurt him. It's hard to stop yourself."

A part of every incident touches a student's underlying anxiety. Sometimes the incident is played down in order to explore underlying issues. The following statements were made by teachers responding to fights in their classrooms or on the playground. In each instance, the teachers built their responses from what the students brought up as they discussed the fights. In these examples the teachers chose to form the central issues around underlying anxieties.

"It's going to be hard to wait for 10 days to see if the judge is going to let your foster parents adopt you." [Issue is abandonment.]

"Tearing up the classroom may not be the best way to get the other guys to be friends with you." [Issue is inadequacy with peers.]

"You said you were an 'idiot,' but what I hear between the lines is a message that maybe with some help from teachers things could be better." [Issue is guilt, self-judged.]

"When your dad told you to turn off the TV last night and you went on a rampage just like the one in class today, it was like the little kid in you. Isn't this what we've been working on, how to handle feelings without having a 'royal fit'?" [Issue is independence-dependence conflict.]

"You're very concerned about Ron being gay and how you're going to act around him." [Issue is adolescent identity.]

In these examples we used each of the basic developmental anxieties discussed previously in Chapter 3. If you still feel uncertain about them, a review of that chapter should be helpful. It is important at this stage in LSCI that you are able to identify these developmental anxieties as they emerge during the discussion and decoding processes that have occurred.

Assess the Student's Perception, Insight, and Motivation To Change. Following a concise statement of the central issue, think through the preceding dialogue to summarize, in your mind, how the student views the incident and the extent of the student's sense of responsibility. From the previous stages, you should be able to see the events as the student has seen and felt them. Some students have extremely restricted social perceptions but others are clearly able to view an incident from another's point of view. It is essential to understand how your particular student views the event. You also should have an idea about the student's view of adult authority and who should solve the problem—the student or the adult (see Chapter 4, concerning the Existential Crisis).

This information will help you evaluate the student's motivation to change and assume responsibility for the crisis. It also will give you an indication of the student's readiness to give up old alibis and rationalizations for new or different behavior in the future. With this information, you and the student are ready to move on to the last process in this stage—selecting a therapeutic goal, based on the student's current perceptions.

If you still feel unsure about how the student views the event and his or her personal role in it, then it is necessary to return to Stage 2 and further expand and clarify the student's perceptions and motivations to change. Decoding a student's words and actions is the single most helpful process you can use to accomplish this.

Select the Appropriate Reclaiming Intervention. Once the issue has been clearly stated, and you have assessed the student's perceptions and motivation to change, the question becomes, "What do I want to happen, now that the student may be open to change?"

Almost every central issue can be managed within one of the six Reclaiming Interventions for troubled children. The labels we use, with the exception of the Red Flag, are Fritz Redl's original therapeutic goals, restated. The original names given by Redl (1959a) are in parentheses. Selection of a particular Reclaiming Intervention is based on the student's current perception of the incident and issue and your assessment of the student's motivation to change. Each goal also has a new, broader insight for the student as its objective. The following is a summary of each type of the six Reclaiming Interventions:

Organize Perceptions of Reality
(Reality Rub Reclaiming Intervention)

Student's Perception:	"I am being treated unfairly!"
Uses:	With students who demonstrate any of the following:

(1) Blocked perceptions of reality due to intense feelings

(2) Misperceptions of reality due to triggering of personal emotional sensitivities

(3) Restricted perceptions of reality due to perseveration on a single event in the sequence leading to the crisis

(4) Private reconstruction of reality as events are interpreted through rigid perceptual filters derived from personal history

(5) Manipulation of reality to test limits

Goal:	To help the student organize thinking so that a more accurate perception of reality emerges; to bring the student to the realization that there is "more than meets the eye;" to help the student begin to understand his or her contribution to the problem
Focus:	Organizes students' perceptions and sequence of time and events; developmentally, the most rudimentary of the therapeutic goals
Student's New Insight:	"Maybe there is another way to look at this situation; I can see how I might have contributed to making it worse, and what I need to do about it."

Identify the Source of the Stress
(Red Flag Reclaiming Intervention)

Student's Perceptions:	"Everybody is against me! No one understands what's going on with me and no one cares! I can't take it any more!"
Uses:	With students who overreact to normal rules and procedures with emotional outbursts; who attempt to create a no win situation by engaging staff in a power struggle which ultimately results in more rejection and feelings of alienation
Goal:	To identify the source of the problem: is it a *Carry In* problem from another setting, a *Carry Over* problem

from another situation within the setting, or did an event in the current setting *Tap In* to emotional unfinished business?

Focus:	Helps students recognize that they are displacing their feelings on others and alienating the sources of support they need to handle their stress
Student's New Insight:	"Someone does understand my real problems and can read beyond my behavior. I need to talk to staff about my real problems and not create new ones here."

Confront Unacceptable Behavior
(Symptom Estrangement Intervention)

Student's Perceptions:	"I do what I have to do even if it hurts others." "I have to take care of 'Number One.'" "I have a reputation to maintain. . . . I have no need to change."
Uses:	With students who are too comfortable with their deviant behavior through receiving too much gratification; those who practice aggression, passive aggression, manipulation, or exploitation of others
Goal:	To make a particular behavior uncomfortable, by confronting the rationalizations and decoding the self-serving narcissism and distorted pleasure the student receives from the unacceptable behavior
Focus:	Helps students realize that they are paying a high price for justifying exploitation of others; they are tricking themselves into believing their cause is just
Student's New Insights:	"Maybe I'm not as smart as I tell myself." "Maybe I've been cruel. . . . Maybe I've been tricking myself."

Build Values To Strengthen Self-Control
(Massaging Numb Values Intervention)

Student's Perception:	"Even when I'm upset, a part of me is saying, 'Control! Stop yourself' . . . but I don't."
Uses:	With students who, after acting out, are burdened by remorse, shame, inadequacy, or guilt about their own failures or unworthiness; those with a destructive self-image; and those who have a negative social role
Goal:	To relieve some of the burden by emphasizing a student's positive qualities; to strengthen self-control and

self-confidence that the student is an able and valued person with qualities like fairness, kindness, friendship, or leadership potential

Focus: Expands student's self-control and confidence by abundant affirmations and reflections about existing socially desirable attributes and potential for future acclaim by peers; developmentally, this goal requires a shift in source of responsibility—from adult to student

Student's New Insight: "Even under tempting situations or group pressure, I have the capacity to control myself."

Teach New Social Skills
(New Tools Intervention)

Student's Perception: "I want to do the right thing, but it always comes out wrong."

Uses: With students seeking approval of adults or peers but lacking appropriate social behaviors to accomplish this

Goal: To teach new social behaviors that student can use for immediate positive gain

Focus: Instructs in specific social behaviors that will have immediate payback in desired responses from others; developmentally, reflects emerging independence and responsibility

Student's New Insight: "I have the right intention, but I need help to learn the skills that will help me make friends, achieve, and get along with adults."

Expose Exploitation (Manipulation
of Body Boundaries Intervention)

Student's Perception: "It's important to have a friend even if the friend gets me into trouble"; or, "I'm going to teach him a lesson!"

Uses: With students who are neglected, abused, scapegoated, isolated, or who seek out destructive friendships by acting out for others; with students who are unwittingly set-up by passive-aggressive peers to act out

Goal:	To help a student see that another student (or adult) is manipulating events in a way that is working against the student's best interest
Focus:	Provides insight into reasons for the behavior of others; views social interactions from the perspective of motivations and behaviors of others; developmentally, this goal requires considerable maturity on the student's part, as the student learns to understand how others think, feel, and behave
Student's New Insight:	"A friend is someone who helps you solve problems and feel good rather than someone who gets you into trouble"; or "I can make my own decisions; I don't need to 'take the bait' when someone is trying to get me in trouble."

Examples of LSCIs using each of these Reclaiming Interventions can be found in Chapters 7 through 12. These chapters illustrate how each of the Interventions uniquely shapes the strategies and content of the remaining stages in every LSCI.

You may be asking, "Why put off selecting a therapeutic goal until Stage 3?" Sometimes, with students we know well, we have an idea from the very beginning about what the student's characteristic perception is, what central issue is involved, and what Reclaiming Intervention is needed. Even so, it is necessary to establish the facts and observations about the crisis and obtain the student's current perception. Without establishing these, the student will not become sufficiently involved to own a solution as it is developed.

Your Role in Stage 3

Stage 3 is perhaps the most difficult for the adult. It requires a lot of decoding, thoughtful observing and listening, and good verbal skills for questioning and interpreting behavior. We have described these processes in the previous stages, but it is necessary to return again and again to the cycle of Stage 2 as you form a statement of the central issue in Stage 3. You will find yourself in an information loop—questioning, interpreting, decoding, and hypothesis building. While sifting through the maze of responses you hear and observe, you also must form your own questions and responses in ways that begin to shape the direction of the LSCI. Your task is to decide upon a particular therapeutic goal.

In Chapter 4 we discuss styles of adult influence and their importance in conveying the type of adult role needed by a particular student. In Stage 3 a clear view is essential about which type of strategies you should use to influence the student. The six types of Reclaiming Interventions are labeled according to the type of action required by the adult. These labels also suggest the style of adult influence needed to accomplish a particular goal. They are helpful guidelines for the roles you might take: identifying the source of stress, organizing a student, confronting behavior, building values for self-control, teaching social behaviors, or providing insight into the behavior of others. The following are examples of statements made by teachers, illustrating each of these adult roles:

The identifier of the source of stress:	"When you come into my classroom angry and wanting to hurt, that tells me you're hurting too. Let's talk about what's troubling you."
The organizer:	"You were standing there on the playground with the ball and feeling angry. Who else was involved? Did they say anything to you?"
The benign confronter:	"You're trying to tease Thomas, hoping he would react to you. But look at what really happened. He is still having fun, and you are in here. Tell me, who has the problem, Thomas or you?"
The builder of values for self-control:	"I can see leadership qualities in you. The others pay attention when you have an idea for the group."
The teacher of social behaviors:	"Maybe if you had a friendly sound to your voice, he might let you use his equipment. Try it out with me."
The provider of insight:	"He must have been really mad to have hauled off and hit you after what you said. Why do you think he got so mad about that?"

The goal and the adult role are closely bound to each other. And it is the student's responses that confirm or negate the validity of the choices you make. As you convey the type of adult role needed to accomplish the therapeutic goal, the flow of the LSCI distinctly turns toward possible solutions.

As You End Stage 3

The third stage transitions when a statement has been made about the central issue and you have chosen a Reclaiming Intervention. With the end of Stage 3, the problem phase ends and the solution stages begin. The following are examples of ways to end this stage and bridge into the next stage:

"This situation is beginning to make sense. When a person understands a problem, it can be solved."

"This has not been a good day for you, but we know what's wrong now, so we can do something about it."

"We know what the problem is, but what are you (we) going to do about it?"

Stage 4: Insight (Choose a Solution)

> **SYNOPSIS OF STAGE 4**
>
> In Stage 3 we made a decision based on what we learned from the student in Stage 2. We determined either (a) the crisis was best managed by a short-term milieu intervention, or (b) the incident offered enough material characteristic of the student's pattern of self-defeating behavior that we would attempt to help him gain insight into the pattern. If we have decided to go forward with a full LSCI, we have selected one of the six therapeutic goals. In Stage 4 our task is to bring the student to insight; that is, to glimpse the rigid patterns of perceiving, thinking, feeling, and behaving that have been driving the inappropriate behavior. This is not an easy task. As students' "ways of living" have protected them thus far in life, they hesitate, even resist, abandoning their old ways. It is somewhat like the person clinging to a life preserver in the ocean, who is afraid to give it up to climb into a rowboat. We are asking the student to trust us to help find new and better solutions to old problems. Table 5.4 illustrates the dynamics of Stage 4.
>
> This stage begins the "how to fix it," or "reclaiming" part of LSCI. The following three questions are to be answered during this stage:
>
> - If a student's crisis is an opportunity to learn new insights into patterns of self-defeating behavior, what would be the message of these insights?
> - How are these insights translated into a plan to change a student's behavior?
> - What will the student see as a satisfactory solution that can be "owned"?
>
> Often there are two solutions to be dealt with: One is the reality issue surrounding the incident; the other is an underlying issue that may have emerged during the previous stages. When possible, the student should come up with alternative solutions and then select the course of action that seems best. If the student is not able to do this, the adult helps the student by providing guidelines, values, or rules. For students to have genuine ownership of solutions, the choices should be ones that they value as beneficial. Stage 4 bridges to Stage 5 when a solution is chosen and the student puts the solution into words.

What Happens in Stage 4?

During this stage the nature of LSCI changes distinctly. The tone is upbeat; the focus is on personal insights and new solutions which make things better. Before this point, LSCI has been diverging, exploring, and expanding for a full understanding of the incident and the central issue behind it. Sometimes it has been painful or confrontational; but now, with a concise statement about the issue out in the open, new solutions become the focus.

TABLE 5.4

Stage 4: Insight

Student	Staff Goals	Staff Skills
Insight	Reclaiming	Reclaiming Skills
Now I understand how I contribute to my crisis and how I make it worse!	What I need to do to facilitate the student's insight into the pattern of self-defeating behaviors: Implementing the selected LSCI	The skills of carrying out the six LSCIs successfully

If a student's crisis were an opportunity to learn a new insight into patterns of self-defeating behavior, what would be the message of this insight? Each of the six Reclaiming Interventions has a specific insight message which the student hopefully will discover as he or she identifies, examines, and reviews his or her pattern of dysfunctional behavior. The interviewer's task is to encourage the student to see this crisis, not as an isolated, one-time happening, but as a chronic pattern of dysfunction that the student turns to when he or she becomes frustrated, angry, and overwhelmed. How an interviewer accomplishes this task is both an art and a skill. However, a student will learn the following from a successful Reclaiming Intervention:

1. The Reality Rub Reclaiming Intervention—"Maybe when I get upset I distort what happened, what I saw, what I remembered, and what I heard; sometimes I come to the wrong conclusions before checking out the facts. Actually I make the situation worse, and I need to stop this pattern of behavior."

2. Red Flag Reclaiming Intervention—"When life gets rough and I get mistreated, I believe everyone is against me. I'm so upset that when I come to school I overreact to the smallest frustration and blow up. What I do is vent my anger at a staff or peer and blame them and not the real people for my anger and sadness. Instead of reaching out to those adults who can help me, I alienate them. I need to change the pattern of beliefs and ask for help instead of creating a new problem at school."

3. Symptom Estrangement Reclaiming Intervention—"Sometimes I find clever ways to justify my aggressive behavior towards peers and staff. I feel powerful knowing that others are scared of me, but lately I am on the hot seat and the staff is coming down on me, so now I'm paying a high emotional price for my behavior. Maybe it's not worth it. Maybe I'm fooling myself into believing I have a right to do what I want, when I want to. Maybe a part of me enjoys the pleasure of threatening and hurting others. Maybe this is not the way to live. I don't want to be cruel—just cool. Perhaps I need to change some of my behavior."

4. Massaging Numb Values Reclaiming Intervention—"When I get upset, I find ways of beating myself up both physically and psychologically. Nobody has to mistreat me, I

have a successful way of doing that all by myself. After all, when I feel like a worm I treat myself like one. But I am learning that I'm not a terrible person. I do have some self-control skills, and others believe in me—believe that I can change and feel better about myself."

5. New Tools Reclaiming Intervention—"I want to have friends and learn, but somehow things go wrong and I'm rejected and feel like a dummy. I have learned I have the right intentions but the wrong behaviors to achieve what I want. The staff recognizes my good intentions, and I am motivated to learn new social skills that will improve my relationships in school."

6. Manipulation of Body Boundaries Reclaiming Intervention—"I want to have friends but sometimes I pick the wrong ones and I end up in trouble. A friend should be someone who helps me and not someone who gets me into trouble. I'm not going to let my friends control what I do anymore! The staff have helped me recognize this destructive peer relationship, and with their help I would like to find new and more rewarding friends. In my case, I have not been aware of how [name of other student] successfully manipulates me to respond to his teasing behavior until I blow up and end up in the time out room. I do not want him to control me in the future, and I need to develop a plan to achieve this goal."

How are these insights translated into a personal plan for improving the student's behavior?

This is the critical step in the LSCI process. If the student's insight into his or her repetitive pattern of inappropriate behavior doesn't lead to a personal plan to change and improve this behavior, the process becomes a hollow intellectual experience. A Reclaiming Intervention mobilizes a student to translate his or her new awareness into a plan to develop new social skills in order to improve self-esteem and interpersonal relationships. During this guided process, the student is encouraged to consider as many alternative plans as possible. Some will be unrealistic and inappropriate; but by discussing the pros and cons of each plan, the student will take responsibility for personal change as he or she practices a problem solving approach.

The interviewer can assist this important process by raising the following questions about the student's plan:

What do you hope to accomplish by using this plan?

How many new skills do you think you need to learn?

Are some of these skills more important than others?

How long do you think you will have to show these new behaviors before your classmates recognize the change?

The student's plan should be realistic and attainable and implemented in degrees, not in expediential leaps.

What Is a Satisfactory Solution? Satisfactory solutions are those that students believe will work to their benefit. The most acceptable solution from an adult viewpoint may not be seen as satisfactory by a student. If a student does not really buy into a solution, the time has been wasted.

There is a general sequence in the development of social problem solving for most students that is based on what they really value. In Chapter 4, Figure 4.1 outlines this sequence. It begins with an orientation that one's own needs are paramount. Any solution that meets these needs is satisfactory. At this beginning level, service to self is the satisfactory solution. Any solution that will work to the student's immediate benefit will be owned. The following are several guidelines for satisfactory solutions at this beginning level of social values that provide for the student's own needs:

- Pleasure-producing results
- Concrete incentives
- Tangible rewards
- Privileges

Gradually, students move from that orientation to a belief that adults' standards are the ones that will bring benefits. At this level, students believe that service to adult authority will protect self and bring benefits. The following are examples of solutions that seek adult approval:

- Accept rules and punishment as inevitable
- Acquiesce to adults as the ultimate power
- Do what gains adult approval
- Accept punishment that restores reputation as a "good" person in the eyes of adults

Development then broadens into the view that justice and fairness are valuable guidelines for problem solving. Social values at this level are oriented to fairness and justice for like-minded individuals. The following are examples of satisfactory solutions involving fairness and similar social values:

- Look out for friends
- Do things for others so they will do things for you
- Demand fair treatment for yourself
- Do what you think will get you a fair deal

Gradually, students embrace values that reflect society's standards for responsibility. Satisfactory crisis resolution for students at this level of social values is derived from concepts about responsibility, reciprocity, and cooperation in a larger, valued community. The following are examples of solutions that reflect this better self:

- Do things to have friends
- Be a good person, so people will like (help, admire) you
- What others think of you is important

Finally, some adolescents may reach the level of social values where responsibility for asserting individuality and independence is blended with responsibility for responding to the needs of others. It requires students to understand the perspectives and feelings of others. It also requires empathy and altruism, sometimes putting the needs of others first. Few, if any, students we work with are at this level of values. When they are, they often can work through a crisis to a satisfactory solution with minimal adult assistance. The following are examples of solutions at this level of care for others:

- Show what you can do to contribute
- Be a responsible person
- Keep your eyes on where you are going
- Be someone who helps others
- Make your life worth something

These five levels embody most of the social value orientations you will find among solutions that students develop. If you can identify the general level in which a student operates, you can be fairly confident that the student will own a solution that fits into that level.

Sometimes it is useful to go beyond a solution that is within a student's current level and challenge the student to consider solutions typical of the next level. This push into a higher level is useful when a student begins to choose solutions in a manner that seems superficial or trivial, or produces little real motivation or commitment to change.

Your Role in Stage 4

Adult responsibility during Stage 4 is to guide. How much guidance you provide should be adjusted to the student's view of adults and who has responsibility for solving problems. (You may find it helpful to review the discussion about the existential phases and styles of adult influence in Chapter 4.) Your influence can widen a student's consideration of alternative ways to solve a problem, or, if you are not careful, you can restrict it without intending to do so. The following are some examples of ways to encourage a discussion of alternatives:

"There are lots of ways to go about solving this problem."
"That's a solution that might work. Can you think of another way?"
"Let's count how many different ways you can think of to handle this situation."

The most important part of being an effective guide in this stage is to see that the student describes as many alternative solutions as possible. The benefits and problems associated with each alternative should be considered. To do this you will need to ask questions and reflect real consequences. The best help you can provide during this stage is to suggest guidelines, rules, and values that are relevant to the incident and alternatives the student is struggling with. Through your responses you can influence the student to carefully consider solutions that the student might not otherwise consider, but that are appropriate to the student's current stage of value development. Consider motivating the student to solutions at the next higher level of values. Some students will be ready to make the leap to the next value level; others will not.

Exercise caution so that you do not jump in too soon and influence the student toward a particular solution. If you provide the solution, or the student sees you as having already made up your mind, the chosen solution will be owned by you and *not* by the student.

As You Transition to Stage 5

This is the point in LSCI when the adult and student begin to merge in agreement about a solution. Among the alternative solutions discussed, one will begin to take shape as being more satisfactory than others. The process is a series of trade-offs. The student is seeking relief from the stress and comfortable resolution of the incident. You are seeking the most constructive solution for the student's perceptions, stage of value development, and the therapeutic goal you have selected in the previous stage. Keep in mind the desired change in student insight that each of the therapeutic goals should produce. New insight is an essential part of a satisfactory solution. The solution also should provide for enhancement of the student's self-concept and confidence to face the people and situations that were a part of the incident. The solution also must really be possible. It must fit into the real situation the student faces, be within the student's capacity to use successfully, and be owned by the student. Stage 4 draws to a close as the student puts the chosen solution into words. Sometimes you may have to summarize it first, and then ask the student to tell it to you again. With other students, you can end the stage with requests such as the following:

> "We've talked about a lot of ways to handle this. Which seems the best to you?"

> "It seems pretty clear that you've considered all the choices. Which will work best for you?"

> "You have thought this through carefully. Let's review the choices."

Stage 5: New Skills (Plan for Success)

SYNOPSIS OF STAGE 5

This is the stage for realistic planning and rehearsal of what will happen when new social skills are learned and used to resolve the central issue of the crisis. The focus is on specific behaviors—what to do when. Both negative and positive aspects are anticipated, and a working plan is formed for putting the solution into action. Table 5.5 illustrates the dynamics of Stage 5.

(continues)

> This stage is used to expand the student's understanding of what new skills the solution will require. The question is, "Will this solution work for the student?" Behind this simple question is the major concern of intervention programs, that there be a carryover effect. Stage 5 is the place to teach the new social skills.
>
> Affirming a student's ability to carry out the plan is essential for success at this stage. It is almost always difficult for students to use new behaviors and new approaches to a problem. Without practice and abundant encouragement, they tend to fall back on old ways of behaving.

Stage 5 ends when new behaviors have been rehearsed, future problem situations have been anticipated, and the student has confidence that the solution can be done successfully and will produce benefits.

What Happens in Stage 5?

Stage 5 is used to help students plan for resolving the current problem and avoiding repeats in the future. It teaches them to anticipate problems and expands their behavioral responses. This stage could be called "rehearsal," for that is exactly what is done.

Rehearse New Behaviors. The adult usually begins the planning and rehearsal by asking questions such as the following:

"You have a good idea here. What will you say to him when we leave here?"
"This is a really good plan. Let's pretend I am that person; what will you say to me?"

TABLE 5.5
Stage 5: New Skills

Student	Staff Goals	Staff Skills
New Skills	**Empowering**	**Cognitive and Behavioral Restructuring Skills**
These are the social skills I need to learn to improve my interpersonal relationships!	This is what I need to teach that would improve the student's self-concept and interpersonal skills with peers and staff.	Prosocial skills
		Self-control skills
		Self-monitoring skills
		Role-playing skills

"It's not always easy to do what we've been talking about."
"This is going to take a lot of courage on your part. How will you begin?"

During this stage you are preparing the student to put the solution into action, to respond to events and people with new behaviors and new understanding. The plan for success may have several parts. One has to do with consequences that have come about as a result of the incident. Rules may have been broken, property destroyed, or offenses committed against another student or adult that must be handled. Preparing the student to accept consequences with responsibility and understanding is an essential part of this stage.

Another part of the plan for success may involve more subtle changes in attitudes and behaviors: resolving the central issue and developing long-range strategies for handling similar problems in the future. Be guided by the individual student, the nature of the original crisis, the nature of the central issue, real consequences that have resulted from the incident, and the Reclaiming Intervention you have chosen.

Anticipate Consequences. Students often fail to anticipate that consequences may result from their behavior in an incident. They often resist thinking about what they have to do, how they will feel, how they will react, and how others will react to them. Such unanticipated problems need to be taught during Stage 5. The following are examples of statements that help a student prepare for the consequences resulting from an incident:

"It's clear you have a good plan. When we go back into the room, he will be expecting you to apologize. What will you say?"

"This talk shows your best qualities. You're going to be able to (repair the damage, handle the suspension, explain it to your parent, face the judge, talk with the principal, apologize)."

"I'm sorry you have to (face the consequences), but once it's over, I know you're going to handle something like this in a better way next time it happens."

Such statements affirm your belief in the student's capacity to face the consequences in a responsible way. They also provide support for the most unpleasant part of an incident, enduring the consequences.

Students also fail to anticipate stress. The next stress may catch them unprepared and resorting to old coping strategies. The following are several examples of statements that help students anticipate problems:

"What will you do if . . . ?"

"What if he doesn't listen?"

"What if she tells you it doesn't matter that you had a reason for breaking the rule?"

"Do you think they'll believe you next time?"

"It will be hard to say no to your friends when they try that again. What will you do?"

"The next time they tell you to do that, you are going to feel just as angry. What will happen?"

"They may ignore you. What then?"

The difficult part of this stage is to balance the amount of reality you expose the student to with the student's capacity to imagine future stress. If a student is just beginning to try new behaviors, it may not be the time to expand the horizon to foresee all possible problems. On the other hand, if a student has already participated in a series of LSCIs with you and there does not seem to be carryover into real-life situations, you may need to spend more time on rehearsal.

Affirm Potential Benefits. The importance of repeatedly affirming and reaffirming a student during this stage cannot be overemphasized. Your support and confidence in the student are the mirror in which the student sees a changed self, using new behaviors to deal with old problems in new ways. Troubled students cannot make this change in their view of themselves by themselves. Your affirmations and belief in the student make real change possible. And without such a change in a student's private thoughts and feelings about self, there will be no real, lasting benefit from LSCI.

Your Role in Stage 5

The adult role in Stage 5 is to simultaneously provide a window of realism while conveying confidence in the student's ability to actually use the solution, and conviction about the benefits that will come to the student for trying out the new solution.

Realism is conveyed through "What if?" questions. Beginning with a future scenario that repeats the present incident, lead the student through a replay while the student describes the new behaviors to be used. Then you can help the student imagine how others will respond. This effort should provide expanded insight into social exchanges, both positive and negative.

Confidence is the fuel for change. It is conveyed through statements such as, "I can see your maturity. . . ." Communicate the value of being responsible. Be convincing in communicating your belief in the good qualities of the student and in the capacity of the student to carry out the plan. Every troubled student is enmeshed in self-doubt. It is not likely that a student can come up with the self-confidence to make significant changes in behavior unless important adults clearly convey confidence.

Benefits must be included in the plan for success. Benefits are not easily anticipated by most troubled students. They seem to live with a sense of immediacy that precludes planning. They also seem to operate under a cloud of pessimism, always ready to see the worst possible side of every person and event. To a large extent, experience has been the teacher, and their experiences have been downers.

Watch for these same qualities in yourself. If you do not convey confidence and approval, you probably will not be successful in helping students to see that desirable things can happen even as they face the consequences of their old behaviors, alter their strategies for dealing with problems, and change the way they view themselves. Teaching students to look at the future with optimism requires optimism and enthusiasm on the part of the adult. The following are examples of statements that convey future benefits:

"If you can do this, people will give you a break. They'll treat you with (respect, fairness, love, kindness, understanding)."

"When you start making these changes, people are going to start saying, 'Wow, I want to be around her.'"

"When you handle things this way, people will say you are a person they can count on."

"Your friends are going to look up to you."

"People will see you as (a leader, a really nice person, a friend, someone they enjoy being with)."

"This will give you the chance to show the really nice things about yourself."

As You Transition to Stage 6

When a student tells how the current issue will be handled and responds constructively to the idea that the issue will come up again in the future, the student is ready for Stage 6. You know that the LSCI has been successful if the student provides constructive and realistic responses to the present situation and future incidents. You will have a sense that the student is realistic about the current consequences and ready to try a new solution, recognizing that it will not be easy to implement but worth the effort in future benefits. The following are examples of ways to end Stage 5:

"This has been tough talk, but it's going to pay off for you!"
"You have a view about this that will really work for you."
"Things will be better when you handle it this way."
"It won't be easy, but I believe you can do it!"
"You can do this, even if it's hard to do."

Stage 6: Transfer of Learning (Get Ready To Resume the Activity)

SYNOPSIS OF STAGE 6

The last stage in LSCI is the plan for the student's transition back into the group. This stage helps the student prepare for reentering and participating in

(continues)

an ongoing activity. It also is important to use this stage to close down private topics or feelings brought out during LSCI. Table 5.6 illustrates the dynamics of Stage 6.

The topic shifts in this last stage. The incident and the central issue have been put to rest, at least temporarily. A solution has been worked out. The discussion centers on where the student will go now, as LSCI ends. Discuss what has happened while the student has been away, what the student will do, and how others will react as the student rejoins the group. Affirmations of the student's new insights and competence for carrying out the new plan are essential if you want to assure that the student is empowered to be successful.

Stage 6 ends when the student is under rational control, has described the behaviors needed for successful reentry, and conveys a responsible attitude for participating in the group.

What Happens in Stage 6?

Stage 6 generally begins with questions such as the following:

"What is your group doing now?"

"When you left the group, they were writing news reports. Do you think they are still at it?"

"We've been in here for quite a while. Do you think your group is still working on that same project?"

"When you go back to your room, what will they be doing?"

TABLE 5.6
Stage 6: Transfer of Learning

Student	Staff Goals	Staff Skills
Transfer of Learning	**Transfer and Follow Up**	**Transfer and Follow-Up Skills**
This is how I need to behave to get more of my needs met when I return to class!	This is what I need to do to prepare the student to return to the classroom and to reinforce his new insights and social skills.	Understanding group forces in the classroom Collaboration skills with significant staff Assisting staff in developing positive reinforcement programs

Such questions shift the focus from the student to another place and other people. The questions are designed to help a student begin to think about the peer group, the activity that has gone on while the student has been away, and the expectations for participation and appropriate behavior.

Like the first LSCI stage, the last stage often is brief because the student usually is eager to put the problem aside and get back to the group. This response is typical of students who believe that there has been a satisfactory solution. These students also have developed some additional confidence in themselves during the LSCI.

The moment of reentry into a group is a powerful one. A student has usually left the group because of crisis and conflict. Now, as the student is poised on the edge of reentry, there is a choice between defensive reactions or participation, with the best possible face put on for the group. An emphasis on participation and looking good in the eyes of peers can do the most for enhancing the reentry process.

The Expectation to Participate. To help a student accept responsibility for participating, review anticipated activities and expectations for participation in detail. We have seen students make substantial progress in highly successful LSCIs, and then lose it all because they had not been sufficiently prepared for the demands made on them when they reentered their group. The fewer surprises the better. The following are examples of ways a student can be prepared for the expectation to participate:

"They are keeping your work for you. You will have time to finish it before lunch."

"The project will be over by now, and they will be working on something new. The teacher will tell you how to do it."

"I know you are sorry to have missed the field trip because of our talk, but we have done something important in here today. They'll want to tell you about the trip when they get back. That will give you the chance to use what we have been practicing in here."

By reviewing the behavior needed for successful reentry and participation before a student returns to the group, the student has increased assurance that the reentry can be handled smoothly and without further embarrassment. When you include affirmations of the student, you increase self-confidence. Without feelings of confidence, students seldom make it back to the door before anxiety floods again and the student is out of control.

Regression and Resistance. Occasionally you may have a student who participates in LSCI with cooperation and collaboration until the talk turns to returning to the group. If a student loses control, appears to suddenly reject everything that has gone on previously, seems reluctant to return to the group, or tries to control the reentry process, something is producing anxiety about the reentry. The student may have one of the following problems:

1. The student may have more to say than has come out in the LSCI.

2. The student may lack the confidence to make the shift back to being a participating group member.

3. The student may have difficulty separating from the interviewer.

Consider each possibility. You may find that you need to go back to an earlier stage to bring out something that has been overlooked. Or you may have to review again the plan you and the student rehearsed in the previous stage, perhaps modifying it to be more realistic about what the student can do successfully. Or you may have to examine the quality of the relationship that has developed between you and the student. The student may be feeling the anxiety that comes with separation from you. Your role in that relationship may be the significant force, fueling resistance to reentry or spiraling negative behavior. We discuss ways to handle this in the following chapter on the helping process and potential pitfalls.

Reactions of the Peer Group. The success of a student's reentry is directly related to how effectively someone deals with the peer group while the student is away. It requires close teamwork to reconnect the student and peers. Too much emphasis on the student's problem in front of peers tends to highlight the deviance, while ignoring the disruption to the group or the discomfort of group members communicates either the adult's desire to ignore it or inability to handle it.

In the complex dynamics of a peer group, the reentry of a member who has been away will almost always cause disturbance in other members of the group. This reaction is intensified dramatically when the absent member left the group under less than pleasant circumstances and may have transgressed against members of the group. Even if not directly involved, members watch a crisis with fascination, closely identifying with trouble and vicariously projecting themselves into the situation.

When the student reenters, it often excites the group again, and these reactions need to be anticipated. Sometimes the reactions will be directed against the reentering student, sometimes against the adult, and often against each other. Anticipating these reactions often heads off trouble.

The adult who remains with the group must deal with the reactions of group members during the time the student is away. Spiraling anxiety can be diluted or avoided by sensitive observation and redirection of each member to something personally successful. During this time group members want to be reassured that they are "safe," the adult in charge is looking after their needs, and the absent student is being treated fairly. The following are examples of statements made by teachers and teacher aides to reassure the peer group:

"You're doing so well with this project that you should be able to show him the finished product by the time he gets back." [The message—Everything is under control, and the student will return to participate.]

"When we see a friend having to leave the room, we wonder what is happening to her. She is okay, and when she works out the problem with the teacher, she will be back." [The message—The student is not being brutalized; she is problem solving.]

"When a problem gets out of hand, it is a good thing to go out with a teacher to talk." [The message—A talk with an adult is the way to solve a problem.]

Your Role in Stage 6

The relationship between adult and student is significant in every stage of LSCI. However, this final stage validates the relationship developed in the preceding stages. If you have not been on target, the student will present some of the problems we have described in the section on regression and resistance. If you have been accurate in identifying and conveying the type of adult role the student needs, using the type of strategies that influence the student, the student will respond constructively to this last stage. The relationship you have established through your adult role should provide the student with confidence that reentry is something that can be handled in a satisfactory way.

The view a student holds about adults changes as a result of increasing emotional maturity. (We discuss adult roles and styles of influence in Chapter 4, and again in Stage 2 of this chapter.) The following are illustrations of how these changing roles are conveyed by adults during Stage 6:

"If this trouble starts again when you go back, remember that you decided to tell the teacher before you get in trouble." [Adults provide protection, power, and approval.]

"I've noticed how you can control yourself even when others are losing it. When you go back, keep your attention on the assignment and you will be the winner!" [Adults' attitudes and views are best, and so they should be imitated and internalized.]

"This is your chance to show the other students your style. When you go back in there cool and calm, they'll know you have the situation under control." [Adult mirrors the student's best self—one who can be independently responsible.]

By the time you have reached Stage 6, you have established a level of trust with the student. He or she has decided to share with you some private thoughts and feelings, trusting that you can help relieve stress and make things a little better. The student has developed a plan, and you have an investment in his or her success. Committing oneself to a goal, especially when it relates to a change in one's habitual behavior, is no small task. Consider what adults do when they set and commit to a goal; for example, the goal of losing 10 pounds: They surround themselves with "reminders" of the goal, such as a calorie intake record, a chart by the bathroom scale, a brown-bag lunch with measured portions. They also engage in positive self-talk ("Nothing tastes as good as slim feels") and reward themselves for incremental weight loss achievements (that CD they've been wanting at 5 pounds, 100 dollars in new clothes at 10). If adults construct such behavioral and cognitive strategies to achieve their goals, it is expected that children and youth will also need support as they attempt to reach their goals.

Ideally, the interviewer will collaborate with other important adults to establish conditions under which the student can practice new skills and enjoy a measure of success as he or she approximates these goals. A wide variety of behavioral and cognitive strategies are available to help the student, including contracts with various adults in the school setting, environmental prompts such as posters and signs, and charts and graphs showing the student's progress towards the goal. If the student is to be successful in changing a repetitive pattern of behaving, our support is essential.

As You End Stage 6

The end of Stage 6 usually signals the end of the LSCI. The student understands that the next stage is to rejoin the group and participate in a responsible way. If the LSCI has been effective, the student's insight has changed, anxiety has been reduced, and self-esteem has been enhanced. The therapeutic goal has been accomplished, and the student is left with changes in emotional memories—a modified private storehouse containing better thoughts and feelings. These are the ingredients of confidence. They carry over as the student leaves the privacy of the LSCI setting and begins to put these changes into action in the peer group and classroom.

The following are statements that end the LSCI conveying confidence that the student can carry out the plan for responsible behavior and participation. We put them in a sequence of students' increasing emotional maturity.

"The next time he starts that stuff, what are you going to do so you won't be in trouble?"

"You've made a lot of progress today. When you go back to the group now, keep thinking about our plan and you will have a good day!"

"You know what to expect from the others when you go back to class. It's going to be tough, but I have confidence that you can handle it now without getting into trouble again. If you spot trouble beginning, let's come out here and talk again before it happens."

"We have some things to continue talking about on another day. When we talk together like we did today, we can work out ways to handle this problem."

At the end of LSCI, you may find yourself wondering, "How long before we have to go at it again?" Don't be discouraged. Each LSCI can be a building block for genuine change, but lasting change comes slowly and in small increments. View each LSCI as one small stage in a series. Each discussion that expands a student's self-confidence, insight, and ability to change behavior is a step toward eventual independent problem solving and emotional maturity.

WHAT WE HAVE LEARNED USING LSCI

- Don't begin LSCI if a student is out of control or emotionally flooding; use behavioral controls or Emotional First Aid instead. (We discuss this topic in the next chapter.)

- Don't begin LSCI if you are overwhelmed by the crisis, the student, or your own feelings; wait until your own reactions are rational, objective, and completely under control.

- Don't begin LSCI if you cannot take the time to go the distance, as needed, through the stages; 30 minutes is about average for a typical LSCI (highly verbal or resistant students may need more time). As the student becomes familiar with LSCI, and you build a relationship and history, the length of time required becomes shorter.

- Maintain a mind-set that crisis is a time for teaching and learning, not judging and punishing, a time of instruction and not destruction.

- You (not the student) must control the pacing in LSCI, spending as much time as is needed with each stage; and you decide when it is over.

- Sometimes LSCI will not occur in orderly stages; you may find yourself cycling back through Stages 2 and 3 several times, to clarify or expand an issue.

- If you have some doubt about a central issue or selecting the proper Reclaiming Intervention, deliberately go back through Stages 2 and 3, and try more decoding.

- Don't feel that you must complete all six stages each time you begin LSCI; if necessary, go directly from Stage 3 to Stage 6, and close down the LSCI with the message that you and the student will talk again.

- Keep in mind that behavior, feelings, and anxieties cannot be changed by a single LSCI; it is through repeated use that lasting changes result.

- Remember the details of each LSCI, so that you can build continuity into the next one with the same student.

WHAT WE HOPE YOU HAVE LEARNED IN THIS REVIEW OF BASICS

- The purpose in using LSCI rather than an alternative behavior management strategy
- What occurs to end Stage 1

- In which stage a student is encouraged to talk, even if what is being said is not particularly truthful or logical

- In which stages you decode and probe for meaning

- The stage in which you finally select a therapeutic goal or Reclaiming Intervention

- The point in LSCI where you switch from talking about the problem to talking about solutions

- The particular statement that you must make before LSCI can shift from discussion of the crisis to discussion of solutions

- The stages in which you use the most probes and interpretations as parts of decoding

- What a student should say before a complete LSCI ends

- Why a cooperative student might begin to be disruptive toward the end of the LSCI

- The purpose of interjecting affirmations of the student into every LSCI stage

Crisis reveals
character . . . ours!

The Helping Process and Potential Pitfalls

6

Now that you have reviewed the six basic stages of LSCI, you are ready to try it. Don't be reluctant to begin. If you are hesitant about your mastery of the background information, keep working on it, but at the same time, begin using LSCI. Nothing is as effective for learning it as actually doing it. As you begin, remember the basics: the name, purpose, insight, and content of each LSCI stage. (We know teachers who actually taped the names of the stages to the wall of a conference room while learning the process.) Remember to decode when a student responds with emotionally laden behavior and, more important, affirm the student as often as you can during every stage, making sure the comment is genuine.

Because LSCI is a helping process built on interactions between you and a student, it requires personal attributes and skills as well as understanding. Perhaps there is no other circumstance that will illuminate your own personal characteristics and style more vividly than LSCI.

The helping process makes huge demands on the adult. In this chapter we take you beyond the basics of LSCI to consider the attributes and skills an adult must have to use LSCI effectively. We first review some basic qualities needed to be effective in the helping process and provide a list of specific skills. Then we describe ways to provide Emotional First Aid to help students who are so flooded by emotion that rational processes are not working and they are unable to participate in LSCI. In the final section of this chapter we describe typical problems that occur when an adult slips away from using these attributes and skills.

ATTRIBUTES AND SKILLS FOR ADULTS IN THE HELPING PROCESS

When working with children and youth in crisis, adults need to acknowledge, accept, understand, believe, and appreciate that emotions are the powerful, personal engines that drive or generate human behavior. Strong emotions are present in every LSCI, and they are generated not only by students, but also by adults. Our emotions and attitudes may (or may not) be hidden, but they are nevertheless active in our behavior. Management of these personal feelings and resulting behaviors may become a central force for many adults during LSCI. (Student crisis can evoke a Conflict Cycle in adults, unless they guard against it.)

To be helpful to a student in crisis, an adult must have a genuine desire to help the student rather than to express personal reactions to the incident. An adult must simultaneously be direct, realistic, clear, and supportive. When adults are caught up in the stress of an incident, their own emotions are added to the crisis, and their energies go into coping with their personal feelings, behavior, and the reactions of others instead of going into the helping process. You cannot be helpful to a student if you are not able to detach your own needs from the incident, the student's behavior, and the associated stress you may feel. We consider Carl Rogers' (1965) descriptions of trust-promoting characteristics for the helping process extremely important in keeping an adult focused on the job of being a helping person during LSCI:

Empathy: Understanding students' feelings and actions
Genuineness: Being consistent, dependable, and real
Positive regard: Conveying caring and interest
Concreteness: Using specific, clear language
Unconditional acceptance: Approving the person but not the behavior

Another resource for adults concerned about being effective as a helping person is Warnock's (1971) four broad guides to universal values. As "ethics of helping" we have found them useful. With some license here, we put them in a context, as guidelines for the behavior of adults who help students in crisis:

• *Don't hurt others.* Keep your words and actions free from psychological hurt or intrusion. Blame, disgust, sarcasm, or dismay have no place in LSCI. Show respect for your students, and don't invade their personal space.

• *Be obviously kind.* Be abundant in your use of affirmation, praise, and interest. Show kindness, especially during the problem phases of LSCI. Convey compassion, acceptance, and respect for the student even while acknowledging the seriousness of the situation and disapproval of the behavior.

• *Be fair to all, not selective.* Let your actions show that you are not selective in your dealings, treating all who are involved in a crisis with the same consideration and fairness. "Fair" should be the adjective students use to describe you, as you help them during crisis. Let them know that fairness is a top priority with you.

• *Don't deceive or distort the truth.* Few adults admit to deceiving or distorting reality or "the truth." But it can happen if adults avoid painful issues, ignore important concerns of a student, or "fudge" on central issues. Present reality in objective ways. Weigh the significance of "the truth" as the student believes it to be and as others perceive it. Then share this insight with the student.

These general attributes and attitudes reflect a lot about the character of an adult. They are the solid foundation for the helping process. How they are put into action during LSCI will influence the eventual success or failure of LSCI.

We turn now to some very specific adult skills that contribute to effective LSCI. Beyond mastery of the basic six LSCI stages, we have observed that effective adults have considerable skills in relationship building and communication. Table 6.1 contains an outline of these essential skills, organized into three categories: relationship, verbal style, and nonverbal body language. We use these three categories as a way to organize the skills into a checklist to guide adults who are learning to use LSCI. (This reproducible checklist is contained in Appendix B for use by adults in training and by their supervisors.) Clearly, these categories overlap. An effective relationship is built on communication skills, while nonverbal body language is a form of communication and is also a major element in building relationship. The important point is that the adult use as many of these skills as possible during LSCI.

You may find it helpful, while interacting with students, to check yourself for these characteristics. Try to identify what you actually do to get across caring attitudes about your students. If you cannot find them in yourself, spend some time experimenting with ways to communicate them to your students. While monitoring your own words and actions, also keep in mind the four fundamental concerns of most students that we described in Chapter 1: protection, gratification, relationship, and responsibility. Your students will be looking for these kinds of reassurances from you throughout the LSCI.

We encourage readers to also seek supervision while learning LSCI. It is not a simple technique but an adventure in teaching, learning, and character building during a time of crisis. It goes far beyond intellectual understanding of the purposes and procedures for the six stages. It requires the adult to have the capacity to relate to the student, to decode behavior, and to accept deeper feelings without becoming defensive, counter-aggressive, or caught up in the Conflict Cycle.

EMOTIONAL FIRST AID

Students in crisis may need immediate help and support when their defenses become ineffective and they are overwhelmed by feelings and the demands of crisis. Flooding emotions distort reality perceptions and dominate behavior. It is not unusual for a student to cling doggedly to the last emotion or perception experienced in a crisis, and this becomes the reality for the student. When behavior is driven by intense feelings, the student is not responsive to rational thinking or talking. A student in this condition is not yet ready for LSCI; Emotional First Aid is needed.

The purpose in providing Emotional First Aid is to reduce emotional intensity to the point that a student can participate in a dialogue. This process requires a shift from behavioral expression of feelings to rational use of words instead. Emotional First Aid also conveys that a student can count on the adult's support and help in resolving the

TABLE 6.1
Skills for Adults Using LSCI

Nonverbal Body Language

Convey support and alliance through body posture.
Use eye contact or the opposite as needed to provide "space."
Vary voice quality and volume as needed.
Use physical stance to convey needed adult role and relationship.
Avoid excessive touch.
Maintain physical proximity or distance as needed.
Stand or sit as needed to convey control.
Convey interest, support, or other messages through facial expressions.

Verbal Style

Use concrete words for clarity.
Use imagery to motivate.
Convey ideas clearly.
Maximize student's talk.
Minimize own talk.
Use a timeline to help student organize events.
Assist student in clarifying an issue.
Assist student in seeing cause-and-effect relationships.
Use reflection effectively.
Use interpretation effectively.
Decode accurately.
Use third-person form to generalize.
Limit use of references to yourself.
Limit use of negative statements.

Relationship

Use active listening.
Communicate respect for student.
Communicate interest.
Communicate calm self-control.
Convey confidence and optimism.
Convey focus and competence.
Avoid intruding into student's private "space."
Avoid value judgments.
Avoid role reversals.
Avoid counteraggression.

crisis. The following are several statements teachers have used to convey this reassuring message:

"It (you) will be all right."
"There is a way to handle every problem."
"I'll bet if we talk about it, we can get a handle on it."
"This situation may not be as serious as it seems."
"I've seen you handle problems like this before, and you did it well."

Redl (1966) describes ways to provide Emotional First Aid, depending on what is needed to assist a student in putting emotions and behavior under rational management. The following material summarizes these five ways of providing Emotional First Aid.

Drain Off Emotional Intensity

Defusing emotional intensity helps students manage frustration or anger by reducing the amount of emotion injected into a crisis. It also is a useful way to intervene early in a potential Conflict Cycle and avoid spiraling emotions. For some adults, defusing emotional intensity, or "drain off" can be difficult. Students overwhelmed with emotion may swear, or say things about other adults that are hard to hear without becoming outraged or angry ourselves. For some students, particularly those who are the most challenging, we have to remember that our goal is to reduce the level of intensity in order to begin LSCI. We cannot allow the student's language to divert us from the goal; an argument about choice of words at this time will intensify the conflict. Instead, we must listen sympathetically, identifying and verbalizing a student's feelings of anger, disgust, fear, or panic regarding cruel, frustrating, or disappointing life events. The following are some examples used by adults to reduce students' emotional intensity, maintain communication, and convey understanding:

"It's really upsetting (unfair, scary, mean, cruel)."

"It's okay to feel like this; it will get better."

"Of course you're angry with him; you believe he embarrassed you in front of the group on purpose. It's understandable that you're upset."

"Other students who have had this same thing happen had those same feelings."

"Sometimes when people feel like this, they think nothing good can ever happen to them again. But there is a way to work it out."

These statements generally assure the student that it is all right to have those feelings and that they will not last forever. In the last two examples, the third-person form is used to convey that others have had the same feelings (and lived through them), and the student is having a very human experience. Use of the third-person form also avoids intruding into a student's personal space. Some students will talk with you about feelings of others when they will not (or cannot) tolerate talk about their own emotions. The following are two teachers' descriptions of how this type of Emotional First Aid was used to reduce emotional intensity.

Bill's Physical Education Teacher. The physical education period was just about over when I blew the whistle and asked the group to stop and put away the trampoline. Bill objected, saying that everybody had had three turns except him and he wasn't going to be gypped. I sympathized with his situation but explained that our time was up and that the best I could do, if he cooperated, was to see that he would be first next time.

Perry's Teacher. Perry had just completed painting his clay horse and was proudly showing it off to the group when Jim shoved Larry who bumped into Perry, causing him to drop his horse which shattered when it hit the floor. Perry was furious and started to attack Larry. When I stopped him, he broke into tears. I said, "This is a terrible disappointment, after all the work you've done! The other guys feel awful about it, too. They thought it was such a neat horse. Let's stop and think about what should be done about this horse now."

The first example illustrates prevention of a blow-up with a simple statement of understanding and concern for fairness; the second conveys understanding and sympathy and offers a rational beginning to problem solving by redirecting Perry away from the boys who accidentally caused the mishap to the problem of what to do about the horse.

Support a Student Engulfed in Intense Emotion

Often an adult stages into a situation that is already out of control. A student's level of panic, anger, fury, guilt, or anxiety is so high that behavioral controls have disappeared. The goal of this type of Emotional First Aid is to protect the student and others from the rage and temporary confusion. Occasionally, this calls for physical intervention until the student's own controls are functioning again. The following are examples of statements adults can make to provide this type of aid:

> "I'll have to protect you until you can help yourself."
> "Teachers are in control here."
> "This is the sort of thing teachers handle."
> "Sometimes kids have to trust adults to take care of problems."
> "There are rules about this situation, and we follow rules here."

Each of these statements provides supportive but firm assurance that external structure, adult authority, and rules guide management of the crisis. The first statement is in first-person form, for situations where a student needs to know that this adult is going to be in charge of the student. The next two statements are phrased in the third person to defuse possible personal confrontation between an out-of-control student and the adult. In the last statement, the plural first-person form is used to convey teamwork—together things will be all right.

The following are two reports, from a teacher and a coach, illustrating their first aid to students out of control and overwhelmed by emotions:

Carla's Teacher. Hearing screams from the corridor, I entered Mrs. Andersen's room and found Vera and Carla in a wild fight. I demanded that they stop, but Carla was too angry to hear. As I separated them, Carla started to hit me, so I had to restrain her physically until she could calm down. I finally talked her down by saying, "Carla, take a deep breath. I'm going to hold you until your breathing comes easy. Then we can talk about what happened."

Charlie's Coach. I heard a muffled sound coming from the rear of the library and found Charlie with his head down in one of the study carrels, crying. I had no idea why. I put my hand on his shoulder and said, "Charlie, let's talk about it. I'll bet between the two of us, we can figure out how to make it better."

Maintain Communication When Relationships Are Breaking Down

In an intense crisis, some students withdraw and become uncommunicative or go into a prolonged anger, sulking and refusing to talk. Unless this defense is penetrated, the world of hostile fantasy can be more destructive to them than the world of reality. The purpose of this type of Emotional First Aid is to redirect students away from this reaction by engaging them in any kind of conversation until they feel more comfortable with their thoughts and feelings. Occasionally gadgets, food, or humor are effective ways of thawing a student from a frozen sulk. The following are descriptions of how two teachers used this type of Emotional First Aid to stay in touch with students until they could be reached for a rational LSCI:

Craig's Teacher. Craig was kept after school to complete his arithmetic assignment. He sat at his desk, folded his arms, looked at me with blazing eyes, and said, "I'm doing nothing and saying nothing. So leave me alone!" When I tried to talk to him, he covered his ears with his hands. So I sat down at the table near him with the materials I was using to make a board game for reading. The pieces were race cars. Although I was silent, I made certain Craig saw them. It wasn't long before he asked, "What's that for?" Now we were in a communication mode and ready to begin LSCI.

Martin's Teacher. Martin kept staring out the window all the time I was talking to him. After many futile attempts to get a response from him, I asked Martin to draw a finger picture on the windowpane and I would try to guess what it was. Halfheartedly he drew a circle that I said was a purple elephant taking a bath in a white Volkswagen. With great effort Martin tried to hide his smile. Then I said, "I'll do one now, for you to guess." Martin nodded that he was interested and guessed my quick design to be an engine falling off a pickup truck and smashing into pieces on an interstate. That imagery made our entry into the first stage of LSCI.

Regulate Social Behavior

Most students quickly learn the rules of a program and are astute at describing conflicting adult standards and contradictions between actions and words, but they often need daily reminders of the rules and regulations if they are to remain in the activity or lesson. The purpose of this type of Emotional First Aid is to provide positive assistance to a student by warning of potential dangers that lie ahead if present behavior is continued. This is an easy form of advice for adults to dispense because it usually is needed before emotions get out of control. The following are several examples:

> "I explained to Sally that in order to stay in the group she would have to keep her hands to herself."

> "Each day I have to remind Bill that he must finish his assignment before he can play softball when the group goes out to recess."

> "When Karen starts complaining in a shrill voice that someone is bothering her, I tell her to use a calm voice and let the person know that it bothers her."

> "Roger likes to make smart remarks to get attention. I remind him that one of our rules is to do things so others can get their work done. This seems to be enough to drain away his interest in getting someone else upset."

Act as Umpire

Often students try to cast an adult in the role of umpire to help settle intense disputes, grievances, or game violations. This form of Emotional First Aid is especially appropriate for students in the preexistential phase of development or going through the Existential Crisis (see Chapter 4). Many important therapeutic gains can be made when an adult assumes this role as a fair and equitable arbitrator. Most students respect and respond quickly to the adult as umpire. Two examples follow:

Ralph's Recreation Leader. Ralph came to me complaining about Peter. It seemed that every time Peter began losing in chess he introduced a new rule. The latest one was that his father told him that the king can move two spaces in any direction once both castles are taken. I explained to Peter that although special rules can be worked out at home, we follow standard chess rules here.

Davey's Teacher. My class was playing dodgeball. One of the rules we agreed on was that if a ball touched any part of the student in the circle, that student exchanged places with the thrower. In this incident the ball skimmed Davey's hair. He claimed that he had not been hit but skimmed. When the group demanded that he change places, he turned to me for support only to hear me rule the skim was a hit and that he would have to change places.

After Emotional First Aid

If Emotional First Aid has been used appropriately, adult authority is established, students are supported, emotions are expended, and rational words replace behavior as the way to communicate. Often, Emotional First Aid preempts the need for LSCI, but if LSCI is indicated, Emotional First Aid helps students to settle down and participate. For those students who are still not able to mobilize themselves sufficiently to problem solve, you may have to end with a decision that reentry and participation in the ongoing activity are the most that can be obtained at the present. When you make this decision, convey clearly what is expected from the student in behavior and participation. Also be sure the student understands that (a) you have judged this to be the best course of action for the present, (b) the student has qualities that will help make the reentry and appropriate participation successful, and (c) there will be other times to talk again.

POTENTIAL PITFALLS IN USING LSCI

Although we ordinarily prefer to use a positive focus when preparing adults to use LSCI, it may be helpful to show how problems arise and provide specific suggestions for what can be done about them. We have identified 13 responses adults frequently use that create unnecessary problems. Everyone makes these mistakes at one time or another when using LSCI. The important lesson to be learned is the value of self-monitoring so that you recognize why a particular LSCI goes astray and what you can do to improve it next time.

Beginning LSCI When a Student Is Not Ready

Never go beyond Stage 1 until the student has given you some verbal response. Don't even think of it! We have described the importance of reducing emotional flooding before you begin Stage 1. We also have suggested the use of affirmations for a resistant student, or the use of gadgets, food, or humor as a type of Emotional First Aid to help a student shift from an emotional to a rational, verbal mode. There will be times when all of these strategies fail to get a student started. If you try all of these strategies and the student remains noncommunicative, wait. Silence can be a powerful device for mobilizing a student toward verbal interaction. There are several ways to use silence effectively as you wait.

Thinking Silence. Some students need time to get themselves under control, to consider how to express themselves, or to consider the feelings and facts surrounding an event. The body language they use is generally not emotion laden. When you suspect this is going on inside a student's head, respect the silence and sanction it with a statement such as the following:

"It's helpful to think about what happened before we talk."

Silence as Confusion. If the student's behavior suggests anxiousness or confusion, it is possible that the student lacks a grasp of what happened or has insufficient verbal ability to get talk started. Sometimes students will pick or twist their fingers, squirm, or kick their feet to convey their confusion or inability to respond. If you suspect this, try tapping into some concrete, key recollection with a statement or question such as the following:

"Tell me what you heard."
"What was the very first thing that happened?"

Such openings from you may help the student connect to a timeline or remember a vivid aspect of the incident that can begin LSCI.

Silence as Resistance. Sometimes silence is used by students to test their independence or resist adult authority. If you have attempted all of the above strategies, or conclude that a student is deliberately resisting your attempts to start LSCI, try one (or two) last attempts to get the student involved with a three-stage sequence of reflection, decoding facts, and a question such as the following:

"When you sit there saying nothing you are missing out on what the others are doing—having fun." [Reflection]

"Sometimes people don't talk because they don't want to get their friends in trouble." [Decoding fact of not talking]

"But right now your friends are having fun and what are they saying?" [Question]

A sequence like this usually evokes at least a verbal response of "I don't know!" You have shifted the student into using a verbal means of interacting with you. If there is no response, go back and try decoding with greater depth, using statements such as the following:

"Maybe students don't talk because they don't trust teachers to understand and help."

"I have the feeling this discussion is upsetting you. It's okay to tell me that you don't want to talk."

"I see it's difficult to continue. I wonder if your silence is connected to something I said."

In the rare instance when these last statements do not produce some verbal response, the student may be (a) developmentally below the level of comprehending your words,

(b) incapable of energizing mental forces (drugs? psychosis? seizures?), or (c) testing you to the limit.

Every adult who works with troubled students has encountered the youngster who "digs in" and refuses to engage in a dialogue or bring a matter to closure. We have two strategies to suggest. Rather than engage in a power struggle, point out that you recognize this issue is difficult for the student to discuss. "It is so hard for you to talk about this that you would rather be silent. Perhaps the issue goes deeper than you are ready to share." Conclude with the hope that more progress will be made at another time, and wrap up by moving to Stage 6. A second strategy is to note the resistance and divert the discussion to relationships which may be at the center of the resistance. "Let's set this aside for now and talk about how you are feeling about me (your teacher, friends, etc.)." The student's refusal to talk may have more to do with a relationship than with feelings about the event being discussed. Ultimately, we have to bring the dialogue to closure, but we want to avoid developing a stalemate. We have plenty of time. Since we have chosen to begin LSCI, the triggering event is representative of the student's rigid pattern of perceiving, thinking, feeling, and behaving, and by definition, will present itself again soon and offer other opportunities for exploration.

Getting Off the Subject

Balancing the extent to which you let a student digress and the extent to which you keep the discussion on the topic is one of the most difficult things to do during LSCI Stages 2 and 3. We have found it helpful to keep in mind the purposes of these stages: for the student, to talk, cool down, and use words rationally; for the adult, to begin to shape the real issue for the next stage in the LSCI.

Sometimes digressions can help the process by giving students an opportunity to communicate on subjects that are not emotionally connected. Digressions also can broaden communication about an incident by indicating information that has significance to a student. We call these signal flares. A signal flare appears as an out-of-context comment. It can signal that a topic appearing to be a simple digression actually has some bearing on the incident, has associated feelings, or is part of a greater anxiety that has found expression through the incident. It may change the course of the LSCI by bringing out a deeper concern. In other instances, a signal flare is used by a student to keep you away from a discussion about the issue. The following are examples of each type of signal flare:

Using a signal flare to bring out a deeper concern. In the midst of a talk about a fight with another boy on the playground, Jeff fires an unexpected question at the teacher, "Are you adopted?" His teacher suspects it may be a signal flare (because Jeff was adopted and has been setting fires at home), but she is not sure whether it indicates a deeper concern or an attempt to get the teacher off the subject of the fight.

The teacher makes a neutral statement and follows it with a question as a preliminary probe, "Adoption is something a lot of kids think about. Do you think about being adopted?"

There is a long silence, and then Jeff quietly says, "Yes, my real parents were killed in a plane crash when I was a baby."

This led to a dramatic shift in the LSCI, to talk about Jeff's thoughts about what happened after the crash, and how a judge found ideal parents for him. Jeff told the story with great detail, intensity, and imagination. It was clear that he had told it to himself many times before. The teacher used this signal flare and continued the story, reflecting that it is important for babies to have parents that care, and how parents show their care. At the end of the story, the teacher decoded for Jeff.

"Boys think a lot about their parents and have high expectations for them. Sometimes, when kids disagree with their parents, they become angry at them, and this feeling stays on the kids' minds and they get into trouble at school."

There was a long silence after that, and then Jeff said, "Yep, that's right."

This was as far as the talk about the deeper concern went for this particular LSCI. The teacher then bridged back to the playground incident and continued through the LSCI stages. She knew that the topic deeply troubled Jeff and needed to be aired, but enough had been done with it for the first time.

Using a signal flare to avoid talking about the issue. Rick was brought to the counselor because his math teacher suspected that he had stolen a watch from another student. As soon as he sat down, Rick began talking.

> R: My math teacher is mean, unfair, and has pets in class. He doesn't know how to do his job. Everyone knows it. It's been going on for years. He should be fired!

What a temptation for the counselor to react to any one of these accusations and innuendoes! But she recognizes this signal flare as an attempt by Rick to keep the LSCI away from the real issue of the watch.

> C: This watch you're wearing is the issue.

When he sees that the counselor does not buy into his attempt to get her off the subject, Rick tries several other signal flares.

> R: I bought this watch from a guy for $1.00 last night at the ball game!
>
> C: Then we need to talk with the person who sold it to you.
>
> R: I don't know who it was—just a guy.
>
> C: When a guy comes to school wearing an expensive watch, and another student reports that his watch is missing, what are we to think?
>
> R: Are you saying I stole it? Didn't you ever take anything when you were a kid? Everybody does it!

In this last example, Rick tries to reverse roles and control the LSCI. When this fails, he tries to divert the focus to the counselor's own childhood. (See LSCI Stage 2 description in Part II for more about signal flares.)

In either case, don't let a dialogue about a signal flare topic continue too long. If it is a real issue from a student's private reality, too much talk may be difficult for a student to handle on a first round. Prolonged discussions on sensitive topics usually result in a student's emotions flooding back again, and you are back to Stage 1 unnecessarily. If the signal flare is a deliberate digression to keep you away from a topic, don't let the student think you have forgotten about the incident. You do not want a student to control the LSCI.

Allowing an Adversarial Climate To Develop

The quality of the relationship between student and adult develops during Stages 2 and 3. Nothing will ice LSCI quicker than letting yourself be cast into the role of the judge, the adversary, or the "supreme being." Often this tone creeps into an exchange without the adult being aware of it. Vetted sarcasm, exasperation with the student, disgust, disbelief, or cynicism may convey such attitudes. Judgments about the generally undesirable nature of a student also may be applied by the type of statements an adult inadvertently makes. An experienced juvenile court worker described the phenomenon this way: "It's like two players in a tennis game. One makes a shot and the other responds. Sometimes your shot is out of the court and doesn't help you. But sometimes you can get in a smashing shot that is right where it should be. Then you've nailed your opponent!" You've won the point but lost your opponent. The obvious innuendo in this scenario is adversarial. Somebody wins and somebody loses. During Stages 2 and 3, the potential is there to set up such an adversarial relationship. The student is determined to win, and so are you. Guard against this; it has no place in the helping process!

When you sense an adversarial tone creeping into your LSCI, try to change it by deliberately breaking into the stream of discussion and interjecting an affirmation of some valuable attribute in the student. This action dilutes the potential for conflict. By deliberately aligning yourself with the student and expressing clear conviction that you have confidence in the student's ability to deal with the crisis, you dilute a potential adversarial position. A posture of fairness for all, which includes the student, is another way to avoid adversarial tones in LSCI. Remember that what we want is a win–win condition.

Reflecting Negatives

As feelings come out during LSCI, it often is the adult who initiates the topic by decoding what a student is feeling. When you do this, guard against reflecting negatives, such as "That was TERRIBLE . . ." "That was OVERWHELMING . . ." "That was a BRUTALIZING experience." These statements only reinforce the student's belief that he or she and the situation are impossible and hopeless.

The intent of the adult is to identify what the student may be feeling and to begin to teach the student that feelings can be put into words. Without the positive addition, the students' unpleasant feelings would be reinforced and their views of themselves as being full of unmanageable feelings would be expanded.

Permitting a Student to Seduce You into Counteraggression

Aggressive students have a way of engaging adults in personal struggles by using words and actions that "push the teacher's buttons." They say things within hearing distance, hoping the adult notices. They choose words and actions that they know the adult will respond to. If the lure is successful and the adult seizes the student's bait, the power struggle is on.

Unfortunately, the battle is one-sided. If the aggressive student wins, aggressive behavior is reinforced. If the student loses, but gets the adult to escalate tension with counteraggression (or open hostility toward the student, or rejection), the aggressive student wins the emotional war by "proving" that adults are hostile toward the student, do not really care, and cannot be trusted.

For the adult caught in this power struggle, the situation seems intolerable. Students' comments, such as shouting "No!" "So what?" "Forget you!" or "You can't make me do it!" beg for aggressive responses from the adult. What complicates the adult's position is that angry feelings and actions in response seem so justified. It seems logical and natural to put these arrogant, hostile, inconsiderate, hopeless students "in their places."

The solution for avoiding counteraggression is to recognize the dynamics of the Conflict Cycle, and to understand that the more an adult struggles with an aggressive student, the more likely it is that the adult will come out on the short end. For the adult to continue counteraggressive behavior is self-defeating. The adult who acts out personal feelings and does "what comes naturally" is perpetuating the aggressive cycle by mirroring the student's behavior and continuing an aggressive model. As a result, the statement "aggression elicits aggression" becomes true, and the aggressive student successfully determines the adult's behavior.

What must adults do to stop this destructive cycle? They must recognize and understand the seductive power of the Conflict Cycle they have been caught in. They must acknowledge that the student is actually controlling the adult's behavior. The adult must use self-control to break off the exchange, separating from personal feelings of righteous rage or the wish to subdue the student and win at any cost. And the adult must not seize the student's bait.

Treating Complex Feelings in Trivial Ways

A common mistake is to ask a student, "How does that make you feel?" before the student has the opportunity to tell his or her complete story. Many of the students we work with would fumble around unsuccessfully if asked such a question. If a student tries to answer this question at all, the typical answer is "I don't know." A student who responds this way has admitted openly to inadequacy. Equally unproductive is an adult's response to a student's answer about feelings that treats the information casually, with marginal compassion, or by trying to minimize the student's feelings. For example, a student may be able to come up with, "It makes me feel terrible," in answer to a question about feelings. If the adult responds, "It's not all that bad," or, "Come on now, it's not worth feeling that bad," the student has been put down and has no next move.

There are ways to teach verbal skills for describing feelings, such as asking the student, how would you show this feeling (e.g., anger, sadness, fear)? What would I see? We believe that teaching basic verbal skills to express feelings should begin in non-crisis situations. The sequence for learning increasingly complex expressions of emotion should be taught systematically.

Failing To Build LSCI Dialogue from a Student's Responses

One of the most commonly heard complaints from adults beginning to use LSCI is, "I don't know what to say!" Adults whose primary concern is their own performance in managing a crisis sometimes listen only to their own voices and their own agendas, and they seldom hear the messages in the student's words and actions. It requires considerable self-discipline and training to become a good listener who decodes and then responds to a student's responses, and resists the impulse to jump to conclusions and solutions.

The easiest way to overcome this problem is to use reflective statements (described in LSCI Stage 1), or to use follow-up questions with some of the student's *exact* words or ideas. An elaboration of this technique is to begin a statement with the words used by the student and then tack on your own new ideas at the end. Such bridging between you and the student conveys that you are listening and hearing.

Invading a Student's Private Space

Probably the most serious mistake made by adults in LSCI is intruding into a student's private psychological space before a student is ready to share it. Unwelcome intrusion usually happens as an adult begins to make interpretations, decoding the student's words and actions. If the interpretation is too private, too bold, or touches a topic too sensitive, a student will close down. Such interpretations often leave a student's private self exposed, without psychological protection. Saving face, like protecting from painful feelings, is a well-developed defense with almost all students. When your words call up these defenses, it is hard to go further, and few, if any, therapeutic gains can be made.

The best approach to a student's private space is an occasional sensitive probe followed by a neutral statement about the topic. A probe is a tentative follow-up question or statement about a topic or idea not touched upon before. Something in a student's words or actions will suggest a probe, although we are seldom certain about its accuracy until we try it. Students' reactions to a probe give you the information you need about its accuracy and their willingness to have that topic included in the LSCI.

Fly-fishing makes a nice metaphor to explain probes. In fly-fishing, the lure is lightly cast onto the surface of the stream. The fisherman casts with some knowledge that this is a likely spot to find a fish. However, there is no guarantee that the fly has landed in the right spot. So the fisherman moves up and down the area, casting again and again, until the connection is made. Probes are used in the same way. An interpretation is "cast" in the general direction you believe may be significant. When you get a "strike," you will know it from the student's response (or notable lack of response). In short, you have interpreted accurately, and the new bit of information goes into your decoding network. As the dialogue with a student continues, your probes take on greater accuracy and you will find yourself decoding increasingly more relevant interpretations about increasingly more sensitive and significant subjects. The student is letting you into that private space. The previous signal flare example with Jeff illustrates a student inviting an adult to share that space.

Carefully gauge a student's willingness to let you into his or her private space. If you sense resistance, or there is an increase of emotional intensity, it may be a sign that the student is not comfortable revealing more at this time. Respect the student's privacy and return to discussing the events of the incident.

Injecting Personal Comments About Yourself

As the personal, private side of a student unfolds, a caring adult often is caught up in compassion and feelings for the emotional suffering of the student. When this happens, it is natural for adults to want to let students know that they share similar experiences and feelings. This is an attempt to support a student by communicating understanding through mutual sharing, but it is seldom interpreted that way by students. When an adult brings personal experience into a discussion, students often see the adult as more centered on self than on the student ("All she wants to do is talk about herself"). This problem occurs more frequently than imagined, and it is usually not recognized or is vigorously denied by the adult. The following are some statements made by adults projecting their own personal experience unnecessarily into LSCI:

> "I have felt that way myself."
> "When I was your age that happened to me."
> "My best friend did the same thing to me."
> "People like that make me angry, too."

A better way to show understanding and compassion is by reflecting positively about the strengths of the student, affirming your confidence in the student's ability to resolve the crisis.

Allowing Students To Reverse Roles with You

Students with strong needs to control adults sometimes use the first three stages of LSCI to test their ability to control adults. Such students usually are skilled manipulators and very verbal. In fact, we have seen students who take charge of their LSCI, controlling the questions, answers, and movement through the stages. They also often try to make the decision about when to stop LSCI. This can happen to anyone, but don't let it happen to you.

The strategy most frequently used by such students is to ask the adult pleasant personal questions or to make observations about the adult's personal characteristics. The following are some typical statements and questions used by students to reverse roles (the student becomes the interviewer):

"Are you married?"
"Do you have children?"
"Are you a real teacher?"
"Your hair (belt, dress, shirt, etc.) is beautiful."
"You have big muscles."

If an adult responds to these harmless questions, the student forms the impression that topics for LSCI can be controlled by the student, and that an adult who can be controlled is a less reliable adult. If the adult actually answers these innocuous questions, more blatant testing of adult authority invariably follows:

"Why are we cooped up in here?"
"Why didn't you take the other guy out?"
"How long do we have to stay in here?"
"You don't understand the situation!"
"This isn't your business; it's between him and me."
"You really don't want to be fair, you only want to get me!"

If you let yourself respond to such statements, the student is testing for social power and controlling the LSCI. Equally devastating is ignoring a student's attempts to control, thereby creating the impression that things get by you or that you do not know how to respond to the remarks. Paradoxically, showing yourself to be inept or vulnerable to manipulation by a student is frightening to the student. The unspoken message is that you cannot control the situation. Students in crisis have to believe that the adult can handle the crisis in an expert fashion and not abdicate authority.

If an adult fails to communicate expertise in handling the minor attempts of students to reverse roles, they almost always continue to pursue the adult, testing for vulnerability until they find it or until they become convinced of the adult's dependability in handling the situation competently. Typically, the role reversals become more overtly confrontational and personal as these students try to exert power over the adult they perceive to be vulnerable to manipulation. The following are some typical examples of students attempting to control adults with personal attacks (notice the implied attempts to elicit counteraggression):

"Your breath stinks!"

"You don't really know what's going on."

"I'm going to get my dad to come down here and tell the principal what a lousy teacher you are."

"I can knock your head off whenever I want to."

"You're too fat to help anyone."

"I'm leaving and you can't stop me!"

By now, your decoding skills should be working, and you should recognize that these are really desperate remarks based on concern, anger, or fear. The student in each instance is asking for the adult to show that the student is not going to be left without an expert adult.

There are several ways to respond to students who try role reversal. The following are possible responses to first attempts, when a student uses innocuous questions or statements to see the extent of your vulnerability:

- Turn the question back to the student, rephrasing it to ask a personal question of the student.

- Use an affirmation to commend the student's interest in others (careful observations, interest in details, responsive to others, good with words).

- Make a statement such as, "What's important in this conversation is you (or what happened)." Then continue the talk about the incident.

If a student continues the intense personal verbal attack, decoding is essential. The student must know that you understand the feelings behind the attack, and that there is another way to help the student out of the desperate situation. The following are several examples of statements teachers have made in response to the previous examples:

"When we're talking about things that are uncomfortable, it doesn't help to try to change the subject."

"I can see how upset you are, but there are ways we can solve this problem."

"It seems to me that you had a choice, and now you regret it."

"What happens to you is what's important, and that will depend on what you do!"

Failing To State the Central Issue Simply and Concisely

As you and a student go through the first three stages in LSCI, developing the background for understanding a crisis from the student's viewpoint, feelings, and insight, it is easy to bog down. The process often rambles back and forth between Stages 2 and 3 for further information and clarification. The adult continually probes for wider and deeper meaning, and decodes the student's responses. It requires mental organization to analyze a large amount of complex and often disparate information. You may not know exactly what it all means, what is important, and what is simply off the track. Yet it is essential to make a concise and clear statement about the central issue before you leave Stage 3.

We find that the best help in this situation is observing the student. Most students' behavior provides an indication of what is truly significant. Test your observations by decoding. The student's response will give you an indication of your proximity to the central issue. Sometimes students protest loudly but then show by body language that they are waiting for your next statement. At other times they will be unusually silent, waiting for you to follow up on the idea. When you sense that you are on the right track, ask the student to put the central issue into words with statements such as the following:

"What is really important in all of this?"

"We've talked a lot. Some of this is really important if things are going to get better for you. Let's list the important points."

"I think what we are talking about gets right to the heart of the problem. Do you agree?"

If the student is not able or willing to respond, try to extract the essential focus from the student's viewpoint with lead-ins such as the following:

"It seems like what we have been talking about really is . . ."
"What I hear in all of this is . . ."
"It is really hard for kids to have to face. . ."

Once you or the student has made a simple summary of the issue, you are ready to move the LSCI into the problem-solving stages. Do not go forward until that concise statement has been made. If you do, you will have no basis for choosing a therapeutic goal and nothing to which you can attach a crisis resolution plan.

Jumping to Solutions Prematurely

Once an issue is out in the open, adults tend to leap to the finish, to "fix it." This same type of reaction also slips into the adult's response when a student describes the incident and the adult says, "Didn't you know that would happen?" Without waiting, the adult often goes ahead and tells the student a better way to handle the incident, or the adult reminds the student of the rules that should have been used to govern the behavior. In either case, the adult is providing the solution prematurely. Neither of these responses is appropriate during LSCI Stage 4, when what is needed is to encourage the student to consider all of the alternative solutions, right and wrong, that might be used to resolve the crisis. Hold off on your opinion or idea about the best solution for two reasons. First, you do not want to preempt the student's process of thinking through the choices. To do so would close off the opportunity to consider the results and consequences of each alternative. This is an essential part of accomplishing the LSCI goal. Second, if you provide the solution (rule, guideline), it is yours, not the student's. You will own it, but the student will not! Remember that the preferred result for LSCI Stage 4 is a student-selected solution. Also remember that you should not leave Stage 4 until the student states (or restates) the solution that has been chosen.

Failing To Consider Negative Solutions and Consequences

It is not unusual to find adults attempting to lead students away from mentioning inappropriate or negative solutions during LSCI Stage 5. This desire to skirt any thought of more inappropriate behavior is understandable, but not useful. By sanctioning a review of the inappropriate solutions, an adult actually helps a student rationally anticipate and weigh the consequences. We have found it helpful with some students to role-play the various choices and vicariously play out the negative consequences.

Consider the reality of actually implementing a resolution to a crisis that involves new behavior. It is likely that the student may try out the new solution with the best of intentions. But the ineptness of the student or the unpredictable nature of the responses of others to the student may produce a failed attempt. To reduce this likelihood, it is helpful to always rehearse the new behavior with the student during Stage 5. Take the role of the potential adversary. When the student tries the new behavior, respond negatively to the student. If the student is overwhelmed, confused, or reacts in anger to your role play, the new alternative has not been sufficiently practiced. You have not prepared the student well enough, or the chosen solution is beyond the student's ability to accomplish successfully. You may have to go back to Stage 4 and reconsider solutions with the student. If the student handles the practice role play, in which someone responds negatively to the new behavior, you have increased the odds that the student can react to the next real incident with the new behavior. The LSCI has been a success.

PRACTICE WITH THE FIVE FORMS OF EMOTIONAL FIRST AID

This chapter has emphasized the challenges to the adult using LSCI. The process is one that requires a constant vigil to preserve an attitude of helping, supporting, and confidence. These qualities are challenging—an adult using LSCI is in a particularly demanding, and often frustrating, position. We must help ourselves before we can help our students.

Because there is so much material in this chapter, it will require frequent reviews as you actually use LSCI. It was difficult for us to select one particular topic to focus on in the final review for the end of this chapter. We selected Emotional First Aid, and gave it a new application—applying it to the helping adult. We did this because it is essential to maintain your own emotional strength to be effective with LSCI. We also believe that if you can take a concept and apply it to your own needs, it will become easier to use with students in similar situations. This material was originally developed by Carol A. Merritt (1981, pp. 18–19), and is reprinted here with minor changes and permission of the author.

 ## Quiz: What Emotional First Aid Can a Teacher Use to Get Through the Day?

1. You have just spent several hours developing what you consider to be a wonderful lesson. As you present it to the class, the students begin complaining and saying, "That's dumb! We're not doing that!" You struggle on, but it becomes more and more apparent that you will be unable to use this lesson. Your stomach tightens and your face turns red. All you can think of is how much time and effort you spent. Which form of Emotional First Aid do you need?

   a. Draining off of emotional intensity
   b. Support when engulfed in intense emotions
   c. Maintenance of communication
   d. Regulation of social behavior
   e. An umpire

(continues)

2. You are angry with a student who has been uncooperative and disruptive all day. However, you notice he has earned just enough points to have free time. Your disgust with the student makes you want to take away his free time, yet he has earned it. When you mention your problem to a fellow teacher, the response is, "Hey, he earned his points. Maybe you need to tighten up your behavioral system in the future." Which form of Emotional First Aid do you need?

   a. Draining off of emotional intensity
   b. Support when engulfed in intense emotions
   c. Maintenance of communication
   d. Regulation of social behavior
   e. An umpire

3. John has been quite verbally abusive and disruptive off and on during the day. It seems that no matter what you try, this behavior continues. At the end of the day, he begins once again. You intervene again, and he spits in your face. Which form of Emotional First Aid do you need immediately?

   a. Draining off of emotional intensity
   b. Support when engulfed in intense emotions
   c. Maintenance of communication
   d. Regulation of social behavior
   e. An umpire

4. Your students are working independently at their desks on an assignment. Suddenly it seems that each student requires your individual help, *now*. You try to meet each student's need, but you can feel yourself becoming overwhelmed and wanting to be somewhere else. Consequently, you begin to withdraw slowly. Which form of Emotional First Aid will help you now?

   a. Draining off of emotional intensity
   b. Support when engulfed in intense emotions
   c. Maintenance of communication
   d. Regulation of social behavior
   e. An umpire

5. All staff members are attending an important meeting. Time is running out, and a decision has not been made. One staff member begins on a new tangent, and others become irritated. The director interrupts her and redirects the group to the task, saying, "Remember, we must reach a decision about our new policy today." Which form of Emotional First Aid is the director using?

a. Draining off of emotional intensity
b. Support when engulfed in intense emotions
c. Maintenance of communication
d. Regulation of social behavior
e. An umpire

(Answers: 1-a; 2-e; 3-b; 4-c; 5-d)

WHAT WE HAVE LEARNED FOR AVOIDING PITFALLS

- Think of LSCI as two-way communication between allies.

- Maintain a positive relationship based on trust.

- Credit a student's good intentions whenever possible.

- Provide simple, genuine affirmations about the student during every LSCI stage.

- Listen to your words and the tone in your voice to be certain that you are conveying respect and unconditional acceptance even though you cannot approve the behavior.

- Always control the movement from stage to stage through LSCI.

- Stay calm and focused.

- Avoid leading a student into "entrapment." (It is not ethical to manipulate students into testifying against themselves.)

- Communicate that change will produce satisfying results for the student.

- Avoid staying forever on the topic of the incident and associated problems. Give equal time to alternative solutions.

- With students who review an incident quickly and concisely, it is essential to decode and push them for greater insight.

- Always have students put the chosen solution into their own words and describe the behaviors they plan to use to accomplish it.

- Let the student know that LSCI is ongoing ("We will talk again.").

WHAT WE HOPE YOU HAVE
LEARNED FROM THIS CHAPTER

- Why LSCI makes such heavy demands on the personal attributes and skills of the adult

- Six basic attributes of an adult that are essential for the adult to be helpful to students in crisis

- Examples of specific adult skills for LSCI in relationship, verbal style, and nonverbal body language

- The purpose in providing Emotional First Aid as part of the helping process prior to using LSCI

- Five general ways to provide Emotional First Aid and the specific purpose of each

- An example of a typical adult statement for each type of Emotional First Aid

- Four outcomes of effective Emotional First Aid

- What to do if a student is not ready for LSCI after Emotional First Aid

- A major problem that sometimes occurs with LSCI Stage 1

- Three ways to use silence

- A time when it is useful to get off the subject of the incident during LSCI Stages 2 or 3

- How to determine when it is counterproductive to get off the subject of the incident

- Ways to avoid developing an adversarial tone in your relationship with a student

- Why it is important to avoid frequent use of negative reflections or statements, and how to turn them into positive ones

- How counteraggression develops and why it is essential to curb it in yourself

- An example of an ordinary question or statement adults often make that trivializes a student's feelings, without intending to do so

- How to overcome the problem of not knowing what to say

- A definition of a probe and how it is used in LSCI to get to deeper concerns

- How you can tell if you have gone too far into a student's private space

- How to avoid personal comments about yourself, and why this is important

- What students are trying to do when they attempt to reverse roles with you

- How to respond to attempts at role reversal

- How to find the central issues during LSCI Stage 3 when you are bogged down in so much information from a student that you do not know what is relevant

- What is lost during LSCI Stage 4 when an adult tells a student what the rules are or provides a solution to the crisis

- Why it is important that a student consider negative or inappropriate solutions as well as appropriate ones during LSCI Stage 5

Applying LSCI to Particular Patterns of Self-Defeating Behaviors

III

In Part III we take you beyond a "standard" LSCI to illustrate how the process is used with six patterns of self-defeating behaviors. During the first three LSCI stages, your task is to formulate the central issue which will become the focus of the Reclaiming Intervention.

You may recall that in LSCI Stage 3, the six types of goals are outlined: identify the source of the stress, organize reality, confront behavior, build values for self-control, teach new skills, and expose exploitation. A specific therapeutic goal is selected from the particular perception a student has about the incident.

The goals are presented in the form of action statements to highlight the adult's role in shaping the therapeutic focus. We present the original perception a student might hold about an incident, which gives you the information you need to choose a particular goal. The goal you select will shape the remainder of the LSCI. It will guide what you do and say, and will structure the way the crisis is resolved. If effective, the LSCI outcome changes the insight the student has about the incident, the student's feelings and behavior, and others' reactions.

The next six chapters illustrate the Reclaiming Interventions used to accomplish these therapeutic goals. You will see that the basic stage-by-stage process is not modified. Neither are the general purposes and contents of the LSCI stages changed. What changes is your approach, the direction of the solution, and the outcome for the student.

The Reality Rub Reclaiming Intervention: Organizing Perceptions of Reality

7

Student's Perception:	"No one agrees with what I know happened!"
Uses:	With students who demonstrate any of the following patterns:
	(1) Blocked perceptions of reality due to intense feelings
	(2) Misperceptions of reality due to triggering of personal emotional sensitivities
	(3) Restricted perceptions of reality due to perseveration on a single event in the sequence leading to the crisis
	(4) Private reconstruction of reality, as events are interpreted through rigid perceptual filters derived from personal history
	(5) Manipulation of reality to test limits
Goal:	To help students organize thinking so that a more accurate perception of reality emerges; to bring students to the realization that there is "more than meets the eye"; to help students begin to understand their contributions to the problem
Focus:	Organizes students' perceptions and sequence of time and events; developmentally, the most rudimentary of the therapeutic goals
Student's New Insight:	"Maybe there is another way to look at this situation. I can see how I might have made it worse, and what I need to do about it."

This LSCI Reclaiming Intervention helps students reorganize and clarify reality by discussing their blurred, distorted perceptions of the incident, identifying what is real versus what is imagined or constructed to avoid reality. These students have been described as having "social blindness" or "tunnel vision," seeing only the part of an event that is personally threatening. They forget the sequence of events, distort reality, separate feelings from behavior, and intensely remember the last hostile action (remark, punch, hit, words) inflicted by a peer. The common characteristic among students for whom this type of LSCI is appropriate is the inability to connect cause and effect in the series of interpersonal exchanges culminating in an incident.

Originally called a "Reality Rub-In" (Redl, 1966), this type of LSCI has its foundation in the characteristic way a student thinks and reacts to an incident. Redl describes the rationale for this therapeutic goal:

> The trouble with some of our youngsters, among other things, is that they are socially nearsighted. They can't read the meaning of an event in which they get involved, unless we use huge script for them and underline it all in glaring colors besides. Others are caught in such a well-woven system of near delusional misinterpretation of life that even glaring contradictions in actual fact are glided over by their eyes unless their view is arrested and focused on them from time to time. More fascinating even, are the youngsters whose preconscious perception of the full reality is all right but who have such well-oiled ego skills in alibiing to their own consciences that the picture of a situation that can be discussed with them is already hopelessly repainted by the time we get there. It is perhaps not necessary to add how important it is, strategically speaking, that such children have some of this "reality rub-in" interviewing done right then and there, and preferably by persons who themselves were on the scene or at least known to be thoroughly familiar with it. (p. 44)

We identify five patterns which signal the need for a Reality Rub Reclaiming Intervention:

1. *Blocked perceptions of reality (Pattern 1)*. Sometimes feelings, such as anger, fear, and depression, become so intense and overwhelming during a crisis that students temporarily block out the ability to process sensory messages. They literally do not see, hear, or remember what is happening around them. They are so angry they "see red." They are so frightened, they are "scared out of their wits." They are so depressed they cannot think, and so anxious they cannot remember what they hear. Until the intensity of their feelings is drained off, they will continue to behave in irrational and suppressed ways.

2. *Misperceptions of reality (Pattern 2)*. This is the most common form of a Reality Rub Crisis. Students come to us with a history which is not available to us until we take the time to hear the student's story. This history colors every situation as it is fil-

tered through eyes, ears, and memory. In many ways, students who misperceive what is happening have a temporary delusional belief. They are convinced that what they saw, heard, and remembered is exactly what actually happened during the crisis. These students cannot be talked out of their convictions and are more likely to believe their own accout of the crisis than any objective evidence.

3. *Restricted perceptions of reality (Pattern 3)*. This pattern occurs when students respond to a crisis by focusing their awareness on one part of the sequence of the crisis. Redl and Wineman (1951) call this process "social myopia." These students only talk about a particular act, as if it represented the entire crisis.

4. *Private reconstruction of reality (Pattern 4)*. The three previously described types of distortions of reality all involve intense feelings that alter the students' perceptions. Logic based on faulty perceptions leads to wrong conclusions. In this case, however, students do not deny, misperceive, or restrict sensory experiences. They are able to describe the interpersonal behaviors with accuracy, but still come to the wrong conclusions. For example, a visitor to Manhattan asks a vendor how to get to Carnegie Hall. The vendor, who is a music lover, hears him correctly but answers, "Practice, practice, practice!" The vendor didn't distort reality, but came to a conclusion that was consistent with his private logic.

5. *Manipulation of reality (Pattern 5)*. Student behavior in this pattern tests the rules and limits of the staff and setting. These students look for loopholes in the classroom management system and use them to justify their behavior. This is not a new concept, but one in which students shape reality to fit their own needs.

THE ADULT'S TASK

With the Reality Rub Reclaiming Intervention, the goal is to correct a student's blurred and distorted perceptions of the incident. To accomplish this goal, the task is to help the student clarify reality by discussing the student's perceptions of the incident and sorting out distortions about what occurred. In the process, you help a student reconstruct the details of the incident, consider the resulting consequences, and organize the new insight into a behavioral plan for future use.

A thorough timeline is essential for a successful Reality Rub Reclaiming Intervention. The adult helps the student reconstruct the incident and the feelings involved. Together, they trace through the sequence of events, identifying who, where, when, and what happened. It can be useful to use a diagram of the Conflict Cycle in reconstructing events during the timeline, as it may bring order to the student's often chaotic recollection of the incident. In doing so students are helped to organize perceptions and learn that their behavior evokes behavior from others. They learn the likely consequences of similar actions, and see the possibility of altering future events by changing their actions.

In a perceptive discussion about the use of this type of LSCI with disturbed adolescents, Robert Bloom (1981) summarizes the importance of maintaining a helping relationship during such LSCIs.

> Challenges to youngsters' perceptions of reality often are emotionally painful to the youths. Much comfort is found in being a victim of events; recognition of their contribution to their pain and misfortune can be vigorously avoided. And, in the typically conflicted adolescent-adult push-pull relationship, an adult on whom all this misfortune and pain can be projected is readily available. (p. 23)

Bloom suggests four guidelines to keep on track: (a) maintain an ongoing relationship, (b) avoid creating a sense of urgency, (c) keep your own hostile feelings under control, and (d) be calm and focused.

EXAMPLES OF STUDENTS
WHO CAN BENEFIT

Of the six LSCI therapeutic goals, the Reality Rub Reclaiming Intervention is frequently needed to organize (and reorganize) students' perceptions about the reality of an incident. Here are brief vignettes about students needing this type of LSCI, in which the focus is to help them see reality in a clearer way, their own role in it, and the way others see the same events.

Perry (Pattern 1)

As assistant principal of an urban high school, I was notified of a fight which occurred in the boys lavatory. Perry, a tenth grader, was assaulted by three students. Perry is a frail, intellectual student known for his advocacy of gay rights. When I saw him, Perry was lying on the floor sobbing. His clothes were torn and there was blood on his face and shirt from a nosebleed. He looked terrible, and appeared traumatized. I stayed with him as the nurse examined him. There appeared to be no serious physical damage, although Perry clearly was psychologically overwhelmed by the group assault. He had difficulty speaking and lapsed into brief periods of silence. I spent the next 20 minutes reassuring him that we would take care of him, notify the appropriate authorities, and deal with the students who attacked him. Even with all this support, Perry was unable to tell us what happened to him in a coherent way. Much to my surprise, he couldn't identify the three students who assaulted him. I realized that Perry was so frightened by this traumatic experience that he had blocked out many of the details. I decided this was not an appropriate time to get an accurate timeline of the incident and that he needed continued emotional support.

Darryl (Pattern 2)

Darryl is a sixth grade student who was brought to the crisis room because of a fight he had had with Warren on the bus. It seemed that Warren was teasing Darryl by calling him "stupid" and "retardo." The teasing got out of hand, and Darryl hit Warren which resulted in Darryl's detention. Darryl was furious and kept pacing back and forth in the crisis room. Darryl and I usually have a good relationship, and this was not the first time I had seen him so angry. As I tried to drain off his feelings, I said "Darryl, I'm wondering if you were thinking clearly today." Darryl exploded and shouted, "Why are you dissing me? You think I'm stupid!" I was taken aback by his comment, which reflected his feelings about the earlier torment from Warren. I tried to explain, but he said that he knew what he had heard and that I was "just like the rest of them." I realized that Darryl's feelings were so intense that he had altered my comments to fit his emotional state. With this awareness, I chose not to defend my comments and moved the discussion back to the incident on the bus by using the Conflict Cycle.

Steve (Pattern 3)

After a fight, all ten-year-old Steve can remember is that Bill hit him and called him a "mother name." He continued to perseverate on this single issue and had no recall of his teasing, provocative behavior toward Bill, which triggered the fight. An accurate timeline was difficult to establish at this time. Only through extensive use of the Conflict Cycle was Steve able to understand the sequence of the fight.

Mike (Pattern 4)

Mike was looking forward to the special activity at the end of the week for all students in his ninth-grade class who completed their homework and earned their behavior points. He did his math homework the night before using a calculator to make sure the answers were correct. However, when his work was checked by the teacher this morning, Mike was shocked to learn that all of the answers were wrong. When he was told that he would need to correct the problems with adult help, Mike exploded. "How could they be wrong? I used a calculator!" The Reality Rub Reclaiming Intervention will help Mike untangle his feelings and assumptions. The goals are to help him understand that (1) use of the calculator does not guarantee accurate answers, (2) the fact that his homework was incorrectly done does not meant that he can't participate in the activity, and (3) his ability to talk through a disturbing situation will help him earn his behavior points. Ultimately, we want Mike to understand that checking out the assumptions that drive his feelings is a better choice than to simply act out his feelings.

Martin (Pattern 5)

After a lot of annoying behavior from the class, Martin's fifth grade teacher tells the class that no one can leave his or her seat without permission for the rest of the period. Almost immediately, Martin gets up, walks across the room, and asks for a pencil. When he is told that he is using the pencil as an excuse to break the rule, he protests that he needs the pencil to do his work. Then he kicks over a chair and screams at the teacher, "You always pick on me! You want me to fail my work!" The issue here is testing the teacher's authority, while the student justifies his behavior as being appropriate.

These vignettes illustrate some of the problems that are suited to the Reality Rub Reclaiming Intervention, the goal of which is to organize reality to broaden students' perceptions and insights. We suspect that you have found some of your own students among these descriptions.

EXAMPLE OF LSCI USED TO ORGANIZE PERCEPTIONS OF REALITY: A REALITY RUB RECLAIMING INTERVENTION

JOANNE: IT'S FRIDAY, AND I WANT OUT OF HERE!

Joanne is a sixteen-year-old student attending an alternative school in a large urban area. Since her parents divorced three years ago, Joanne lives with her mother who has a hard time managing Joanne's demanding, self-centered behavior. Because Joanne is so oppositional, her mother seems always to be directing and correcting her—pleasant conversation has all but ceased to exist. Joanne has poor impulse control, saying whatever comes to mind without filtering her thoughts for the effects her words may have on others. As a result, she can infuriate adults and peers and engage them easily in Conflict Cycles. Joanne is attractive and clever, and a source of great amusement to her peers. At school she often finds herself in trouble for "mouthing off." When confronted, Joanne can become verbally abusive and sometimes leaves the classroom or the building without permission.

It is Friday afternoon, 30 minutes before school is dismissed. Joanne has had a trying day, finding it difficult to follow directions and complete her work. Yet she has managed to stay just short of receiving disciplinary action. As the group completes a history assignment, Ms. Foster goes from desk to desk, checking each student's work. When she reaches Joanne, she finds her reading a magazine, her completed worksheet sitting on her desk. Ms. Foster checks the answers and finds that the first five are correct, but the second five questions are not. The following dialogue takes place between the teacher (T) and Joanne (J).

T: You did these pretty quickly, Joanne. It looks like the first five are correct, but did you look up the answers for the other five?

J: (Without looking up from her magazine) I didn't have to look them up—I knew the answers.

T: Please put away the magazine and get out your history book. I would like you to look up the correct answers and finish the assignment before you leave.

J: (Angrily) I told you I don't have to look them up—are you deaf or something?

T: Joanne, the last five are wrong and you need to correct them.

J: That's bull! Those answers are good enough and you know it. I did the work so just get away from me. (With increasing intensity) You people around here are pathetic! All you want to do is hassle us. Then you think you can tell us we got problems! (Stands up and begins to pace) I've got a problem all right—putting up with your BS! Every day it's the same damn garbage! (Shouting) I'm not taking it anymore! (She walks out of the room into the hallway. Ms. Foster follows, and asks the classroom aide to take over monitoring the group. Joanne is leaning against the wall.)

T: Take it easy, Joanne. I don't think there needs to be an argument here.

J: Can't you understand f___'in English? I said leave me the f___ alone!

▶ **Stage 1: Drain Off**

T: Joanne, it's Friday afternoon; think about what you're doing. Do you really need more problems right now? OK, so you're upset—let's try to work something out. You don't need to take it beyond this level.

J: Yeah, like you don't want me in as much trouble as you can get me in.

T: You think I want you in trouble.

J: Don't give me that innocent act. You know exactly what's going on.

T: Give me the benefit of the doubt, just this once—OK? Help me understand what happened because, although it's been a long, rough day, you've been staying out of trouble. You don't want to have trouble now, so let's take a minute and work through this. Now, how were you doing when we started history?

J: Fine. When history started I was thinking that I had less than an hour before I could get away from you.

T: (Ignoring the personal remark) So you were looking forward to finishing the day and starting your weekend.

▶ Stage 2: Timeline

J: Yeah.

T: You weren't angry or upset then, just wanting to finish up the day.

J: Right.

T: Then I handed out the assignment sheet and said that it was due at the end of the period. How were you feeling then?

J: I started it, didn't I?

T: Yes, you did—I noticed that you got to work on it right away. Was the work difficult?

J: That's baby stuff and it's boring as hell!

T: So you were having some thoughts about the assignment. You were thinking that it was busy work and you were feeling bored.

J: Who cares about Ohio history anyway?

T: I can understand how you might not find it the most interesting thing to read. So you got bored after looking up the answers to the first five questions?

J: Hell yes! What do you think?

T: So what did you do?

J: I'm not dumb, you know. I just answered the other ones from what I remembered from class.

T: So you were bored with looking up the answers and you decided to give the last five your best shot from memory. Then I came to your desk and saw that your paper was finished and you were reading a magazine.

J: Yeah, I was done. You always say don't bother anybody when you finish your assignment, so I wasn't.

T: That's true, you were keeping to yourself and not bothering anyone. So I looked at your work and told you the last five were wrong and I wanted you to correct them. Is that right?

J: Oh, you're conveniently leaving out the part where you threatened me. Of course, you don't remember that, do you?

T: I threatened you?

▶ Stage 3: Central Issue

J: You said you were going to keep me after—and it's Friday!

T: So that explains it! Joanne, think about it— what I said was that I wanted you to finish the assignment before you left. You had plenty of time to do it, and you know how you are with homework—you don't do it on weekends. So I just was trying to get you to finish it up now. That's all—I had no intention of keeping you after school today.

J: Yeah, right.

T: Have I ever kept you after because your work was not done correctly?

J: You make me miss breaks and be late to lunch to correct work.

T: True, but have I ever caused you to miss the bus because of it?

J: No, I guess not, but who's to say you weren't going to do that today?

T: Then tell me, where's the evidence that I was going keep you after today?

J: Well, it sure seemed like that's what you meant.

T: You know, in a way, I'm kind of glad this happened.

J: What do you mean?

T: Because it's a great opportunity to learn something. Do you see how you jumped to a conclusion before you had evidence that your conclusion was right?

J: Maybe.

T: Think back, what was going through your mind when I told you to finish the assignment correctly before you left?

J: You don't want to know.

T: Give me a clue—with respect, please.

J: I was thinking how rotten it was of you to keep me after on Friday just because of five questions.

T: And how were you feeling when that went though your mind?

J: I was mad as hell!

T: And how did you show me you were "mad as hell"?

J: Well I didn't throw anything or leave the building, did I?

T: That's true, you showed some control for someone that angry. Do you remember what you said?

J: I said something about all you teachers are sick.

▶ Stage 4: Insight

T: That's right, and you left the room without permission. And all of this because of what you "assumed" I was saying. Do you see that you let your emotions get the better of you? Instead of thinking it through and asking me if you would have to stay after, you just let your feelings take over.

J: (Silence)

T: Has anything like this ever happened before?

J: (Slight smile) Once or twice.

T: That smile tells me you know this is a problem—jumping to conclusions, getting angry?

J: Yeah, well, I have a hot temper.

T: But that hot temper has to be controlled by a cool head or it gets you into a lot of trouble.

J: Tell me about it.

T: Do you see how you have a tendency to make your problems bigger? Do you see that today you almost created a problem that could have gotten you suspended?

J: Yeah, I guess.

T: Joanne, if you could solve this problem—avoid jumping to conclusions and acting on your emotions, life would be so much easier for you. Think of how smoothly your afternoon would have gone if you had not jumped to conclusions. What can you do to work on this?

J: I don't know because when I'm doing it, I don't know I'm jumping to conclusions. I just get mad.

▶ Stage 5: New Skills

T: That's an observation we could work with—the fact that you feel yourself getting mad. And when you get mad, what happens?

J: I just get mad.

T: What do you do when you get mad?

J: Whatever—I'm like on autopilot.

T: So when you feel yourself getting mad, it's kind of like a warning?

J: I guess.

T: What does that warning feel like?

J: Everything rushes to my head and I just want to get away.

T: So your body gives you a signal that you're about to lose it—everything goes to your head. It's great that you recognize the signal, because you can use it like a traffic signal to stop—before things get out of hand.

J: Yeah, sometimes I do.

T: So you have already practiced this, and how have you done?

J: Depends; not that great, really.

T: What can you do, then, when you feel that warning anger coming on?

J: I could tell myself to chill, or something. I could tell myself to shut up so it won't get any worse.

T: Sounds like a pretty good strategy. When you feel yourself getting angry, what will you say to yourself?

J: I don't know, something like, "Chill—don't talk" Something like that.

T: Do you think it would help to count to ten before saying anything?

J: I don't know—maybe.

T: And when you have your emotions under control, might it be helpful to check out your conclusions, maybe to ask the person what they meant? That way, you will know for sure what the person intended instead of just assuming you know what they meant.

J: What do you mean?

T: I mean, check it out. For example, today when I told you to finish the work before you leave, you might have asked, "Do I have to stay after if I don't finish it?" Then you would have known that you wouldn't have to stay. If you had known that, would your reaction have been different?

J: I guess I wouldn't have been so mad.

T: Exactly. So what you're saying is that in some situations you can actually feel yourself getting angry. When that happens you will . . .

J: Tell myself to relax and be cool.

T: Then when you have your emotions under control, you will ask the person . . .

J: I'll ask the person, "What do you mean?"

T: Yes, you'll get more information—you'll check out your assumptions. Can you do it?

J: I'm going to try.

► Stage 6: Get Ready To Resume the Activity

T: OK, you've got a plan and you can try it out right now. When we go back to the room everyone will be finished with their work, but I'm going to give it to you as homework. Can you handle it?

J: Yeah.

T: What are you going to do if you feel yourself getting angry?

J: I'll just chill and count to ten and not say anything, then I'll make sure I know what's going on.

T: OK—let's see how you do. You know, I have to say that I'm impressed with the way you were able to handle this talk. You really want to do well and you want to manage things for yourself; that's half the battle.

J: Thanks, Ms. Foster.

Ms. Foster transformed a potential crisis into a learning opportunity for Joanne. She recognized this event as another example of Joanne's tendency to misperceive reality due to stress or anxiety. She also recognized through the timeline that Joanne's vital interest was being able to leave on time. One can see how quickly Joanne's perception of the situation, and subsequently her feelings and attitude changed, when that threat to her freedom was nullified. Ms. Foster understood the hostility she received from Joanne was associated with the problems she is experiencing in her relationship with her mother. Ms. Foster decided that she would not decode this openly for Joanne, as displacement was not the central issue. Yet she acted on this awareness by consciously avoiding Joanne's attempts to draw her into a power struggle through sarcastic comments and swearing. Additionally, in her role as mediator, Ms. Foster took into account Joanne's developmental stage and readiness to contribute to the plan to change her behavior. She guided the planning in Stage 5, but invited Joanne's suggestions and incorporated them into the plan. As Joanne is regularly supported in acting on the plan, and helped to recognize when she is not using the plan, her ability to "think twice" will improve. As it does, conflicts with adults will decrease in frequency, and, ultimately, her perception of herself as a competent young adult will be strengthened. This is the goal of the Reality Rub Reclaiming Intervention. For additional examples, see Long and Pincione (1992); Long (1993); Fecser and Martin (1995); Ryan (1997); and Walker, Long, and Brendtro (2000).

WHAT WE HOPE YOU HAVE LEARNED FROM THIS CHAPTER

- The primary purpose in using the Reality Rub Reclaiming Intervention

- The common characteristic shared by all students who can benefit from the Reality Rub Reclaiming Intervention

- Characteristics of students for whom this form of LSCI might not be applicable

- What essential process is used by adults to provide the structure for achieving this goal

- The importance of using small details in this form of LSCI

- Why a helping relationship must be maintained by an adult to conduct the Reality Rub Reclaiming Intervention effectively

- Why abundant affirmations are essential for students with whom you use this form of LSCI

- Four guidelines to aid adults in being effective with the Reality Rub Reclaiming Intervention

- Why this form of LSCI is most frequently used with students when they first begin a program

- How a student's insight changes if the Reality Rub Reclaiming Intervention is successful

- What indications suggest that different therapeutic goals should be used with a student

The Red Flag Reclaiming Intervention: Identifying the Source of the Stress

Student's Perception:	"Everybody is against me! No one understands what's going on with me and no one cares! I can't take it any more!"
Uses:	With students who overreact to normal rules and procedures with emotional outbursts; who attempt to create a no win situation by engaging staff in a power struggle which ultimately results in more rejection and feelings of alienation
Goal:	To identify the source of the problem; is it a *Carry In* problem from another setting, a *Carry Over* problem from another place within the current setting, or a *Tap In* to a personal unresolved emotional conflict?
Focus:	Helps students recognize that they are displacing their feelings on others and alienating the sources of support they need to help handle stress
Student's New Insight:	"Someone does understand my real problems and can read beyond my behavior. I need to talk to staff about my real problems and not create new ones here."

The Red Flag Reclaiming Intervention was not one of Redl's initial LSI therapeutic interviews. It arose from the Reality Rub, as professionals using LSCI observed a commonly occurring theme in the course of the interview. The theme has to do with the dynamic of displacement. During the timeline, the interviewer often discovered, after considerable exploration, that the source of the stress the student was feeling at the moment was not grounded in the immediate setting or the immediate events, but rather in some past experience which had left residual unfinished business. The student had an emotional "sore spot," and when an otherwise innocent comment or occurrence bumped up against that sore spot, it set off an onslaught of impassioned dumping. The unfortunate victim who happened to be available became, in the student's eyes, the source of the stress and received the full wrath.

163

We have discovered three types of Red Flag conditions: the *Carry In*, the *Carry Over*, and the *Tap In*. The *Carry In* situation occurs when a student has had a recent negative encounter or experience which occurred *before entering* the setting in which the crisis develops. There has been an argument or incident at home, in the community, or on the bus which the student was unable to resolve satisfactorily. Often the student is in a position in which real feelings cannot be expressed to the offending party for fear of retaliation or punishment. So rather than telling stepfather that he is angry at being accused of stealing money, or telling the bully on the bus he can no longer tolerate his abuse, the young person comes into the classroom loaded with feelings and explodes at the slightest reasonable request from the staff.

The second type of Red Flag, the *Carry Over*, is very similar to the *Carry In*, except that the offending event has occurred within the same setting as the following expression of emotion, in another class, or in an exchange with someone else throughout the course of the day. Again, instead of telling Mr. Bruno, the no-nonsense physical education instructor, that derogatory remarks about lack of coordination are not appreciated, these feelings are bottled up, awaiting an opportunity in a safer place to be unleashed.

The third type of Red Flag, the *Tap In*, is somewhat more complex as the issue for the student is a much deeper one. In this situation, an old wound exists as a result of abuse, abandonment, neglect, or trauma. Many troubled and troubling children suffer from post-traumatic stress disorder and are hypervigilant and hypersensitive. When one has been a victim, it is common for strong instincts for self-preservation to develop. Protection becomes the filter through which life is viewed, and everything is evaluated for its threat potential. Just as a person with a painful physical condition will be sharply attuned to anything in the environment that might stimulate that pain, so are these children constantly monitoring all that goes on around them that they may act to protect themselves from further suffering. When that old pain is stimulated, students will react with an intensity incomprehensible to the uninformed observer.

THE ADULT'S TASK

The Red Flag Reclaiming Intervention is the most frequently used LSCI in urban schools. It requires a good deal of skill on the part of the interviewer, as most students are not inclined to approach an adult and announce that something is bothering them. Rather, students characteristically adhere to the old adage, "If the only tool you have is a hammer, everything looks like a nail." The communication tools our students typically have are limited indeed. In fact, there are those who know only one way to engage adults—make them angry. The irony is that most students really do want to tell their story to an adult who can help, or at least understand. Yet these helping adults are the very ones the student drives away with disrespectful or even abusive comments and behaviors. To be successful, the adult must avoid being drawn into a conflict which will arouse counteraggressive feelings. Our goal is to discover the true source of the stress and make known to the student the pattern of displacement and its damaging effects on efforts to solve or cope with the real underlying problem.

The first task the adult faces in confronting a Red Flag situation is to stay calm and avoid becoming counteraggressive. This is not easy, as frequently the crisis will occur early in the day, or early in the class period, and there will be few, if any, observable antecedent events that might explain a behavioral response of such great magnitude. The most innocent comment or request, such as, "Please open your math book" might ignite the explosion. For the adult, it doesn't add up. Furthermore, our good relationship with the student, which helps so often in dispersing tension in other situations, seems to have evaporated. The young person rages against every effort of the adult to help and to understand, and even the most patient adult begins to feel anger creeping into nonverbal messages. The impulse is to administer consequences to address the surface behaviors, and if we do this, we might be successful at restoring temporary order, but we will not have helped the student understand the feelings and learn better ways of acting on them. Instead, we must stay with the student's irrational tirade, drain off the intense emotions, and restore the young person to a level of clearheadedness. This is done by maintaining a composed demeanor, acknowledging the feelings, and communicating to the student that you are truly interested in the situation.

As you enter the timeline stage, it is important to work backward in time until you reach a point at which the student was not feeling upset. You might ask, for example, "Did anything unusual happen before you arrived at school this morning?" or "Did anything unusual happen during the night?"

You are trying to establish the most recent point of relative calm, and trace events forward until you find the first moment of distress. This process is a delicate one, as students usually will not come right out with the problem. They will, instead, drop hints or clues (hence the name "Red Flag"), and wait for you to decode them. A skilled interviewer will recognize these as "offers" to the adult to ask the kinds of questions that will enable the student to ease into the sensitive topic. With support the student will reveal the true source of the stress, and when this happens, it is important to provide abundant affirmation. This serves at least two purposes: (1) it brings a sense of relief that someone else knows the problem and is supportive, and (2) it encourages the continuation of the interview.

Carry In and *Carry Over* issues can range from mild to quite serious situations. They can be as irritating as a teacher giving a detention to a student who doesn't feel it is deserved, or as disturbing as witnessing a physical confrontation between parents. *Tap In* issues are usually more intense as the student shares past traumatic events and seeks to be supported in personal pain, grief, or fear. (These issues are explored further in the discussion of the Massaging Numb Values Reclaiming Intervention in Chapter 10.) The student shares the problem with the interviewer in the hope that a way will be found to make things better. The student has taken a risk, and the adult now has a responsibility to support the student. Support comes in many forms: acting as a confidante to help the student through a difficult situation; seeking help from other professionals such as the school social worker, counselor, or psychologist; or in cases where abuse is suspected, notifying Children's Protective Services. Our goal at this point is to reassure. The student does not have to handle the problem alone. It is very important to note that solving the complex problem is not a goal of this Reclaiming Intervention. There are times when the life issue is so urgent there is a tendency to forget the therapeutic goal and begin immediately to assemble the team to address the problem. Remember that the therapeutic goal of the Red Flag Reclaiming Intervention is to help the student recognize the dynamic of displacement. We need to make the student aware of the damage caused to good relationships when pent-up feelings are unleashed on friends and supporters. We need to help the student understand that the very people who can be counted on for relief from the real problem are the ones this behavior is driving away. This goal is just as important as the goal of beginning to work on the complex life problem. What plan can work if the student unwittingly continues to "bite the hand that feeds"?

EXAMPLES OF STUDENTS WHO CAN BENEFIT

Ray

Ray is a 9-year-old boy who is small for his age and fears other older or larger students. He comes to school in a van with Chris, who has recently been victimizing him on the morning ride to school. Chris takes Ray's lunch box, selects what he wants, crushes the remainder, and returns it to Ray. Ray arrives at school feeling weak, miserable, abused, ashamed, and angry. In the safe environment of the classroom, he seeks any excuse: the work is too difficult or too easy, the teacher is ignoring him because she doesn't respond to his raised hand immediately, a classmate swears and the teacher doesn't do anything about it. Ray explodes, acting out his feelings about the incident in the van. (*Carry In*)

Rick

Rick is 16 years old and has been attending an alternative high school for about six months. Usually he enters the building, greeting the attending staff and removing his baseball cap according to the school rules. On this morning, however, he does not greet the staff and refuses to remove his cap. When he is told to report to the office, he swears at the staff and continues to walk down the hallway toward his classroom. A teacher gently takes Rick's arm to redirect him and Rick becomes violent, attempting to punch the adult. He is physically restrained, during which he uncharacteristically screams, swears, and struggles. When Rick has finally been restored to calm and the teacher begins a timeline, Rick reveals that his stepfather and mother got into a terrible argument the previous evening, and when Rick stepped in to protect his mother, his stepfather pushed him into the wall. His mother left the house with Rick and his younger sister. They spent the night at a neighbor's house, and when Rick left for school this morning, his mother told him not to go home at the end of the day. She would call to tell him where they would spend that night. (*Carry In*)

Jamal

Jamal, a 15-year-old student with a learning disability and a behavior disorder, takes social studies in a regular classroom with a teacher who is sensitive to his difficulties and supportive of his efforts. On this day his teacher is out sick and a substitute teacher is in charge. The substitute teacher decides that students will read aloud from the textbook, not realizing that Jamal has great difficulty reading. When it is Jamal's turn to read, he is torn between trying to read aloud and embarrassing himself before his classmates, or choosing a diversion that will relieve him of reading. He decides to say "Pass" when he is called upon to read, and the substitute gives him a detention for refusing to follow directions. Jamal is furious, but says nothing in class. The next period he enters his special education classroom, and when his teacher tells him to work on his journal, he explodes in an angry torrent of curses and accusations. (*Carry Over*)

Michael

Michael, a brooding 12-year-old boy, lives with his father who is a steelworker. About a year ago, Michael's mother abandoned the family following the death, due to cancer, of Michael's brother, who was twelve. The previous evening, Michael's father brought a woman home for dinner for the first time since Michael's mother left. Michael was rude to her, refusing to answer questions or look at her. During dinner his father yelled at him and sent him to his room for the rest of the evening. There was no mediation, and Michael woke the following morning, prepared himself, and came to school. Ms. Taylor's class was finishing the book *Old Yeller* and reading aloud the last chapter in which Old Yeller is put to death. When it was Michael's turn to read, he threw the book across the room and screamed at his teacher that he was not going to read and that it was a stupid story. He continued to scream and ran out of the room, telling Ms. Taylor that he wished she was dead. (*Tap In*)

Sylke

Sylke is fourteen years old and has been struggling with dyslexia all of her life. Her parents, who immigrated from Eastern Europe, cannot understand why Sylke reads at a third grade level, and despite explanations from the school psychologist, they still believe she is just not trying. They admonish her for her poor performance, and allow her brother to refer to her as "Stupid." They tell her that if she doesn't like to be called stupid, she should work harder in school. Although Sylke does poorly with academics, she is coordinated and athletic and excels in sports. During gym class, the group is playing volleyball and it is Sylke's turn to serve. She uncharacteristically botches the serve, placing the ball right in the middle of the opposing team's court. It is set up for a slam and the other team scores. A competitive boy on Sylke's team turns to her and says loudly, "You stupid idiot, why did you do that?" Sylke attacks him violently, knocking him to the floor and brutally striking him in the face. The teacher has to physically hold Sylke until she regains control. (*Tap In*)

EXAMPLE OF LSCI USED TO IDENTIFY THE SOURCE OF THE STRESS: A RED FLAG RECLAIMING INTERVENTION

 ## STEVEN: TAKE ME OUT TO THE BALL GAME

Steven is a 12-year-old only child who resides with his mother in a working-class suburb of Cleveland. He was placed in an alternative middle school for at-risk students with his mother's enthusiastic support, due to his low grades and frequent disciplinary referrals during the previous school year. It was during that year that Steven's father moved out of the home to live with another woman and gradually discontinued all direct communication with Steven.

It is Monday morning and Steven is in his first-period language arts class. A few minutes before the bell is to ring, Ken, a student who sits directly behind Steven, suddenly stands up and shouts at him, "Hey, man, where are my tickets?" "I don't know nothin' about your damn tickets!" Steven yells back. The teacher, Mrs. Hicks, quickly intervenes and asks the boys what's going on. According to Ken, he had won two tickets to an Indians game from a local radio station, and he and his father were going to the game this weekend. Ken brought the tickets to school to show around, and Steven, his friend, had asked to see them. He gave the tickets to Steven and went to sharpen his pencil. When Ken returned, his tickets were nowhere to be found. Steven insisted he didn't have them. Mrs. Hicks asked Ken to check his pockets and book bag carefully to make sure he had not misplaced the tickets. Steven looked on as Ken searched his pockets and desk to no avail. Mrs. Hicks then asked Steven to empty his pockets and search his belongings as well. When given this direction, Steven exploded, shouting that he was no thief and that Mrs. Hicks had no business accusing him of stealing. He continued, saying he was sick of all the "garbage" he had to go through at school, and that Ken was a "dumb ass" because he had the tickets right in front of his face. He then reached over to Ken's desk and flipped open his science book. There were the tickets. Steven had placed them there while Ken was sharpening his pencil. Before Mrs. Hicks could say more than, "Steven," he yelled, "Why don't you just shut up!" The bell rang, as if on cue. Mrs. Hicks dismissed the rest of the class. Steven didn't have to be asked to stay behind, as he had laid his head down on the desk.

Mrs. Hicks got Steven some tissues and sat down beside him. The following interview took place between Mrs. Hicks (T) and Steven (S).

▶ Stage 1: Drain Off

T: (Placing her hand on Steven's shoulder) I can see it's not been a good morning for you; can you try to take a few deep breaths? Maybe that will help you feel a little better.

S: (Silence, tries to control crying)

T: You know, you and I have worked out problems before.

S: (Silence. Steven has stopped crying and is sitting with his head on the desk.)

T: The fact that you are here now, managing to get yourself calm, tells me that you are trying to be responsible. You are willing to work on solving your problems. Can you help me figure out what just happened between you and Ken? When I came over, Ken was saying that his tickets were missing.

S: I didn't steal his tickets. I'm not a thief. (Straightening up in his desk)

T: No, you're not. I saw the tickets in Ken's science book—you did not steal them. Can we back up a little? I noticed during class that you had your head down on your desk for a while, and you seemed kind of distracted during the lesson.

S: Well, you know, I really didn't want to even come 'cause I was feeling kind of mad to begin with.

▶ Stage 2: Timeline

T: You were feeling kind of mad when you came to school today?

S: Yeah, I felt like I was gonna go off, so I just decided that I was going to put my head down mostly, so nobody would mess with me today.

T: It's good to know that you were able to understand yourself so well. Putting your head down was probably a good decision. While you had your head down, can you tell me what you were thinking about?

S: I don't know, just stuff. Personal stuff mostly, about my dad.

T: I've met your mom and I know you live with her. Tell me about your dad. Do you see him often or talk to him?

s: Nah, he never calls. Well, if he does, it's not to talk to me. I haven't seen him in months, but, well, I did see him Saturday, but it was like by accident. He didn't come over or anything like that.

T: I understand; it wasn't planned. You just sort of ran into him somewhere.

s: Yeah, at the mall with my mom. We were walking through Sears and there he was, at the jewelry counter.

T: How did you feel when you saw him?

s: Well, I was kind of excited at first.

T: Did you have a chance to talk with him?

s: Not really . . . I was gonna go up and say hi, but he turned around and looked at me before I could. The he turned right back around like he didn't see me.

T: That must have been quite a letdown.

s: Yeah, but I handled it OK. I mean, I didn't cry like a baby or anything. I just kept walking with my mom.

T: Did you and your mom talk about it later?

s: Nah, we both just acted like it never happened, but she was real quiet over the weekend. She spent a lot of time in her room.

T: You didn't talk about it, but you've been thinking about it.

s: Yeah, a lot.

T: It was on your mind all weekend, and today, when you came to school you were still thinking about it.

s: Yeah, you don't really forget something like that.

T: Listen, what you experienced would be hard for anyone, and I want to thank you for telling me about it. Now I understand why you were on edge this morning. It makes sense to me, and I recognize the courage it takes to come forward with it.

▶ Stage 3: Central Issue

T: Anyone who had the experience you had, Steven, would be thinking about it a lot. When something like this happens, it helps to talk through it. Otherwise, you just keep turning it over in your mind and it's like one of those wheels in a hamster cage. Lots of spinning, but the hamster never gets anywhere. Who do you think would be a good person to talk to about this?

s: Probably my mom.

T: Would it be OK with you if I called your mom today and told her about our conversation? I know that when she learns this has been bothering you, she will want to talk with you about it. What do you think?

S: Yeah, I guess.

T: OK, I'll give her a call. Maybe both of you could benefit from a good talk together. I really admire how you were able to tell me about how you felt and she would appreciate knowing it too.

S: Yeah, I would kind of like to get it over with.

T: OK. There's just one more thing—can I try to summarize? You came in with a lot on your mind this morning and decided to try to keep to yourself. Then Ken showed you his tickets. Is that right?

S: Well, I had my head down, but Ken was all happy and kept going on about his tickets. So I asked him to let me see them.

T: Did Ken know you were bothered by something?

S: No.

T: And here he was, kind of bragging about his tickets. I guess he must have been pretty happy that he won them, huh?

S: Yeah, he was obnoxious.

T: So he was being happy, and that bothered you because you were unhappy. That's understandable. So what did you do?

S: Well, after he showed me the tickets, I put them in his science book, but I was kind of having fun watching him get all frantic when he couldn't find them.

T: You know, Steven, I think I see what happened now. You really didn't mean any harm, but you wanted Ken to get a little upset because here you were all upset about your dad, and Ken was acting all happy about his Indians tickets. It seemed off balance and you wanted to tone down his enthusiasm so you could tolerate it.

S: Yeah—it was pretty mean; I mean, I would have been happy if I had won the tickets.

T: That's a very mature insight.

S: I was going to show him where I put the tickets, but then you came over and you were suspecting me of stealing them.

T: What makes you think that I suspected you of stealing them?

S: Well, you made me empty my pockets and everything.

T: Sure, but I made Ken do the same thing. Mistakes happen. Everybody misplaces things. Hasn't that happened to you? Was there ever a time when you swear you put something in a certain place and it wasn't there?

S: Yeah, sure.

T: Well, that was why I asked both of you to search everywhere—because I thought the tickets might have been misplaced—not because I thought you stole them.

S: Well, I felt like you were accusing me.

T: Do you feel that way now?

▶ **Stage 4: Insight**

S: No, I see what you were doing.

T: Do you remember what you said to me?

S: I guess I was pretty nasty, huh?

T: You swore at me and told me to shut up.

S: I'm sorry, I really didn't mean it.

T: I know you're not really angry with me, and you're not really angry with Ken either, are you?

S: No.

T: You're right. But you are angry with someone—who?

S: My dad.

T: But you could not communicate your anger to him, so instead, who did you give it to?

S: Well, I guess it was Ken and you.

T: Yes, you got it. Has this ever happened before?

S: Maybe; my mom says that when I get mad I am mad at everyone.

T: And when you get mad at everyone, does it help solve the real problem?

S: No.

T: In fact, think about it, the people you dump your anger on—your friends, your teachers, maybe your mom—are the very people who like you; these are the people who are in your corner. Do they deserve to have your anger unloaded onto them?

S: No—not really.

▶ Stage 5: New Skills

T: So what can you do to turn this around? How can you keep from dumping your anger on the people who want the best for you?

S: I don't know; I don't really mean to cause so much trouble.

T: Well, you have shown remarkable maturity and responsibility in the discussion we just had. You are very good at putting your feelings into words, and that's the best way to deal with problems. Is there anybody here at school who you think you could talk to when you're feeling bad?

S: I talk to Mr. Andersen sometimes.

T: Can you think of a way you could touch base with Mr. Andersen on a regular basis?

S: Well, he told me he's always in his room early and I could check in with him at the beginning of the day—right when I get off the bus, if I could get permission from the security guard.

T: That sounds like a good plan. May I discuss the idea with Mr. Andersen?

S: Sure.

▶ Stage 6: Get Ready To Resume the Activity

T: Steven, you have taken a bad start and turned it into something good. Let's review what we've decided to do. First, I will call your mom and tell her about our talk. Then, I will talk with Mr. Andersen to see if you can check in with him when you arrive so you can tell him how you're doing. You have made some great plans and I'll be checking in with you too to see how it's going—OK?

S: OK.

T: Well, you've missed the first 20 minutes of your English class. I'll walk you down there and tell Mr. Johnson that you've been with me. He will probably have make-up work for you to do at home. Can you handle that?

S: Yeah, I'm ready.

Mrs. Hicks guided Steven through the six stages of LSCI and effectively defused a situation which may have exploded into a classroom crisis. Once she drained off his feelings, she used well-developed listening, responding, affirming, and decoding skills to understand the situation through Steven's eyes. Like most students under stress, Steven wanted to tell his story, to be understood and respected. Unfortunately, many students like Steven have had experiences with teachers who are not open to hearing and understanding their stories. As a result these students develop a rigid way of thinking about teachers and do not discriminate between most teachers who want to help and those who are indifferent. Students in stress often don't cooperate initially because they fear humiliation and derision. As a result their stress is expressed through conflict.

This Red Flag Reclaiming Intervention is a *Tap In*, as the stress he experiences about Ken's tickets touch Steven's feelings about his father. Had he not encountered his father just two days before, he may have been less resentful of his friend's good fortune. What is important in this interview is that the teacher took the time to work through the situation, to discover the source of the stress, to offer him some measure of relief, and to expose to Steven his self-destructive pattern of displacement.

Our thanks to Mary Hicks for submitting this example of a Red Flag Reclaiming Intervention. For additional examples of the Red Flag Reclaiming Intervention, see Long and Dorf (1994); Fecser and Long (1997); Cholden and Long (1998); Koenig and Long (1999) and Hill and Long (1999).

WHAT WE HOPE YOU HAVE LEARNED FROM THIS CHAPTER

- The goal of the Red Flag Reclaiming Intervention
- The three types of Red Flag Reclaiming Interventions
- The critical adult task early in the onset of a Red Flag situation
- Why this particular LSCI is called a "Red Flag" Reclaiming Intervention
- At what point the adult must give abundant affirmation
- The impulse the adult must avoid in encountering a Red Flag situation
- Why it is important to avoid being sidetracked from the goal of the LSCI

The Symptom Estrangement Reclaiming Intervention: Benignly Confronting Unacceptable Behavior

9

Student's Perceptions:	"I do what I have to do even if it hurts others." "I have to take care of 'Number One.'" "I have a reputation to maintain." "I have no need to change."
Uses:	With students who are too comfortable with their deviant behavior, who receive too much gratification from their aggressive behavior, and who can justify their behavior in a guilt-free way
Goal:	To make a particular behavior uncomfortable, by confronting the rationalizations and decoding the self-serving narcissism and distorted pleasure the student receives from the unacceptable behavior
Focus:	Helps students realize that they are paying a high price for justifying their exploitation of others; they are tricking themselves into believing their causes are just
Student's New Insight:	"Maybe I'm not as smart as I tell myself." "Maybe I've been cruel." "Maybe I've been tricking myself."

Unlike other types of LSCI, this Reclaiming Intervention is used to confront behavior by increasing students' anxiety about what they are doing and saying. The Symptom Estrangement Reclaiming Intervention is used with students who typically have highly skilled ways of protecting themselves from feelings of guilt by shifting responsibility and fault to another student, the program, or adults.

These students generally receive so much reinforcement from their peers that they do not believe anything is wrong with the way they behave. Therefore, they have little motivation to change or give up their power position in the peer group or with adults they can control. They use their verbal skills to avoid talking about an incident and the feelings evoked by it. They try distractors, role reversals, and other ploys to divert the adult from the issue (see LSCI Stage 2 in Chapter 5, and "Getting Off the Subject" in Chapter 6). Often students switch from one tactic to another until they are successful in confusing and frustrating the adult. A singularly consistent strategy among such students is their attempt to control adults and the focus of the LSCI through alibis and rationalizations.

We have discovered three basic justifications students use to divert adults from the focus of the intervention:

- Basic Justification No. 1: "He Started It"

  "It would never have happened if he had left me alone."

  "He was staring at me."

  "He was laughing at me."

  "He touched me first."

  "He was looking for trouble and he found it."

- Basic Justification No. 2: "It's No Big Deal"

  "You're making a big deal out of nothing."

  "We were just playing around."

  "I guess he didn't get it; I was only kidding."

  "It was an accident."

  "What's the big deal? I didn't use the (stolen object)."

- Basic Justification No. 3: "No One Would Have Done Anything"

  "I didn't tell staff about it because I knew they wouldn't do anything."

  "I'm not a baby. I don't run and tell the teacher. I handle my own problems."

  "I have a right to take care of myself."

  "My father said if anyone messes with me, I should slug him first and ask questions later."

  "Every man has a right to protect his reputation."

Unlike other types of LSCI, the therapeutic goal here is to confront this behavior, increasing students' anxiety about what they are doing and saying to the point that they have some understanding and motivation to change their behavior. Fritz Redl (1966) described this type of LSCI as a "Symptom Estrangement" interview. Here is his description of what is needed by these students and why:

> Our children's egos have, in part, become subservient to the pathological mechanisms they have developed. They have learned to benefit from their symptoms (behaviors) through secondary gains, and therefore are in no way inclined to accept an [adult's] idea that something is wrong with them, or they need help. . . . We use many of their life situations to try to pile up evidence that their pathology [behavior] really does not pay or that they pay too heavily for what meager

secondary gains they draw from it. It is not a simple matter of arguing these children into letting go of their symptoms [behaviors]. We must enlist part of their "insight" into wanting the change. . . . And, our actions [adults' daily behavior and values] have to be well attuned to our words in this interview more than others. (pp. 44–45)

THE ADULT'S TASK

The first task of the adult is to keep the focus on students' inappropriate behavior and to avoid being led astray by students' verbal barrages or attempts to control or camouflage their behavior. The next task is to develop anxieties in students' perceptions by decoding their alibis and behaviors to show them how a part of them justifies and enjoys their "righteous aggression."

Through a successful Symptom Estrangement Reclaiming Intervention, students learn that they are no longer fooling themselves or others by their behavior and that it is not bringing about the benefits they desire. When this level of insight has been achieved, these students usually need follow-up LSCIs with a change in therapeutic focus to learn substitute social skills for achieving what they need from others in more appropriate ways. It also is essential that the environment and the adult's own behavior do not continue to reinforce the student's unacceptable behavior. It also takes many, many LSCIs, but the message will get through!

EXAMPLES OF STUDENTS
WHO CAN BENEFIT

The following vignettes illustrate typical problems of students who can benefit from LSCI that confronts their behavior and disallows its continuation by revealing the student's inner feelings of "enjoying" the reactions, discomfort, and confusion of others.

Peter

A model race car brought to school by Jim for a fifth-grade group project has disappeared. After discussion with the group and a search of the room, the model still cannot be found. As the students get ready to leave for the day, the teacher notices a sizable lump in Peter's coat which turns out to be the model car. As the subsequent LSCI begins, Peter shows no remorse or guilt about taking the model from his friend. He calmly defends himself by saying, "I was planning to return it. It's no big deal." When the teacher continues to probe for the details in LSCI Stage 2, Peter changes his response to, "Jim shouldn't have brought it to school in the first place. Everything gets ripped off around here." During Stage 3, as the teacher begins decoding Peter's behavior, his responses change again: "Someone stole my model about 3 weeks ago."

Peter's teacher sees the necessity of benignly confronting Peter's defenses (it's no big deal, it's Jim's fault, and everything gets ripped off at this school) by pointing out that he is deceiving himself if he believes he can take somebody else's possession and say it is okay.

Dick, Jim, and Bob

In the hall, near the middle school boys' restroom, Bob flips Dick's pen out of his pocket. Dick demands that Bob pick it up and return it to him. As Bob starts to do so, Dick grabs the pen out of his hand, and Bob retaliates by calling Dick "an egg-sucking dog." With this insult, Dick starts chasing Bob. As they run, Bob bumps into Jim who is watching from the sidelines. When this happens, Jim grabs Bob's hand and twists it until Bob drops to the floor in pain. When Bob is on the floor, Dick comes over and kicks him in the ear. The teacher hears the commotion and finds Bob rolling on the floor, crying and rubbing his ear. When asked what happened, Jim and Dick reply that Bob has been teasing them, that Bob started it, and that Bob finally got what was coming to him. They show no concern about their cruel tactics, but actually seem pleased about it.

Their teacher takes all three boys to the conference room for a group LSCI that focuses on the event and the inappropriate behavior of each boy. The therapeutic goal for this LSCI is to confront their defense that they had the right to abuse Bob because he started it. The necessary insight is that their justification, that he started it, is only the rationalization for their pleasure at being cruel to Bob, while feeling no guilt for wrongdoing.

Wayne

During sixth-grade social studies class, a new boy in the group, Anthony, is working on a map project. Wayne raises his hand for help. As the teacher starts over to Wayne, Anthony says, "You'll help that white boy when you won't help me." The teacher ignores the remark but moves toward Anthony, sensing the need for proximity control. Before she gets there, Wayne jumps up and hits Anthony in the face. The teacher grabs Wayne, who justifies his behavior, saying "I solved the problem because I knew you would have done nothing about it."

This is a complex issue since Wayne's aggressive behavior and Anthony's racial comment need to be addressed. The focus for Wayne, however, is to confront his justification that he had the right to take the law into his own hands since the teacher would do nothing about it. After a review of the timeline, the teacher should ask two questions: Who is in charge of this class, and what is the difference between the law of the street and the law of the school? The goal is to create some anxiety in Wayne by pointing out that he is not a mindreader and that he didn't know what the teacher would have done had he told her. Instead he used this justification to sanction his cruel behavior without feeling guilty; he brought the law of the street into the classroom.

Bill and Joe

Bill, a fifth-grade student, was in a rotten mood and seemed to enjoy it. His friend Joe came by and flipped him the "bird." Bill jumped up and punched Joe in the ribs. Suddenly the two were in a violent fight filled with screams and kicks. The teacher yelled for them to stop and grabbed Joe while another teacher held Bill. Ten minutes later they were in the conference room, controlled enough to talk about the incident. Bill's interpretation was that Joe was asking for a beating. He had taken Bill's prize pen, cheated in Monopoly, tripped him in the gym, and called his mother a name. He deserved to be punched out, and he was lucky the teachers broke it up or Joe would be a bloody stump by now. Joe's perceptions were entirely different. He had an explanation for each event. "It's true, I gave him the 'bird,' but what's the big deal? We do it all the time. It's like saying hello. I don't know what got into Bill today. We usually get along, but today he acted like a crazy man." Bill's angry response was, "For a week you've been picking on me, and I should beat you up four times instead of one time!" After some review of the sequence of events, Joe seemed to understand Bill's feelings but Bill continued to stick to his story—"Joe got what he deserved!" The teacher sent Joe back to the room and began LSCI with Bill to confront his unacceptable behavior. (This LSCI is described in full by James Tompkins, 1981, pp. 26–28, in an insightful article about the Symptom Estrangement. It is summarized here with permission of the author.)

These examples show how difficult confronting unacceptable behavior can be. When conducting this type of LSCI, adults have to keep focused, maintain communication with the student, control their own emotions and reactions, and avoid moralizing, while clearly conveying disapproval of the behavior. Adults must be quick thinking and verbally facile. The aim is to decode the behavior, revealing feelings students are protecting or gratifying. To this end we are exposing students' defenses to themselves. There is always the risk that they cannot hear it, and will close down or defend more vigorously. When this happens secondary interpretations of the denial are required (see Chapter 3 on decoding). The other task is to illustrate how these students pay too heavily for the small gains they get from their behavior. There are more gratifying ways to obtain what they want (and to feel better).

EXAMPLE OF LSCI USED TO BENIGNLY CONFRONT UNACCEPTABLE BEHAVIOR: A SYMPTOM ESTRANGEMENT RECLAIMING INTERVENTION

ERIC: HIGH NOON AT THE SOFTBALL GAME

Eric is an overweight 14-year-old boy attending a middle school in a tough part of the inner city. He has had a weight problem most of his life, and is very conscious of his inability to compete with his peers in sports or athletic activities. Since his pre-adolescent years, Eric has developed a low tolerance for heckling by other students, and has been known to retaliate with violence. He has a reputation for being a dangerous character, and most of the other students stay out of his way.

On a beautiful spring day Mr. Brown, the physical education teacher, took the class outside for a game of softball. As he usually does, Mr. Brown selected two students to serve as team captains. Each captain alternately selected one student at a time to form the two teams. As their names were called, the students would join the captain who had selected them, and the growing groups loudly advised each captain who to select or not to select from the dwindling group. Eric hated gym to begin with, but he was further humiliated when Mr. Brown chose to select teams this way, as he was almost always the last one called. On this day he again was the last to be selected, and as he quietly walked over to join the team who was stuck with him, Mason remarked, "Now for sure we're going to lose with him on the team." Eric glared at Mason, but said nothing. The game went on and each time Eric was up to bat, Mason would make another disparaging remark. Ultimately, Mason's prophecy came true and his team lost. As the group walked back to the gym, Eric overheard Mason comment to another student, "If it wasn't for that fat ass, we would have won."

When the dismissal bell rang, Eric made sure he was the first one out of the locker room. The students poured out into the crowded hallway, and as Mason came through the door, Eric grabbed him by the front of his shirt and slammed him against the lockers. He then struck Mason hard in the throat with his forearm, throwing Mason off balance. As Mason fell to the floor choking, Eric began kicking him in the face and upper body. When Eric saw the security guards coming, he stepped away and put his arms in the air. "No need to get rough—I've got no fight with you," he said. As one guard attended to Mason, the other escorted Eric to the office where he was to meet with Mr. Byrd, the assistant principal. The following interview took place between Eric (E) and Mr. Byrd (T).

▶ **Stage 1: Drain Off** (Practically nonexistent)

  T: Eric, let's start by telling me what happened.

E: What happened is that jackass got what he deserved. That's it. That's all.

T: You're saying that Mason deserved a beating? Can you explain that to me?

E: He thinks he can run his mouth like that, it's gonna cost him.

T: OK, you're going to have to help me out. What did he say that got you so angry?

E: He's talkin' about me, that's what.

▶ **Stage 2: Timeline**

T: Where was he talking about you, in the hallway?

E: No, in gym.

T: Can you tell me what he was saying?

E: He was saying the team would lose because I'm no good. He was making all kinds of disrespectful remarks he wishes he hadn't made now.

T: Did Mr. Brown have the class divide up into teams?

E: Yeah, and Mason was telling everybody not to pick me on the team.

T: That must have been pretty hard for you to take. It's embarrassing to have that kind of attention called to you. It's understandable that you were angry about it. What did you do?

E: I just looked at him hard.

T: You didn't say anything, you just looked at him?

E: Yeah, but he saw me—he knew what that look meant.

T: What did the look mean?

E: It meant shut up or I'll kick your ass.

T: How do you know Mason understood that when you look at him it means, shut up or I'll kick your ass?

E: He knew—everybody around here knows that when I give them that look they better keep quiet.

T: So you have a reputation as a guy who will fight if he feels someone is disrespecting him.

E: That's right. I don't take no stuff from nobody.

T: So Mason was making disrespectful remarks about you, and you gave him a look. He saw you, you believe he knew your look was a warning, and he kept on making comments?

E: That's right, so I busted him.

T: But you didn't bust him right then.

E: No, I waited until he came into the hall, then I jumped him.

T: Why did you wait until he came into the hall? Why didn't you bust him right when he was making comments?

E: See, that's what I have to do. I can't get around as good as Mason, so I have to wait till he comes to me.

► Stage 3: Central Issue

T: I think I'm beginning to understand. Tell me if this is correct. You were in gym, Mr. Brown had the class divide into teams, and Mason was telling his captain not to pick you. That made you angry so you gave him your look, and figured that was a warning to him to stop. But he didn't stop. During the game, he made other remarks about you making the team lose. You were furious and decided that since Mason didn't heed your warning look, he deserved to be beaten up for disrespecting you. So since you can't get around as well as Mason, you waited in the hallway to jump him. Is that right?

E: Yeah, that's right. I warned him, he disrespected me, he's hurting.

T: You know, Eric, I'm kind of surprised that you didn't go off on Mason right there in gym. You could have found a way to get close enough to bust him, but you didn't. Instead, you gave him a look which you thought was a warning. A few months back, do you think you would have given him a look, or do you think you might have busted him right there?

E: I probably would have just busted him.

T: But this time you didn't; you showed some self-control. This time, you planned your revenge. Tell me about that.

E: I moved up to the door so I could be the first one out in the hall, then I waited for Mason to come out.

T: That was a pretty clever plan. That way you could be sure to grab him before he had a chance to run.

E: Yeah, that's right. I was making sure he was going to get what he had coming to him.

T: So when he came out into the hall, did he see you?

E: Yeah, he saw me, but he didn't know I was going to kick his ass.

T: So you took him by surprise; you didn't give him a chance to fight back.

E: No, I clocked him right away. That boy went down!

T: So you jumped him and hit him hard—can you tell me where you hit him?

E: In the throat.

T: In the throat—how hard did you hit him?

E: I gave him a good shot—not as much as he deserved though.

T: So you hit him hard enough to be sure to hurt him. What happened after you hit him?

E: He went down.

T: You mean he fell?

E: No, man, I dropped him. Boy was hurtin'!

T: So he was in a lot of pain. What did you do after he went down?

E: I kicked him a few times so he'll remember not to mess with me any more.

T: So after you hit him hard in the throat, and he fell down, was he choking?

E: Yeah.

T: So while he was lying there choking, you kicked him? Where did you kick him?

E: Wherever, I don't know.

T: In the face?

E: Yeah, maybe.

T: So according to your description, it was a pretty brutal attack and Mason never even had a chance to defend himself because you jumped him.

E: So what? He attacked me too! I was settling the score.

▶ Stage 4: Insight

T: There's no question that Mason should not have made disrespectful comments about you, Eric, and it's understandable that it would make you angry, but as I listen to your story, there are a few things I don't understand—maybe you can clarify them for me. You were in gym class and Mason made a negative remark about you; you looked at him to warn him, but he didn't seem to get it because he made several more remarks, is that right?

E: Yeah, he kept on even after I stared him down.

T: What Mason did was wrong. We have a rule here that says everyone has the right to be treated with respect and dignity, and Mason violated that rule. Did Mr. Brown hear him?

E: I don't know.

T: Well, Eric, here's the part I don't understand. If Mason violated a school rule, and the teachers are here to enforce the rules, why didn't you tell Mr. Brown about it?

E: (Laughing) Tell Mr. Brown? What for? He wouldn't have done anything.

T: How do you know he wouldn't have done anything? Can you read Mr. Brown's mind?

E: Man, Mr. Brown likes those jock guys. He wouldn't have done one thing.

T: But how do you know? You never gave him the chance. How do you know that today he wouldn't have done something?

E: I just know.

T: Well, Eric, I have an idea why you didn't tell Mr. Brown. You didn't tell him because you were concerned that he might do something to stop Mason. And if he did, you wouldn't have had any reason to beat him up. And what you wanted was a reason to make him hurt. In some ways, a part of you seemed to get some pleasure out of causing pain to Mason. You decided not to follow the rules of the school, and instead you followed the law of the street; get the guy when he doesn't expect it and do as much damage as you can before you're stopped. See, what you did, hitting Mason in the throat and kicking him in the face when he was down, was a cruel and brutal act. And you are sitting here telling me that it's OK because he made some comments about you. You are tricking yourself into believing you had a right to brutalize another person, and you don't. Think about this, Eric, you've been beaten on before. You know what it's like to be hurting—you don't like it, and you are telling me that it's OK for you to cause that kind of pain to others. As long as you keep fooling yourself into thinking you did nothing wrong, you'll find that you are the one who is paying a high price for the momentary pleasure of getting back at someone in a brutal way. What do you think the consequences of your actions today will be?

E: I don't care.

T: There you go, fooling yourself again! You might be expelled, and you might be facing assault charges in juvenile court. Do you really expect me to believe you don't care about that? You can say that to yourself, but you know what you are really thinking.

E: Shut up!

▶ Stage 5: New Skills

T: Sure, it's hard to hear, but you know what, Eric, it doesn't have to be this way. You have a lot on the ball. You're intelligent and creative. You have a whole lot going for you. And I'm not saying you shouldn't get angry when someone says disrespectful things about you. But do you see how you create huge problems for yourself when you hurt others?

E: (Silence)

▶ Stage 6: Get Ready To Resume the Activity

T: Your silence tells me that you're thinking about the choices you made. That's good, because you've shared your pattern of self-defeating behavior, Eric. Every time there is an incident in which you take the law of the streets into the classroom, we're going to remind you of this pattern and what it will cost you. We want to see you make choices that will make your life better, not worse. I want you to stay here and think about what we have discussed today, and I will be back to discuss the consequences of your behavior.

E: (Silence)

Mr. Byrd has used this crisis as an opportunity to help Eric see his actions as brutality rather than bravado. If Mr. Byrd had simply administered the consequences without helping Eric gain some measure of insight, Eric would be adding the school officials to the list of people who are devaluing him. This LSCI makes it troublesome for Eric to hold on to his comfort with causing pain to others, and that is the goal of the Symptom Estrangement Reclaiming Intervention. For an additional example, see Beck (1998).

WHAT WE HOPE YOU HAVE LEARNED FROM THIS CHAPTER

- The primary purpose in using the Symptom Estrangement Reclaiming Intervention
- The common characteristic shared by students who can benefit from this therapeutic goal
- What is done deliberately in this form of LSCI that is not done in any other LSCI

- What process is used frequently by adults to change students' insight during this LSCI

- What new insight a student should have as a result

- One follow-up problem that must be avoided if the results are to be lasting

- The essential message that should be conveyed to both overtly aggressive and passive-aggressive students when using this form of LSCI

- How a carefully detailed timeline helps this form of LSCI

- Why the Symptom Estrangement Reclaiming Intervention can be particularly difficult for adults

- Why this form of LSCI also can be particularly difficult for a student

The Massaging Numb Values Reclaiming Intervention: Building Values To Strengthen Self-Control

10

Student's Perception:	"When I'm upset, I do terrible things, and I feel guilty."
Uses:	With students who, after acting out, are burdened by remorse, shame, inadequacy, or guilt about their own failures or unworthiness, and who seek out punishment
Goal:	To relieve some of the burden by emphasizing a student's positive qualities; to strengthen self-control and self-confidence as an able and valued person with qualities like fairness, kindness, friendship, or leadership potential
Focus:	Expand student's self-control and confidence by abundant affirmations and reflections about existing socially desirable attributes and potential for future acclaim by peers; developmentally, this goal requires a shift in the source of responsibility from adult to student
Student's New Insight:	"Even under tempting situations or group pressure, I have the capacity to control myself."

The Massaging Numb Values Reclaiming Intervention is used to help students who are burdened by anxiety about guilt or inadequacy, yet do not use controls at the right time. These students experience anxiety at the wrong times and in the wrong proportions. Their remorse or guilt usually is felt after the fact, which is emotionally destructive and not helpful to them in controlling their own behavior. Their remorse is often so intense that they seek punishment (set themselves up to be caught and punished). Students who have been physically or sexually abused often develop this self-abusive response and make degrading comments such as the following:

"I'm no good!"
"It must have been my fault."
"I wish I was dead."

"Go ahead, hit me!"
"I guess I'm just a loser."
"I can't do anything right."
"It was a stupid picture." (after tearing up a drawing)

Initially the adult is sympathetic toward such students, since they are so distressed about the results of their behavior. They promise to be good, never do it again, write confessions, make new resolutions, and shed abundant tears. However, like a tempting bag of popcorn, their intentions do not last long. It is not that they deliberately defy or ignore rules and regulations. The problem is that they are easily stimulated, lack adequate self-control, are sensitive to what is happening around them, and then become unproductively guilty when they are caught in the Conflict Cycle.

The therapeutic goal for these students is to strengthen their self-control by building up their self-esteem. If they have sufficient belief in their own capabilities and attributes, they will be more likely to use control and put on brakes *before* they react to stress with impulsive, unacceptable behavior. Adults often mistakenly believe that these students can control themselves if they want to do so. It is essential to understand that these are students who do not like their own behavior but, because of weak self-control skills, they cannot use the constructive values they have internalized. Fritz Redl (1966) called this form of LSCI "Massaging Numb Values" to convey the point that the values are there, within the student, but are not in use. According to Redl, unless they are reinforced and expanded such values lie dormant or atrophy:

> No matter how close to psychopathic our children may sometimes look, we haven't found one of them yet who didn't have lots of potential areas of value appeal lying within him. . . . Admitting value sensitivity, just like admitting hunger for love, is quite face-losing for our youngsters. There are, however, in most youngsters some value areas that are more exempt from peer group shame than others. For instance, even at a time when our youngsters would rather be seen dead than overconforming and sweet, the appeal to certain codes of "fairness" within their fight-provocation ritual is quite acceptable by them. Thus, in order to ready the ground for "value arguments" altogether, the pulling out of issues of fairness or similar values from the debris of their daily life events may pay off handsomely in the end. (p. 45)

THE ADULT'S TASK

The first task for adults is to see through the smoke screen of aggressive behavior and provide affirmations of the student, reflecting on positive qualities and leading the student into also acknowledging them. Use of a timeline in LSCI Stage 2 is helpful in focusing the student on details that bring out examples of positive attributes, no matter how small these may be. (Any strategy that creates more inadequacy, shame, remorse, or guilt in these students only complicates the problem.)

The method is to highlight and magnify the flickering signs of control. When examples of constructive behavior and positive qualities become part of the LSCI discussion, decode to help students gain insight into why they succumb to behavior they know is not acceptable. Then connect this insight to the underlying positive values it represents (see Chapter 3 for decoding strategies and Chapter 4 for a review of developing values). In Stage 4 shape the central issue around the positive behaviors that have been observed and the values they represent. Finally, in Stage 5 use these qualities as part of the plan to resolve the crisis, and reinforce values to guide behavior choices in the future.

Anthony Werner (1981) offers a major caution for adults using this type of LSCI:

> Responding to this pupil's acting out behavior in punitive or moralistic ways does not help the pupil learn and grow but only creates additional problems. . . . He will either feel that he has "paid the price" and lose contact with his feelings of guilt and the desirable values behind them, or he will feel increased guilt and will act out more intensely. (p. 31)

Werner goes on to describe the particular qualities needed by adults to make this type of LSCI effective.

> The effective interviewer is one who is able to be supportive, compassionate, and empathetic. With these qualities and skill in LSCI, this interviewer can become an advocate for the child. He [or she] can help turn a specific problem incident into a valuable experience for the child. (p. 31)

EXAMPLES OF STUDENTS WHO CAN BENEFIT

The following vignettes illustrate three types of situations in which students respond to the Massaging Numb Values Reclaiming Intervention. The goal is to strengthen students' self-control by recognizing and emphasizing existing values the students reveal in their behavior. When selecting this therapeutic goal, it is important to avoid using it in a way that will reinforce unacceptable behavior. This is less likely to occur if you base your own responses on (a) a student's level of development about who should take responsibility for control of behavior (the existential phases discussed in Chapter 4); (b) the type of developmental anxiety with which the student is struggling (discussed in Chapter 3); and (c) the general level of values the student currently uses and the possibility of challenging the student to rise to the next level (discussed in Chapter 4). In the following illustrations, we show how the adult adjusts responses to avoid reinforcement of unacceptable behavior, and we summarize the diagnostic cues which guide the interviewer to select a Massaging Numb Values Reclaiming Intervention.

Doug

During free time, Tom, age 13, talks Doug, age 12, into helping him let the air out of a car tire in the staff parking lot at the middle school. Doug is very upset when they are caught and spontaneously says, "It was a dumb thing to do." In the LSCI they discuss exactly how the incident developed and who had the idea. Doug says that he refused to go along with Tom twice before he agreed to help him. With this information the teacher is able to support Doug by saying, "When you were able to say no twice, it shows me that a part of you is trying to stop doing something you know is wrong." Doug is surprised but pleased that the teacher supports his flickering attempt at control rather than punishing him for his impulsive behavior.

The teacher selects this intervention with Doug to protect him from any self-abusive behavior, because she recognizes that his behavior in this incident was not up to his level of conscience development. He showed traces of self-control and a value system that should have been operating before the incident occurred.

Jack

Jack, age 10, has special reading instruction three times a week with his favorite teacher, Mrs. Beyer. Mrs. Beyer is patient and caring and tolerates Jack's hyperactivity better than any other adult in the school. During the last session, Mrs. Beyer was called out of the room for a moment, and Jack stole 10 dollars from her purse. The theft has gone undetected for 2 days and Jack's feelings of guilt are beginning to grow. When he is called to reading instruction today, he refuses to go. This is uncharacteristic of Jack, and the adults, including Mrs. Beyer, are confused. When his classroom teacher orders him to go to reading, he clings to his desk and screams, "I ain't goin'!" Jack ends up in the principal's office where he is about to receive a detention. Jack does not protest, and the principal recognizes that he seems to want the punishment. As the principal begins LSCI, Jack is nervous, but as he begins to talk and the timeline unfolds, Jack confesses to the theft. The principal affirms him for telling the truth and taking responsibility for his poor choice. Jack visibly relaxes as he plans his apology to Mrs. Beyer.

EXAMPLE OF LSCI USED TO BUILD VALUES THAT STRENGTHEN SELF-CONTROL: A MASSAGING NUMB VALUES RECLAIMING INTERVENTION

MIKE: THE RED MURAL DISASTER

Mike is a very large 16-year-old student who lives with his father, a policeman, and his mother, a grocery store clerk. Almost since birth he has been an active and impulsive child, described by his parents as "hard to handle." Mike has been diagnosed with Tourette syndrome, which manifests as sudden flashes of emotion coupled with spontaneous behavioral responses. He is taking medication that helps reduce the intensity of the condition. Though his parents are well meaning, his father has resorted to physical means to control Mike which have sometimes left bruises. Child Protective Services and Mike's parents have worked out a very satisfactory arrangement in which Mike lives for most of the week at a nearby group home and stays with his parents on weekends. Mike receives education and mental health services at a day treatment center, and in his classroom of ten students, Mike stands out. His peers tolerate his clumsiness and immaturity, but leave him out of conversations and activities. One of his goals is to improve his relationships with peers.

Today is a special day for Ms. Minner's class. For the past month they have been working with an artist in residence, on loan from the Ohio Arts Council. He helped the group design and paint a large, colorful mural on the wall of the building lobby, and today is the final day of painting. The dedication of the mural is a gala event scheduled in just three days, and everyone is relieved that they met the deadline.

Mike had to stop at the nurse's office for his medication and had been delayed. He joined the group almost 25 minutes late. As he entered, some students were painstakingly touching up the last of the details. Mike asked Rick, the artist, what he should paint, and was told that the work was finished and there was no more painting to be done. Mike argued that others were painting and he wanted to do the same. Rick and Mr. Ray, the aide, explained the situation again to Mike, and told him that his help was needed in the next step, removing paint from the floor where it had splattered during the project. Mike angrily refused this task and insisted that he paint his name on the mural. He was told that he would be permitted to do that with the other students later. Mike turned and stormed away angrily. In his path was a can of red paint about one-third full, and as Mike approached it, he kicked it violently. The can flew, spinning into the air and spattering red paint all over everyone and onto the mural.

Mike froze, realizing what he had done. The response of the group was immediate and intense. Enraged, they screamed at Mike and berated him. A very aggressive student, Chris, had to be physically restrained as he attempted to attack Mike. Chris was shrieking threats at Mike and struggling against the staff who were holding him. Mike began escalating in response, screaming repeatedly, "Let him go! Let him kill me!" As Mike was escorted to the office, he was crying and very distraught. At one point he purposefully slammed his fist hard into the brick wall causing bleeding across his knuckles. Upon entering the office, he threw himself into a chair, sobbing and holding his head in his hands. He refused any treatment or aid for his bleeding hand, and as he cried, he repeated under his breath, "I'm a sick f__ -up."

Ms. Minner arrived and was briefed about the incident by Mr. Ray. She put her hand on Mike's shoulder and the following dialogue developed between Ms. Minner (T) and Mike (M).

▶ Stage 1: Drain Off

M: Get away from me, Ms. Minner.

T: Mike, it's probably hard for you to hear right now, but it's going to be OK.

M: Just leave me alone. There's nothing you can do. I don't want to talk about it. My father's right, I'm a dumb-ass f___-up. So just leave me alone.

T: After what just happened, Mike, anyone would feel upset. The way you feel now is perfectly understandable.

M: (Silence)

T: You made a mistake, but it's not the end of the world.

M: (Silence)

T: Right now you're feeling awful about what happened, and you don't know what to do about it.

M: They should have just let Chris kill me, then I would be dead and everyone would be better off, including me.

▶ Stage 2: Timeline

T: Right now, it seems like one of your darkest moments, but maybe it's not as bad as it seems. Mike, let's go back and review what happened so we can understand it better. Maybe we will be able to figure out a way to do something about this. You went to get your medication, and I know you joined us late.

M: Yeah, the nurse was looking for bugs or something in a bunch of kids' hair and I had to wait till she was done.

T: What were you thinking about while you were waiting?

M: I was thinking, "Come on, come on," I was getting impatient.

T: So you were impatient because you were held up. How were you doing when you finally joined the group?

M: Well, when I first got there, pretty good. I knew we were finishing today and I was anxious to paint.

T: So you were pretty excited about helping to finish the mural; you were really eager to paint. What happened next?

M: I asked Rick what I should paint and he told me it was already done.

T: That must have been a letdown.

M: Yeah, I was mad because I was looking forward to this all day.

T: That's understandable, of course. So what happened next?

M: Well, other kids were painting and I didn't see why I couldn't, so I argued about it.

T: What do you mean, "argued"?

M: You know, I kept saying I was going to paint anyway.

T: You were pretty disappointed and angry, and you tried to get Rick to let you paint.

▶ **Stage 3: Central Issue**

M: Yeah, and then Mr. Ray told me to get the turpentine and clean the paint off the floor. That really made me mad. I felt like I was going to go crazy, so I decided to go back to the classroom so I wouldn't lose it and that's when I came up on that can of paint. I don't know, I just kicked it and I ruined the mural. Then everyone started screaming at me, and Chris was going to hit me until Mr. Ray stopped him. He should have just let him go.

T: There were some strong feelings. Mike, let me ask you something: Is this the worst thing that you've ever done?

M: It's one of them.

T: So there have been other times when you have felt this way—like everything's messed up?

M: Yeah, lots of times. That's what I mean. I'm a screw-up—I've always been a screw-up.

T: So a lot of things have gone wrong in the past, but somehow you've gotten through them. You've been able to put them behind you?

M: Yeah, that's what screw-ups do; they wait till the next day and screw something else up.

▶ **Stage 4: Insight**

T: You made a mistake today—a pretty bad one—but it was a mistake. You've made mistakes in the past; everyone has. But it doesn't mean that everything you do is a mistake. It doesn't mean you're a bad person. In fact, I've seen you do some things that were pretty admirable recently. Yesterday you loaned Todd some money for lunch, and last week you helped Mr. Johnson mop the hallway. You didn't have to do those things.

M: That's nothing; look what I just did. You can't tell me that I didn't screw up big time.

T: No, you're right, you screwed up. My point is that this doesn't mean you *are* a screw-up; it means you made a mistake. Sometimes you make some pretty good choices and sometimes you make mistakes. Nobody's perfect. Take Babe Ruth. Did you know that he struck out hundreds of times? Did that make him a lousy player?

M: (Silent, looking at the floor)

T: It was a pretty intense moment out there in the hall today, but you know, as you tell about it, there's one part I don't understand. One part of the whole story doesn't seem to fit. Tell me if this is right. You have been working on the mural all month and you were really looking forward to finishing it and signing it today. When you went to the nurse's office for your medication, you had to wait because she was dealing with some other kids. You were feeling impatient, but you got through it and finally joined the group. Then you were told that the mural was already finished and you would not get to paint after all. You were disappointed and angry. How angry were you?

M: Real angry!

T: So, on a scale of one to ten?

M: About a nine and a half.

T: OK, so you're about as mad as you can get because now, it's the second thing that's gone wrong. But it's not over yet. Next, Mr. Ray tells you to start cleaning the paint off the floor. By this time you're really steamed. In fact, you're so angry you told me you felt like you were going crazy. Is that right?

M: Yeah, I lost it.

T: Well, that's the part I don't understand—if you were so angry, and you "lost it," how come you stopped after you kicked the can of red paint? There were lots of cans of paint out there. If you lost it, and you were so crazy and so angry, how come you didn't kick a bunch of cans?

M: (Thoughtfully) I don't know.

T: I have an idea about why you stopped yourself. You stopped yourself because a part of you was saying, "Control yourself." You didn't go crazy or out of control. In fact, do you remember what you told me you were thinking when Mr. Ray said you should clean up the floor?

M: What?

T: According to you, you decided to go back to the classroom so you *wouldn't* lose it. Is that right?

M: Yeah, I was on my way when it happened.

T: You actually had a plan to keep yourself in control. It's hard to believe under the circumstances, but that's progress, Mike. When you first came here, would you have ever thought of trying to leave to avoid a problem?

M: Probably not . . . but I still kicked the can of paint.

T: Yes, let's talk about that. When you turned and headed toward the classroom, what was going through your mind?

M: I don't know, something like, "I'm out of here!"

T: And you were feeling . . .

M: Mad as hell!

T: Did you think, "I know how to get them back for making me mad as hell—I'll kick that red can of paint and it will splash on the mural"?

M: (Apologetically) No, that part, kicking the can, that just sort of happened. I didn't even think about it.

T: I agree. But if you could replay the situation, would you have chosen to kick over the can?

M: No, but I did.

T: So part of you was in enough control to try to leave the situation, but another part of you acted out impulsively, and what we have to work on is making the control part stronger so it can overcome the impulse part.

M: That's impossible.

T: No, actually it isn't. You've already started to work on it. Remember, you tried to walk away. Did I understand that correctly?

M: Yeah, I was going to go to the classroom.

▶ Stage 5: New Skills

T: Right, you had a solution to the problem—walk away—but you couldn't get beyond your impulse to kick the can. In fact, Mike, there are a lot of people struggling with impulse control problems and we know about some things that have helped. I remember two students who graduated from here who did very well. They used different ways of managing their impulsiveness. One used what's called "visualization." He discovered that usually when he acted out impulsively, it started with his feeling angry. He started to notice the signs of anger, you know, impatience inside, fists clenching, and so on. Then he trained himself to really notice those signs, because they were warnings that he might act out and be sorry later. What he did was, when he noticed those signs, he visualized, or imagined, a gigantic red stop sign and at the same time, he yelled inside of his head as loud as he could imagine, "STOP." He would do that while walking away. For him it made a big difference. The other kid did something similar. He became familiar with his signs of anger too, but instead of visualizing, he used self-talk. He decided what he was going to say to himself and practiced when he wasn't angry. Then, when he got angry, he concentrated on his self-talk, something like, "Walk away, don't listen to them, you can do it," and with a lot of practice, he really started to bring his impulsiveness down. Is any of this worth a try in your case?

▶ Stage 6: Get Ready To Resume the Activity

M: Maybe, but right now everyone wants to kill me and the mural is wrecked.

T: OK, let's see what Rick says about the mural. I'm sure there's a way to fix it, but you might have to pay for it or work it off some way.

M: I would do anything to make the mural OK.

T: And I'll talk with Mr. Ray and Chris and the others and see how we can get everyone to calm down. They might think you deserve consequences for what you did.

M: I do.

T: You have a lot of fine qualities, Mike. You are willing to accept responsibility for yourself and you are willing to work on your problem. I really respect that.

M: I just want all of this to go away.

T: You can make it better. Let's go see Rick. Later we'll talk about trying out some strategies to help you strengthen your controls.

Ms. Minner used cognitive restructuring through this Massaging Numb Values Reclaiming Intervention. At the beginning of the interview, Mike believed himself to be a worthless "screw-up." By the conclusion, Mike sees that he is accepted by Ms. Minner and that things can get better. He recognizes that he has already made some gains, and that there is reason to hope that he can continue to grow. Developmentally, Mike still needs and wants a good deal of adult guidance, and may well benefit from a cognitive-behavioral intervention implemented with close supervision by a trusted adult. For additional examples, see Long & Wilder (1993) and Hewitt & Long (1999).

WHAT WE HOPE YOU HAVE LEARNED FROM THIS CHAPTER

- When an LSCI therapeutic goal should focus on a student's values

- Characteristics of students who benefit from the Massaging Numb Values Reclaiming Intervention

- The type of insight such students have about their own behavior

- When and how these students typically show their values

- How you can improve a student's self-regulation of behavior by reinforcing latent values

- The four sequential tasks for adults using this form of LSCI

- Two strategies to avoid in this form of LSCI, and what happens if they are used

- Three types of information you need, to avoid reinforcing unacceptable behavior while using the Massaging Numb Values Reclaiming Intervention

- The common characteristic shared by all students who benefit from this form of LSCI

- How this therapeutic goal can be used with older students to help them face, in a responsible way, the serious consequences of their unacceptable behavior

The New Tools Reclaiming Intervention: Teaching New Social Skills

11

Student's Perception:	"I want to do the right thing, but it always comes out wrong."
Uses:	With students seeking approval of adults or peers, but lacking appropriate social behaviors to accomplish this
Goal:	To teach new social skills that the student can use for immediate positive gain
Focus:	Help the student realize he or she has the right attitude and intentions, but the wrong behavior. Since behavior is easier to change than attitude, the student can successfully learn new social skills.
Student's New Insight:	"I have the right intention, but I need help to learn the skills that will help me make friends, achieve, and get along with adults."

Teaching new skills to students who lack successful social behaviors is a major way for adults to help students manage and change socially inappropriate behavior. Most troubled students use inappropriate or dysfunctional patterns of interpersonal social behavior. Yet many of these same students have appropriate intentions and feelings.

These students want to belong to a peer group, have friends, achieve, be acclaimed as a person others admire, and have a close relationship with someone. Although they have such positive feelings and good intentions, they lack the acceptable social behaviors that could result in greater fulfillment of their desires. The behaviors of these students often produce quite the opposite reactions in others. They want to be friends, but they communicate this by shoving, hitting, bragging, touching, or making negative remarks about others. They want adult approval, but they try to achieve this by overreacting, contradicting, directing adults, boasting, covering up for inadequacy or failure by disavowing interest, posturing as know-it-alls, or clowning. Adolescent students often take on negative, alienated postures toward adults and peers as defensive covers for their social and interpersonal ineptness and their failures to achieve approval or affirmation.

Using this form of LSCI, an adult can support a student's good intentions and desires and teach new social behaviors. The therapeutic goal is to change a student's ineffective, unacceptable behaviors by teaching substitute behaviors that bring about desired reactions from others. To accomplish this goal, the adult helps students realize that their current ways of expressing feelings and needs do not bring the results they hope for. Then a connection must be made between the student's desire for acceptance, and behaviors that will bring about these desired results.

Fritz Redl (1966) describes this form of LSCI as widening students' "adaptational skills." In crisis and under stress, students' defensive behaviors often break down or change form. Redl sees this as a significant time to make therapeutic gains:

> Use many of their life experiences to help them draw visions of much wider ranges of potential reactions to the same messes. . . . Even the seemingly simple recognition that seeking out an adult to talk it over with is so much more reasonable than lashing out at nothing in wild fury may need to be worked at hard for a long stretch of time with some of the children I have in mind. (p. 46)

THE ADULT'S TASK

A trusting relationship with the helping adult is essential to the effectiveness of the New Tools Reclaiming Intervention. For this reason it is rarely used during the initial stages of students' programs, when they typically spend their time defending against adult help and support. Once beginning trust develops and a student wants to learn and have friends, the adult can serve as a model for the student and use a range of techniques to teach prosocial behavior.

Perhaps the hardest part of the New Tools Reclaiming Intervention is to initially identify a student's genuine feelings and desire for socially rewarding results. This is the task during LSCI Stages 2 and 3. With the help of decoding, you can validate these intentions, if a student is not able to convey them directly (see Chapter 2). Then it is important to support and affirm the student by reinforcing the idea that what the student wants from others is desirable and achievable. Throughout the process, providing empathy, warmth, and real concern for the student's feelings is essential.

The next task in LSCI Stage 4 is for you and the student to review alternatives for achieving desired results. There are numerous ways to evoke changes in others' reactions (see breaking the Conflict Cycle in Chapter 2). From the alternatives discussed, help the student select new behaviors that are realistic and achievable. Keep the choices simple and achievable in small, sequential stages. Then in Stage 5 let the student rehearse the new behavior in role play with you. Be sure to include simulations of situations in which uncomfortable feelings may recur when others say or do things that fail to acknowledge the student's "new look."

While these tasks require a fairly straightforward effort to teach new social skills, Leonard Sanders (1981) offers an important caution when a student's behavior is so outrageous or frustrating that it is difficult to attribute any "good intention" to the student: "Take care not to destroy the good intentions and growing positive attitudes of the pupil. The goal is to hook up the pupil's desire for acceptance with acceptable behavior" (p. 32).

This is an important point. New skills are taught on the premise that the student has shown good intentions and wants different results. Clearly, if an adult belittles or fails to recognize the student's intentions (however obscured they may be by unacceptable, negative social behaviors), the foundation for building solid new behaviors may be lost.

When a switch to new behavior is agreed upon by student and adult, behavior can begin to change. But don't be discouraged if change does not occur rapidly. Change will be gradual. It is difficult to quickly change old coping strategies that typically have developed from defensive maneuvers to protect the student from feelings of rejection, alienation, or inadequacy.

EXAMPLES OF STUDENTS WHO CAN BENEFIT

Al

Whenever Al wants help with his math assignment, he taps his pencil on his desk. If the teacher ignores him, he calls out disruptively, "Come over here! . . . I said, 'Get over here!'" Versions of Al's irritating and somewhat disrespectful behavior toward the teacher are fairly commonplace whenever adults make assignments for students to do work independently. What is Al's intention? His intention is to accomplish the task successfully, but it is obscured in his defensive attempts to capture the teacher's attention and reassurance without appearing to need help. LSCI that builds on this intention should be successful in motivating Al to change the way he tries to enlist aid from the teacher.

Kathy

A seventh-grade class is engrossed in a project, designing a group game about environmental issues. Kathy is asked to join a group of four other students in which Matthew, a student she likes, is a member. Matthew smiles at her, and she says, "It's not my idea to join this group." Matthew reacts and responds, "Looks like 'Acid Rain Kathy' is here!" The group laughs and Kathy says, "I'm *not* joining this group! Nobody tells me what to do, and I'll damn well do what I please!" Then she stalks away.

After getting Kathy's story, the teacher chooses to emphasize that Kathy had the right idea and was trying to relate to Matthew, but had the wrong behavior. This therapeutic goal is chosen because the teacher knows that Kathy wants to be an accepted group member and to be liked by others. When Kathy feels good about herself, the teacher has observed that she is kind and protective toward younger or smaller students in the class. The teacher uses these past observations to build on Kathy's good intentions to be a helpful, valued member of the group. Once Kathy realizes that her teacher acknowledges her desire to have friends and can see beyond her inappropriate behavior, Kathy is willing to learn new friendship skills.

EXAMPLE OF LSCI USED TO TEACH NEW SOCIAL BEHAVIORS

JEREMY: HELLO, TIFFANY!

Jeremy is an impulsive 16-year-old student with little social awareness. Although he is bright and creative, he drives away both peers and adults with outrageous antics he employs to amuse himself and to impress others. He has few close friends, but one of them is Chico, a 15-year-old student in Jeremy's class. Chico is more socially competent than Jeremy, but he enjoys Jeremy's sense of humor. They ride the bus to school together and often share a seat. Recently Tiffany moved into the neighborhood and Chico has taken a liking to her. She rides the same bus to school.

One morning Jeremy boards the bus and is surprised to find that his usual seat next to Chico is occupied by Tiffany. They are talking and pay no attention to Jeremy as he takes the seat behind them. Without saying a word, Jeremy leans forward and snatches the pick from Chico's hair. (Part of Chico's "look" is a red pick stuck in his hair just above his right ear.) Chico whirls around and screams at Jeremy, "Give that back, fool!" Jeremy smiles and sticks the pick in into his pants just behind the buckle of his belt and says, "Come and get it, sucker!" Chico is enraged. He jumps out of his seat, grabs Jeremy by the jacket, and hauls him to his feet as the bus monitor intervenes. Jeremy is shocked and surprised at Chico's response and swears at him as the bus monitor moves Chico to a new seat. When the bus arrives at school and the students get off, Chico is waiting for Jeremy, and the two begin a verbal volley of insults which escalates into a fight. Staff intervene, and the boys are separated. Jeremy is taken to the office of the assistant principal, Mr. Sheppard, who has just spoken with the bus monitor and staff on duty. Mr. Sheppard (T) conducts the following New Tools Reclaiming Intervention with Jeremy (J).

▶ **Stage 1: Drain Off**

T: Jeremy, it's pretty early in the morning to be getting into fights.

J: I know! Tell Chico about it! Man, he's crazy today!

T: What do you mean?

J: Like he's gone nuts! He's an idiot! I'm gonna kick his ass!

T: A lot has happened here in just a few minutes—let's try to calm down and figure it out.

J: I'm not going to take that mess from him! He's crazy!

T: What do you mean, he's crazy?

J: He's acting all tough and everything, tryin' to fight me. He knows I can take him if I want to.

T: When did all of this start? I saw you guys when you left yesterday and it looked like you were OK.

▶ **Stage 2: Timeline**

J: It started on the bus. He got all pissed off for no reason.

T: So at the end of the day yesterday, it was OK between you guys. Then what happened on the bus this morning?

J: He gets on before me, right? So when the bus comes to my stop, I get on and I sit behind him.

T: Did you say anything or did he say anything to you?

J: No, I just got on and took a seat.

T: Do you have assigned seats on the bus?

J: Not unless you get a pink slip.

T: So you can sit wherever you want?

J: Yeah.

T: Is that where you usually sit, behind Chico?

J: No, I usually sit next to him.

T: Why didn't you sit next to him today?

J: Because Tiffany was.

T: So let me see if I've got this straight. It's a regular morning, nothing going on between you and Chico, and you get on the bus and see that Tiffany's sitting next to Chico where you usually sit, right?

J: Yeah, so I sat behind.

T: So you were taken a little by surprise?

▶ Stage 3: Central Issue

J: What do you mean?

T: Well, you were expecting to sit in your usual seat, and you saw it was taken by Tiffany, so you must have been a little surprised by that.

J: What are you trying to say? It's not like I'm gay or something!

T: I'm just saying that when you have a certain seat every day you kind of get used to it, and when it's not available, it can be a little bit unsettling because now you have to make a decision you don't normally have to make—where to sit. It was sort of a habit, sitting with Chico, and sometimes it's hard to break habits. Know what I mean?

J: Yeah, I guess I was a little surprised.

T: Sure—how did it make you feel to see that your seat was taken?

J: At first I was kind of pissed off.

T: Pretty understandable feeling under the circumstances. So you decided to take the seat right behind. What happened next?

J: I was just sitting there.

T: Was anyone sitting next to you?

J: No.

T: So while you were sitting there by yourself, what were you thinking?

J: I was thinking how bored I was.

T: You were bored because usually you talk with Chico and today there wasn't anybody to talk to. What was Chico doing?

J: He was talking to Tiffany.

T: And ignoring you?

J: Yeah, he could have at least said hi or something.

T: Chico and Tiffany were talking, and Chico didn't even say hi to you. What kind of reaction did you have to that?

J: Well, it made me kind of mad. He was dissing me.

T: So here you are, sitting there alone, feeling angry and disrespected . . . so what did you do?

J: Well, I decided to have a little fun with Chico, so I grabbed his pick out of his hair.

T: You just reached over and grabbed the pick . . . you didn't say anything?

J: No, I just took it as a joke, you know?

T: You took the pick as a joke, expecting what?

J: That he would laugh.

T: Are you telling me that what you really wanted to do was strike up some conversation with Chico?

J: Yeah, I didn't want it to be a big deal.

T: Well, Jeremy, that's really good to hear! You were trying to be social, to talk to a friend. Your idea was not to cause trouble—you didn't want trouble, you wanted conversation. You wanted to be involved in a positive way! You had the right idea—but something went wrong. You expected Chico to laugh, and then you would start talking. But he didn't laugh. What did he do?

J: He told me to give it back to him.

T: So did you?

J: No.

T: What did you do with it?

J: (Somewhat embarrassed) I stuck it down my pants and told him to come get it—but I was just kidding. He knew I was kidding; we always goof around.

T: Tell me about Chico's reaction.

J: He went nuts! He grabbed me out of my seat like he was gonna bust me or something and then the bus aide made him go sit behind the driver.

T: Were you surprised by Chico's reaction?

J: Yeah, why does he have to go and make a federal case out of it? I wasn't gonna keep the stupid pick!

▶ **Stage 4: Insight**

T: That's an excellent question. Let's see if we can understand Chico's intense reaction to what you think of as a little goofing around. Now, this might be tough because it will require you to do a little perspective taking. That means putting yourself in the other guy's shoes. Let me ask you this, why do you think Chico was sitting with Tiffany this morning?

J: I don't know, maybe he likes her.

T: So you think he is attracted to her?

J: Probably.

T: What kind of an impression do you think he wanted to make?

J: A good one.

T: What makes a good impression on a girl when a guy likes her?

J: He wants her to think he's cool.

T: Your joke this morning, did it make him look cool?

J: I guess not.

T: How do you think he felt when you snatched the pick out of his hair?

J: Pretty mad, I guess.

T: And if he was pretty mad, and maybe embarrassed, how do you think he felt after you shoved it in your pants?

J: I get your point.

T: What is it?

J: That I was just kidding, but he took it serious because he was trying to make a good impression on Tiffany. He's pissed off at me because I made him look like a jerk.

T: You have such a clear understanding of what happened, Jeremy! I'm not saying that Chico was right in threatening you, but you can understand why he'd be upset. You had the right intention, to join the conversation, but you went about it in the wrong way. Partly, I think, because you were a little offended and you didn't know how to handle it. What might have been a better way to handle it?

▶ Stage 5: New Skills

J: I guess I knew he wanted to talk to her so I probably should have stayed out of it.

T: That's one possibility . . . anything else?

J: I could have said hi to both of them.

T: Yes, and that might have started a conversation, or it might not have, but it's a friendly way to let people know you want to talk. What would you say if you tried that and they said hi back to you?

J: You mean what would I talk about?

T: Yes, what would you talk about?

J: I don't know, maybe the game last night or something else.

T: So conversation isn't the hard part; it's how to get started.

J: I knew I was goofing around, I just didn't think it was going to get out of control.

▶ **Stage 6: Get Ready To Resume the Activity**

T: So what are you going to do now about this problem between you and Chico.

J: I guess I'll say I'm sorry and explain that I didn't mean to embarrass him.

T: What do you expect his reaction to be?

J: He'll still be mad.

T: It might take him some time to get over it. How will you handle it if he says he doesn't want anything to do with you?

J: I'll just leave him alone.

T: For now that's probably a good plan. It takes a lot of energy for people to stay angry; he'll probably be more willing to let it go after some time has passed . . . provided, of course, that you don't embarrass him again. Do you want me to set up a meeting with Chico and you after lunch?

J: Yeah, I guess.

T: Jeremy, I can see you feel bad about the incident, and I really admire how mature you are being in trying to make it better. Go on to your first-period class and I'll call you down after lunch and we will review new ways of talking with Chico.

J: OK.

Jeremy is an excellent example of many students who seem blind to the social environment of which they are a part. Developmentally, he has not reached the level at which peer approval is a strong need, and he remains unaware of how others judge his behaviors. Mr. Sheppard has helped Jeremy take a step in that direction by reviewing the incident in detail and highlighting his good intentions and teaching him the appropriate social skills. This is the goal of the New Tools Reclaiming Intervention. For additional examples, see Koenig (1997) and McCarty (1998).

WHAT WE HOPE YOU HAVE LEARNED FROM THIS CHAPTER

- The primary purpose in using the New Tools Reclaiming Intervention discussed in this chapter

- The common characteristics shared by students who benefit from the New Tools Reclaiming Intervention

- Why it is often difficult and important to identify a student's good intentions

- The new social skills students should gain as a result

- Why this form of LSCI is rarely used when a student first begins a program

- Three characteristics students have that indicate readiness for this form of LSCI

- Three major processes adults use to accomplish this goal

- One potential problem an adult can cause, if caution is not exercised

- Where the New Tools Reclaiming Intervention fits in the logical sequence of goals for LSCI, as a student's insight expands and grows

The Manipulation of Body Boundaries Reclaiming Intervention: Exposing Peer Exploitation

12

Student's Perception:	"It's important to have a friend even if the friend gets me into trouble"; or, "I'm going to teach him a lesson!"
Uses:	With students who are isolated and rejected and who seek out destructive friendships by acting out for others; with students who are unwittingly "set-up" by passive-aggressive peers to act out
Goal:	To help a student see that another student is manipulating events in a way that is working against the student's best interest
Focus:	Provide insight into reasons for the behavior of others; view social interactions from the perspective of motivations and behaviors of others; developmentally, this goal requires considerable maturity on the student's part, as the student learns to understand how others think, feel, and behave
Student's New Insight:	"A friend is someone who helps you solve problems and feel good rather than someone who gets you into trouble"; or, "I can make my own decisions; I don't need to 'take the bait' when someone is trying to get me in trouble."

Peer friendship is a complicated relationship. It is based on a mutual trust and respect in which neither student consciously exploits the feelings or resources of the other. Friendship is essential to a student's self-esteem and promotes a feeling of belonging. It is an emotional bond which creates rewarding interpersonal relationships. Friendship means closeness, sharing secrets, and emotional support. Peer friendship is an important source of psychological support for students over 9 years of age, and making and keeping friends is a major activity of adolescents.

The primary issue of this Reclaiming Intervention is the dynamic of peer vulnerability to the influence of exploitive students. Two different patterns of self-defeating behavior have been identified in students.

PATTERN 1—THE DYNAMIC OF FALSE FRIENDSHIP

This pattern of self-defeating behavior involves isolated and rejected students whose emotional needs make them vulnerable to the influence and control of exploitive peers. For these students, the need for friendship or peer acceptance is so great that they seem willing to pay any psychological price to obtain it. A false friendship develops when an exploitive student recognizes the isolated or rejected student's need to be accepted. Under the guise of friendship, he or she reaches out to the vulnerable student in a manipulative way by saying something like, "Come on over and have lunch with us," or "Hey, cool jacket!" The needy student is so pleased by receiving interest from the more powerful student that he or she readily accepts any invitation or compliment. However, the unstated contract of this new friendship is that it will last just as long as the needy student is willing to carry out the wishes of the exploitive student. Over time, the needy student becomes a psychological pawn or puppet in the exploitive student's game plan. The more powerful student will bid the needy student to carry his or her contraband, take responsibility for his or her misdeeds, or do his or her homework. The exploitive student stays out of trouble while the needy student becomes the unlucky fall guy.

Fritz Redl (1966) vividly describes this type of dynamic:

> From time to time one invariably runs into a child who exhibits a peculiar helplessness toward a process we like to refer to as group psychological suction. Quite vulnerable to even mild contagion sparks, he is often discovered by an exceptionally brilliant manipulator . . . and then he easily drifts into the pathetic role of the perennial "sucker." (p. 46)

PATTERN 2—THE DYNAMIC OF BEING SET UP BY A PEER

This pattern of self-defeating behavior usually involves a bright, highly verbal passive-aggressive student who enjoys exploiting a less bright aggressive student. The passive-aggressive student sets up the aggressive student in two different ways. First, he or she makes fun of the aggressive student by questioning his or her sexual, intellectual, or personality attributes, but only if there is a staff person nearby who will protect him or her when the aggressive student gets out of control. Second, he or she painstakingly and cleverly creates scenarios in which the aggressive student is led to believe that another peer is taking advantage of or disrespecting him or her. The passive-aggressive student continues to fuel the conflict until the aggressive student, again, is out of control.

What is fascinating about this dynamic is that the aggressive student is unaware of how he or she is being manipulated and controlled by the passive-aggressive student. The outcome is predictable: The aggressive student takes the bait, acts against the other peer, and ends up with disciplinary consequences. Meanwhile, the passive-aggressive student has been thoroughly entertained and remains consequence free.

The therapeutic goal with such students is to expose to them the self-serving control of the instigator and to show how he or she gets power and pleasure by setting them up, while they get nothing but trouble (the perceived "friend" does not really care about them).

THE ADULT'S TASK

Foundations for a successful Manipulation of Body Boundaries Reclaiming Intervention depend upon a carefully constructed timeline in Stage 2, based on what has happened, in detail. With this information you should be able to find specific descriptions of the behavior of the instigator that can be identified as exploitive toward the victimized student. A student who has been manipulated this way will almost always defend the "friend," so it is not useful to openly cast the instigator in a negative light. Wait until your student has described the incident in such detail that the conclusion is obvious. Your exploited student's "friend" was looking after himself or herself, and the exchange was not an act of genuine friendship or caring. When conducting an LSCI where "false friendship" is the issue, it is often helpful to have both students present, as one of the objectives is to arrange for the manipulation to present itself in the interview, thereby revealing it in its clearest form. When conducting a "setup" LSCI, it is best to see the aggressive student or the exploited student alone.

Once the facts of misuse and self-service have been established, be sensitive to the sense of loss your student will be experiencing. A significant friend—no matter that it was an abusive relationship or a false friendship—has been lost. Your second task is affirmation and support of the student's insight into the relationship, even though he or she feels like a victim, without support or friends. During LSCI Stage 4, this affirmation and support can be done as you reinforce the student's need to have and maintain healthy friendships. This would be an ideal time for a New Tools Reclaiming Intervention.

The third task, also begun during LSCI Stage 4, is to provide some hope for discovering alternative behaviors the student can use to obtain support and relationship from others. Because these students have so few social skills with peers, it is often necessary to emphasize that "to have a friend, you must be a friend." This theme leads to a review of specific proactive social skills that build friendships.

Your final task is to conduct a second LSCI, this time with the student who did the manipulating and exploiting. You probably recognize that the most fitting therapeutic goal for students who are instigators is to confront them with their unacceptable behavior. We attempt to show them that manipulation does not benefit them; it backfires when others see through it. (Chapter 9 describes this type of LSCI, the Symptom Estrangement Reclaiming Intervention.)

Another type of manipulation often occurs which does not involve "false friendship"; instead it involves the student being "set-up." A clever, passive-aggressive student sets up a trap into which a less bright, usually aggressive student falls. The "victim" takes the bait while the manipulator sits back and enjoys the action. For example, Tom, an awkward and uncoordinated but bright 13 year old, does not like Sam who makes fun of him regularly. During a game of baseball, Sam is pitching and his rival, a strong, athletic, but rather dull student named Paul, is at bat. Tom stands behind the backstop well within earshot of Paul. The first pitch comes in low and Paul takes his first strike. Tom says to him, "He's trying to make you look like an ass, Paul. He told me he was going to make you eat dirt today!" With the second pitch, Paul has to step back to avoid being hit by the ball. Tom says, "He's doing it now! Look how he's trying to hit you. He's making you look a fool out there! Are you going to take that from him?" Paul yells out, "Hell no!" He then directs a question to Sam, "Come on man, you want a piece of me?" Sam throws a high pitch, and Paul swings wildly at it, taking his second strike. Tom says to Paul, "He's laughing at you! He wants to make you look like a butt! I can't believe this! I never thought I'd see the day a punk like him would do you so bad!" The third pitch is right over the plate. Paul swings and strikes out. Enraged, he throws the bat and charges at Sam. By the time the staff reach the pitcher's mound, Sam is dazed and bleeding, and Paul is standing over him swearing and shouting threats.

When we conduct the LSCI with Paul, the goal is to make him aware of how he was set up to lose his temper and receive the consequences. We also want to teach him ways of avoiding giving away his self-control to the manipulative student in the future. The use of analogies is often helpful to make the point. We want Paul to realize that he is the master of his own choices, so we may use as examples of manipulation a puppeteer and a puppet, a remote control and a television, a light switch and a lightbulb, and so on, to demonstrate how he is being controlled.

EXAMPLES OF STUDENTS WHO CAN BENEFIT

The name given by Fritz Redl to this form of LSCI, "Manipulation of the Boundaries of the Self," highlights the characteristic problem common to all of the students who can benefit from this therapeutic goal. The psychological boundaries of their personalities are so vulnerable to influence and manipulation by others that they are unable to form a confident or self-assertive presence. They have such a marginal sense of self-esteem and personal worthiness that they allow someone else to "pull their strings." It is easy to see how such students fail to develop responsible, independently directed acceptable behavior. The following are two examples of students who are typical of those who can benefit from LSCI that helps them see that they are being victimized.

Bob

George is extremely clever in getting Bob to blow up in the classroom. He knows Bob is very sensitive and is having trouble completing an assignment. After a few minutes, George says in a loud voice, "I'm all done! The teacher gave me the easy job!" (smiling and looking over to see Bob's reaction). This is enough to trigger an explosion from Bob. He leaps out of his desk, throws his chair in George's direction, and shouts, "You're a dumb ass!" As the teacher moves in to avert further disaster, George says in her direction, "Bob's really out of control; how can we work with all this noise?" ("Set-up")

In the LSCI that followed, Bob was able to recount the sequence of events. He also was able to describe alternative behaviors that are more acceptable ways to handle anger. On several occasions he had lost control after George had fueled a situation with his incendiary remarks. The teacher recognized that Bob was not aware of how he was being manipulated by George. So the teacher chose the therapeutic goal of exposing George's manipulation and focused the LSCI on helping Bob consider how his behavior resulted in his being in the time-out room, while George was in the classroom, enjoying seeing Bob in trouble. This was a new idea for Bob!

Doug

Doug is an unsophisticated 14-year-old loner. His best "friend" and idol is a 16-year-old-student named Russ, who is slick and streetwise. Wherever Russ happens to be, Doug can be found hanging around. One day Russ brings a bag of marijuana to school, and word gets around that he is selling it. Being streetwise and a predator, Russ is very tuned in to the environment and senses that things are getting hot. He already has a court record and doesn't want another offense, so he asks Doug to do him a favor: Would Doug hold the marijuana for him until after school? Doug is honored to be entrusted with the task and willingly takes the bag and shoves it into his pocket. When the principal calls Russ into his office on the basis of the rumor that he is selling drugs, Russ is happy to comply with the principal's request to empty his pockets. However, the principal knows Russ too well to be fooled by his "innocent act" and tells him that he is going to call a detective to interview students because there is too much in question for the principal to be satisfied that Russ is not involved. Russ "breaks down" and tells the principal that he's got the wrong man. It's true that there is marijuana in the building, but he is not responsible. Doug is the one he's after. Russ is secretly gambling that Doug will take the rap for him in the spirit of "friendship." (False Friendship)

The LSCI follows, after Doug has been brought to the office and the marijuana has been found in his pocket. The principal sees both boys together and begins the interview with Doug. Doug is sticking to a story that he found the marijuana on the way to school that morning, but the principal's careful structuring of the timeline reveals so many inconsistencies in Doug's fabricated account that it becomes clear he is lying. At the point where it looks like the story is about to break down, Russ pipes up, telling Doug that he doesn't have to say anything to the principal and that he is better off shutting up and saving it for the detective. Doug is scared, but he plays his loyal role, becoming defiant and refusing to answer any more questions. It is at this point that the principal reveals to Doug how he found out that he had the marijuana; Russ told him. Doug is crushed and in disbelief. The principal goes on to point out how Russ is really no friend to Doug and will gladly cause him great trouble and pain if it saves his own skin. The truth is out, and Doug is hurt and ashamed. After dismissing Russ, the principal does a second timeline, and the truth comes out. The principal encourages Doug and tells him that he will help him out of the trouble he is in by speaking with the detective and with the judge if necessary.

EXAMPLE OF LSCI USED TO EXPOSE PEER EXPLOITATION

ALEX AND LEON: WITH A FRIEND LIKE YOU, WHO NEEDS AN ENEMY?

While the teacher is out of the classroom, Alex shoots off a cap gun belonging to Leon. As the teacher returns, he hears the noise and walks in to see the smoke. When the teacher confronts Alex, he simply says, "It's not mine. It's Leon's." Knowing that Leon is a smart, sophisticated streetwise sixth grader, who has the reputation of being clever and verbal, the teacher wonders why he gave the gun to Alex, a lonely, insecure student who acts impulsively at times and seems to always be on the fringe of the group. He chooses to do LSCI with the two of them together since the incident involved Leon's cap gun. Whenever there is a crisis, Leon seems to be at the center, but always manages to escape responsibility. The teacher suspects that Leon may have instigated this latest event. We selected this LSCI to illustrate how the teacher (T) managed the topic of exploitation with both the victim (A) and the manipulator (L) present.

▶ **Stage 1: Drain Off**

T: This is the most interesting gun I have ever seen. It has no handle or barrel . . . just a trigger and a firing cap. Whose gun is it?

L: It's mine!

T: Where would you get a gun like this? It's so unusual!

L: I found it in an alley when I was riding my bike.

T: You must have sharp eyes to see such a small gun. I bet you were happy to find it.

L: Yeah!

T: Are you always this lucky?

L: Sometimes.

T: Did you have to clean it up to make it work?

L: Well, I took it home and got it working.

T: Did you have any caps at home or did you have to buy them?

L: I had to buy them.

T: Did you get the roll kind or the stick kind?

L: The stickum kind.

▶ **Stage 2: Timeline**

T: It seems you got the right kind. When did you first bring this special gun to school?

L: Today.

T: Where did you keep it?

L: In my pocket. (Looking relaxed and enjoying the discussion)

T: Did you have it in your pocket this morning?

L: Yeah, I had it all day.

T: Who did you show it to before Alex got it?

L: No one.

T: What! (Showing surprise) You mean you had this neat cap gun in your pocket all day and you didn't show it to any of your friends? Is that true?

L: Yeah.

T: That's amazing. I'm very surprised. You must have excellent self-control! Most kids who had a neat cap gun like that would have shown it to everyone—most kids wouldn't be able to keep it in their pocket all day.

L: (Begins to look uncomfortable)

T: Alex, now you tell me how you got to use Leon's cap gun.

A: I sit in front of Leon and while we were cleaning up to leave, Leon tapped me on the shoulder and showed me this cap gun.

T: I'm sure you were surprised to see it. So what happened next?

A: Leon said I could hold it.

T: I assume then that you are friends. Tell me, are you two real good friends, good friends, or just friends?

A: Well, we are good friends.

T: Is that true for you, Leon?

L: Yeah, we're friends.

T: I see. So, as a friend, you gave Alex your prize gun.

L: That's right.

T: Then what happened?

A: Well, I was playing with it, and Leon said you were out of the classroom so it was OK if I wanted to shoot it off.

T: That must have been very tempting for you. Here a friend gives you his cap gun and then tells you the teacher is out of the room.

A: I told Leon I better not shoot it.

T: What did Leon say?

▶ **Stage 3: Central Issue**

A: He said if I didn't want to, Bill would shoot it.

T: Let me guess, Alex. You looked around the room, didn't see the teacher, and you shot the cap gun. When I came back, what did you do with the cap gun?

A: I put it in my desk.

T: How did I know you had done it?

A: (Looks very nervous and starts swinging feet) There was smoke coming from my desk.

T: Looking at you, Alex, you seem very upset and worried about this problem.

A: A little. (Clearly upset)

T: What I don't understand, Leon, is why you didn't shoot the gun?

L: Well, Alex is my friend so I let him go first.

T: I see, but help me understand why you told Alex to shoot the gun or you would give it to Bill. Is that right?

L: Well, Bill said he would do it, and I didn't think Alex would do it.

T: Oh, you didn't think Alex would do it! So you were kidding him or teasing him?

L: Yeah, I was just having fun.

T: That's right. You were having fun because you are a very smart person! You knew that the guy who shot the gun would be in trouble. Since you didn't shoot the gun, then we can all agree that you are very smart. Alex, if Leon is very smart what does that make you?

A: (Deep silence) Dumb!

▶ **Stage 4: Insight**

T: Your friend Leon gives you the gun, tells you the teacher is out of the room, calls you a chicken, and then tells you he was only kidding and he didn't think you'd be dumb enough to pull the trigger . . . (Long silence) . . . Alex, let me ask you an important question. Is a friend someone who helps you or hurts you? Is he someone who gets you into trouble or someone who helps you stay out of trouble? Think about it. Remember, Leon is a very smart guy. He has excellent self-control. He can keep his gun in his pocket all day; but when he takes it out, who does he get to fire it off in the classroom?

A: (Looks uncertainly at the teacher while Leon is looking anxious and angry) I'm not sure . . .

T: Alex, it is important to have friends, and I want you to have friends. But you need friends you can trust, not friends who take advantage of you. For example, if you fell out of a boat, would your friend give you a helping hand and save you, or would he push you away from the boat so he wouldn't fall out?

A: (Silence)

T: I know what kinds of friends I want. Maybe it is different with you. Maybe you enjoy being used for Leon's pleasure and fun. If so, you are free to continue, but don't trick yourself into believing you have a trusting friend. It's your choice.

A: Leon does get me into trouble. Even my mother doesn't want me to play with him.

T: You have a difficult situation to think about, but it sounds as if you have a new idea about friends. It is important to have friends, but they need to be helpful, not hurtful, to you.

A: Yeah, Leon can get me into trouble.

▶ Stage 5: New Skills

T: You've got a good insight there. How should this change what you do around Leon?

A: Well . . . maybe I ought to stay away from him.

▶ Stage 6: Get Ready To Resume the Activity

T: You have a difficult situation, but it sounds like you have the right idea! Tomorrow we can talk about it some more, and perhaps develop a friendship program for you, OK?

L: What about me?

T: We have much more to talk about.

L: It's unfair; I didn't do nothing!

T: I hear you, but we still need to talk about how you treated Alex.

You probably recognize the need for a second, follow-up LSCI with Leon, with a different therapeutic goal—to confront him about his unacceptable behavior (see Chapter 10). Our objective in conducting a Symptom Estrangement Reclaiming Intervention with Leon is to show him that he used Alex; he got pleasure out of Alex's getting in trouble. If he continues to treat his "friends" this way, he will soon find himself without them.

You also may have noticed that the teacher selected Alex's exploitation and need for friendship as the central issue, rather than the incident itself. In this LSCI Alex was able to understand the dynamics of his relationship with Leon and how he is being influenced and used by this false friend. Alex will need additional assistance in follow-up LSCIs to learn new social skills for making and keeping friends. Social communication instruction, along with other social skills training, will all be helpful to Alex. In addition he probably will need reinforcement of his values from time to time (see Chapter 10) to strengthen his self-control.

The success of this LSCI was in large part due to the interest the teacher showed in the gun and the care with which each detail of the incident was brought out. The initial focus on the gun reduced Leon's defensiveness and made it possible to move the students freely into a discussion about the sequence of events. By bringing out the small details as he worked through this LSCI, the teacher was able to show Alex the facts. The timeline developed in Stage 2, through questions about "Where? What?" and "Who?" provided these facts without the teacher having to make accusations which would have heightened the students' defensiveness and made this LSCI more difficult. For additional examples of the Manipulation of Body Boundaries Reclaiming Intervention, see Long and Gonsowski (1994) and Dawson (2000).

WHAT WE HOPE YOU HAVE LEARNED FROM THIS CHAPTER

- When the LSCI therapeutic goal should focus on exposing a student's exploitation by others

- The common characteristic of students who benefit from the Manipulation of Body Boundaries Reclaiming Intervention

- The role friendship plays in the events that lead to exploitation

- A common characteristic of students or adults who exploit others

- Why some students allow themselves to be abused by adults

- Why you shift the central issue from the incident to the exploitation during this form of LSCI

- What painful feeling results after a student realizes that he or she has been exploited by a "friend" or adult

- Three tasks for adults using this form of LSCI

- Why a carefully constructed timeline during Stage 2 is essential

- When it might be appropriate to move slowly and avoid excessive details while doing this form of LSCI

- Another, inevitable, LSCI that must follow when you use the Manipulation of Body Boundaries Reclaiming Intervention

The Double Struggle Reclaiming Intervention: The Adult's Role in Perpetuating the Conflict

13

(continues)

Staff's New Insights:	"Now I understand the situation from the student's point of view and I recognize how I contributed to the problem."

A battleship was among a fleet of smaller ships participating in training maneuvers at sea. One cloudy, dark night, a thick fog settled over the fleet, making visibility poor. As the fog thickened and the seas grew heavier, a lookout on the battleship reported, "Captain! Light bearing on the starboard bow!"

"Is it steady or moving astern?" the captain questioned from the bridge.

"Steady, sir. We're on a collision course!"

The captain's response was quick, "Signal that ship: 'Advise you change course 20 degrees.'"

"Aye, aye sir!"

Almost immediately a signal flashed back to the battleship through the fog: "Advise you change course 20 degrees." The captain's eyes narrowed as he called out again, "Signalman, send this message: 'You had better listen to me. I'm a captain. Change course 20 degrees.'"

Within seconds another signal flashed back: "I'm a seaman, second class. Change course 20 degrees." By now the captain was furious. "Send this message and fast," he ordered the signalman: "I'm a battleship. Change course 20 degrees." Back came the flashing light, "I'm a lighthouse." The captain changed course.

Anyone who works with children and youth has felt like the captain on many occasions. Most of us were raised to respect authority and we expect students to do the same. This expectation is appropriate, and the majority of students live up to it. However, in every group there are those students who appear to be "unclear on the concept." They do not recognize your age, your education, or your position. They disregard the rules of the game; they will not follow your direction, heed your advice, or keep their opinions to themselves. They are defiant and disrespectful, and they will not respond to authority. Adults who rely on authority rather than relationship as their primary management style are quickly frustrated by these students. These adults are often baited into Conflict Cycles which leave them feeling helpless and incompetent. As a result, some staff develop a strong dislike for challenging students. Rather than perceiving them as struggling with their emotional issues and in need of support and guidance, they perceive these students as troublemakers who need punishment or even exclusion. Because these adults are inept at dealing with troubled and troubling students, they fall back on the only tactic they know: proclamation of authority, which results in challenges and, ultimately, in punishment. The parallel is interesting. Troubled students are troubling because they possess a rigid and limited range of relationship skills. They know only a few responses to stressful situations, and these responses tend to escalate problems rather than bring them to resolution. The same is true of some adults. Again, the old adage applies: If the only tool you have is a hammer, everything looks like a nail.

No one enjoys feeling incompetent, so it is understandable that adults can become outraged by the predicaments they find themselves in with challenging students. What they need is a new way of understanding the dynamics of conflict and new skills so they can begin to have successful experiences interacting with troubled students. We can help our colleagues begin to develop new skills through the Double Struggle Reclaiming Intervention. In this intervention we use the paradigm of the Conflict Cycle to subtly suggest how well-intentioned adult intervention may escalate an incident. Through a discreet dialogue, we help staff understand that the problems students cause are not the causes of their problems.

THE INTERVIEWER'S TASK

Working with troubled and troubling children and youth can be a daunting undertaking. When staff are daily, even hourly in some cases, confronted with students' stresses and conflicts, it is not surprising that their own psychological armor wears thin. Students stir up counteraggressive feelings, and for some staff who are not trained, these feelings surface as hostility. Some staff become entrapped in a Conflict Cycle and unwittingly contribute to the crisis. When this happens emotions run high for several reasons. Real anger toward the student may be present along with anger at one's self for "taking the bait," as well as embarrassment and feelings of incompetence. When we choose to benignly confront staff who contribute to student crises, we must be mindful of the staff person's need to protect self-esteem and save face. Defenses will be up, and tact and skill are required to disarm them. Remember that our goal is to help the staff person take a fresh view of the situation. At the onset of this Reclaiming Intervention, the staff person may believe that the student is fully responsible for the incident and may feel "righteously indignant" about justifying his or her own actions. At the close of the intervention, we hope the staff person will understand how good intentions went awry and ended up fueling the crisis. If we are successful, the staff person will arrive at this insight feeling respected and nondefensive and willing to think about the student with a depth of understanding that was not present before.

EXAMPLES OF STAFF WHO CAN BENEFIT

Mrs. Williams

Mrs. Williams is a very competent professional who approaches her work as a reading instructor very seriously. She carefully assesses and plans for each student and has a high rate of success. Although recognized as a successful teacher, Mrs. Williams is not satisfied with her current position. Her goal is to continue her education and to eventually teach at a university. Yet after five years, she has not taken steps toward making her goal a reality, and she is bothered by her own procrastination. This year Mrs. Williams has a nine-year-old student, Janis, in her special education classroom. Janis has a high IQ, but refuses to achieve, no matter how creatively Mrs. Williams tries to work with her. After several months without success, Janis has frustrated Mrs. Williams beyond reason. Mrs. Williams finds herself in frequent power struggles with Janis and, uncharacteristically, is using the classroom management system to punish and restrict her. Janis responds by acting out and Mrs. Williams is becoming increasingly counteraggressive.

A Double Struggle Reclaiming Intervention with Mrs. Williams would help her to understand that her frustrations about Janis's refusal to work up to her potential are interfering with her ability to help the student. In fact, her reaction is making learning more distasteful to Janis, and Mrs. Williams's behavior is working against her own objectives for the student.

Mr. MacArthur

Mr. MacArthur is a conservative man who has been teaching physical education at the middle school level for over 20 years. He is known for keeping an orderly tone in his gym classes—bordering on the military—and has little interest in students' opinions about his style. Mr. MacArthur commonly complains about today's students and their lack of respect for authority. He has no tolerance for those who "march to the beat of a different drummer." This year Mr. MacArthur is particularly outraged by Adam, a brooding student who keeps to himself, has spiked hair, and dresses in black. Adam hates gym class and despises Mr. MacArthur, who seems to go out of his way to make life miserable for Adam. He openly humiliates Adam, who is not afraid to take a stand against the teacher. Mr. MacArthur easily becomes entangled in Conflict Cycles with Adam, who is more than happy to be suspended from gym class.

An adult who chooses to engage in a Double Struggle Reclaiming Intervention with Mr. MacArthur would be wise to prepare for a good deal of venting. Mr. MacArthur may have difficulty seeing how he contributes to the crisis, and his feelings about Adam may derive, in part, from his value system. Yet even Mr. MacArthur, more likely than not, does not want to do damage to the students he has dedicated his career to teaching. Support for the struggle he is experiencing and recognition of his good will are important in this dialogue. Once the supervisor has affirmed Mr. MacArthur's good intentions and Mr. MacArthur has accepted them, the following question might be asked: Given Adam's level of resistance and difficult behavior, what actions are you taking that might make the situation worse for him?

EXAMPLE OF LSCI USED TO BENIGNLY CONFRONT STAFF ABOUT THEIR CONTRIBUTION TO A CRISIS

 TOM: WHAT ARE YOU LOOKING AT?

Tom lives with his mother, older brother, and sister in a trailer in a rural area. Life at home is turbulent, and issues of money, privacy, and alcoholism are ever-present. From his elementary school years, Tom's teachers have characterized him as defiant and challenging, and when he began attending the middle school two years ago, he was diagnosed as emotionally and behaviorally disordered. Now age 14, Tom is a student in Ms. Keller's special education classroom, and he is mainstreamed for two classes a day. He has made progress this year with Ms. Keller's help, but he still distrusts adults. Only those who take the time to get to know him and pass his "tests of tolerance" can recognize that Tom is a student who is struggling to overcome many pressures. The demands of school are formidable, and Tom is trying to be successful given the hand life has dealt him.

On Monday morning Tom was having a particularly difficult time. He appeared distracted and Ms. Keller was unsuccessful in getting him started on his work. He seemed absorbed in his own thoughts, and while the rest of the group was completing desk work, Ms. Keller asked Tom to come with her to a quiet room which is accessible from the classroom and has a separate door which opens into the hallway. In the quiet room Ms. Keller began a timeline, and Tom disclosed that he had been thinking about his sister's girlfriend, who had been killed in an automobile accident about ten days ago. The story was in all of the papers, but Ms. Keller didn't realize until today how well Tom had known the girl and how much a part of his life she had been. Just as the discussion reached its most sensitive moment, Mr. Riley, Tom's art teacher, passed the quiet room door as he walked down the hall. Mr. Riley doesn't have much patience for Tom and, when he saw him talking with Ms. Keller, immediately concluded that Tom must have been causing problems in class. He stopped outside the door and stared at Tom through the window. The following exchanges occurred among Ms. Keller (K), Mr. Riley (R), and Tom (T).

T: (Loudly, to be heard through the door) What are you looking at?!

R: (Opening the door) You don't talk to me like that!

T: Get out of here!

R: Keep it up—you'll be down in the hole (term used for in-school suspension room in the basement) before you can say "It's unfair."

T: "It's unfair!"

R: That's exactly what I expect from you! You have no respect for yourself or anyone else! I'll let Mrs. Andersen (the school principal) know there will be another loser in the hole tomorrow!

T: (Sarcastically) Oh, so you'll be in the hole tomorrow?

K: It's OK, Mr. Riley; I can handle it. Tom, please.

R: You may be able to handle it, Ms. Keller, but I won't take that kind of disrespect from any student! I don't want him in my class today, and we'll have to talk about whether he should ever come back.

K: OK, I'll keep him with me today, and I'd like to talk to you later.

R: It's a waste of time.

K: I'll get back to you.

R: (Shaking his head and looking at Tom, Mr. Riley leaves the room.)

Ms. Keller used Emotional First Aid to drain off Tom's intense feelings about the art teacher. She returned to the subject of Tom's grief, and conducted a Red Flag *Tap In* Reclaiming Intervention to help Tom understand that he was displacing the anger he felt about his friend's death to Mr. Riley. She helped him understand that the feelings he was having, though unpleasant, were a normal, expected response to a tragedy. She told him she would be available if he wanted to talk further and, feeling a little more grounded, Tom returned to class, where Ms. Keller helped him get started on his work. She then arranged to see Mr. Riley later in the day. The following dialogue ensued.

▶ **Stage 1: Drain Off**

K: (Mr. Riley enters the conference room where Ms. Keller has been waiting for him.) Hey, thanks for coming; I was beginning to wonder if you were going to show.

R: I'm here, but it's a waste of my time and yours.

K: Well, that was quite an encounter this morning.

R: Yes it was, and I'm sick and tired of his garbage behavior! He can't get away with talking to me that way!

K: Tom needs to think before he speaks; that's one of the many issues we're working on right now.

R: Well, I think you're being way too easy on him. If he doesn't have consequences, you might as well tell him it's OK to do it. Everybody else has to follow the rules; why not him?

K: It doesn't make his behavior OK, but he is a very troubled young man; he's really struggling—you know what he has to live with. And there's something else you need to know to put what happened into perspective.

R: All I know is that you let him get away with murder, and then you get upset when I put my foot down.

▶ Stage 2: Timeline

K: Listen, I agree that he has to have limits. I am constantly setting limits for him in class, and he has been more accepting of them in last couple of months. He's mainstreamed for two classes now, and he's making it in one of them. But you need to know what was going on this morning that set off the conflict between you two. When Tom arrives in the morning, he's usually loud and talkative. No question about it, everybody knows when Tom is here. But today he was unusually quiet and withdrawn. It was pretty obvious something was wrong, so I asked him to come to the quiet room to talk. As it turns out, the girl who was killed in that accident a week and a half ago was a good friend of his sister. Tom saw her almost every day, and he considered her practically a member of the family. She was one of the few people in his life that he felt really liked him; she enjoyed his sense of humor and, to use his words, "she treated me like I was somebody."

R: That's too bad, but it doesn't give him the right to be disrespectful to teachers and carry on the way he does.

K: I agree that he does need learn how to talk to staff; he won't get anywhere if he continues to be defiant and act out. Part of what's going on is that he is hurt and angry, and he doesn't know what to do with those feelings. Any little thing can be a trigger; that's what happened this morning. The anger wasn't really about you—it was an expression of his anger about the death of his friend.

R: So I'm supposed to walk on eggshells with him because he's having problems?

K: No, I'm asking you to recognize that there's more to Tom's outburst than meets the eye. Tom was wrong today, no question. He made the first mistake, saying to you, "What are you looking at?" You didn't start this conflict, he did.

R: That's right; it never would have happened if he hadn't opened his mouth.

K: When you stopped and looked at him through the window, he was right in the middle of telling me this about the death of his friend. He was choked up and it was hard for him to say. When he saw you stop, he knew you believed he was in the quiet room because he had been a behavior problem. That thought triggered his anger, and he showed it by making that remark.

R: So what was I supposed to do?

K: Now, in this situation, you couldn't possibly have known what was going on, so I have to give you the benefit of the doubt. You didn't start it, but you did keep it going. You responded to his surface behavior and you gave in to your immediate impulse—punishment. Tom doesn't need any more punishment.

R: What, it's my fault that he talked to me that way?

▶ Stage 3: Central Issue

K: What I'm saying is that you allowed yourself to be drawn into a Conflict Cycle. Each time Tom made a disrespectful remark, you countered it. The effect was to keep the cycle going until you threatened him with suspension and called him a loser. He already believes he's a loser; that's the self-concept we're all working to change. What he does, though, is he baits adults into these conflicts where we end up accidentally reinforcing his idea of himself as a loser.

R: You know, I'm not out to get him, but we can't tolerate that kind of behavior. It's not good for us and it's not good for him, no matter what's going on at home.

K: I don't mean to suggest that you are against him; if I thought that I wouldn't be here now. I'm bringing this to you because I do believe you want to see Tom make it; you want the best for him.

R: So how do you handle it when he starts mouthing off like that?

▶ Stage 4: Insight

K: The first thing I do is tell myself to stay calm, and then I observe how he tries to make me angry. As soon as he begins to say or do something designed to draw me into a conflict, I point out to him that it appears he is trying to make me fight with him. I decode the behavior for him. For example, last week he came in and erased the morning assignment from the board. My first impulse was to lecture him, but instead I said to him, "Tom, when you come in here and the first thing you do is something you know is going to upset me, that tells me something is upsetting you, too."

R: What did he say to that?

K: He didn't say anything. He went to his desk and sat down. I said to him, "I'm going to put the assignment back up on the board, and then I'll check in with you." He still didn't say anything, but he stayed at his desk. After I finished rewriting the assignment, I went over to him and asked, "What's bothering you today?" He said, "Nothing." I told him I wanted to see him during the morning break. He answered, "Maybe." As it turned out, he did talk to me during break, and he apologized for erasing the board. We discussed what else he could do when he came in to school with a lot on his mind, and he agreed to check in with me. He was OK for the rest of the day. I think he just needed to know that I recognized his stress and that I cared about him.

R: Once again, no consequences!

▶ Stage 5: New Skills

K: There were consequences; I talked to him and he apologized. What you mean is that there was no punishment. I decided that since he apologized, and the apology appeared genuine, I would let it go at that. That's not to say he never has to pay the price for poor choices; I've charged him points for some things and he has paid for vandalism in the room. In this case, though, adding a punishment wouldn't have helped teach him anything.

R: I'm not so sure I agree. Anyway, you might get by with that in a special ed class, but not out here in the real school. How long do you think it would be before we had mass chaos, if I excused a blatant act like that? The kids are all watching to see who's in charge.

K: If something like that happened, and you were in a position in which you had to set a limit, you might send Tom to me instead of to the office. The other kids would see that he had a consequence, having to leave class, and maybe you and I could discuss it with him together. After all, what's the goal here? If he could be convinced that we're in his corner, the defiance will begin to fade. Every time we fight with him, he comes away believing we're all against him and he hasn't got a chance. What do you say we give that a try?

▶ Stage 6: Get Ready To Resume the Activity

R: I've got to tell you; I don't like the idea of spoon-feeding kids who don't follow the rules. It really goes against my grain. If I try this and it doesn't work, we'll be talking.

K: If you don't allow yourself to be drawn into a Conflict Cycle, things will get better between you. Tom's life is complicated—he has a lot of emotional baggage. More often than not, the real source of his stress is not the school or the teachers, it's all the other issues. We have to teach him a better outlet for his stress than taking it out on us, and that means gaining his trust.

R: Well, you can't win an argument with him anyway so why get into it. You better know, though, that this is going to eat up a lot of my time and I'm not real happy about that.

K: It'll be worth it, because you'll be one of the few that makes a difference in a life that needs a lot of kindness.

R: OK, you're doing a good selling job; I'll give it a shot.

K: Thanks. See you tomorrow.

Ms. Keller may have made a significant contribution to Tom's chances of success in Mr. Riley's class. Like most regular education teachers, Mr. Riley was not trained to work with troubled and troubling students. They make him angry and threaten his position of authority in the classroom. It is also true that, like Mr. Riley, most teachers want to see students succeed, and are willing to try new approaches if they are supported. Follow-up by the special education teacher is as important for staff as it is for students when new skills are being learned. Our thanks to Mary Ellen Fecser for submitting this example. For additional examples of the Double Struggle Reclaiming Intervention, see Long and Kelly (1994) and Long and Brendtro (1996).

WHAT WE HOPE YOU HAVE LEARNED FROM THIS CHAPTER

- Staff perceptions when students draw them into a Conflict Cycle

- How to acknowledge the staff person's good intentions in dealing with the crisis

- How to support the staff person with affirming statements

- The dynamics which lead to conflict between certain staff and some students

- How trained colleagues can help staff understand the Conflict Cycle and how a well-meaning person can fuel a conflict

- If you change the way an adult thinks about a student, you've changed the way that person feels and behaves toward the student. Only then can new alternative of helping a troubled student be considered.

SUMMARY

Having worked your way through this book, we hope you have developed a perspective about crisis as occurring when students are not able to manage their own feelings and behavior in ways that bring about the results they desire from others. We hope you have an understanding of LSCI as a process you can use for supporting and teaching children and youth in crisis.

We also hope that you view your roles and responsibilities during LSCI as changing to adjust to the particular crisis, behaviors, anxieties, and developmental needs of each student. The roles and messages you will be required to deliver are complex. The variations are endless. Sometimes you will have to be an adult authority who enforces rules, order, and justice. At other times you will be the benevolent nurturer, the teacher, the sympathetic supporter. Sometimes you will protect a student from situations too overwhelming to handle; at other times you will back off from a central role to allow experience ("the great teacher") to teach the hard way. Through it all, the adult remains the source of support and respect for the student. When this happens, every student, regardless of age, behavior, or complexity of problem, will gain life's essential ingredient, the knowledge that "I'm not in this alone."

The Future of LSCI

14

There is nothing more powerful in life than an idea whose time has come. We are living in an era when most professionals in the business of helping at-risk and troubled students agree that the task of helping and healing is multidisciplinary. No longer do we refer children for psychotherapy with the hope that this single intervention will result in lasting change. Today the therapist is one in a collaboration of professionals who create systems of care for children and families. The social worker, probation officer, clergyperson, and teacher are all important members in the ecology of the child and family. The boundaries between the helping professions are blurring, and this is why LSCI is so important a skill in our contemporary human services systems.

Community-based care for children and youth with emotional disturbances demands that professionals be competent in managing the critical needs—and crises—these young people present. Crises do not happen by appointment, and we cannot wait for the scheduled 30 minutes with the therapist when they occur. Professionals must be able to provide on-the-spot support and must be prepared to prevent urgencies from becoming emergencies. Nowhere is this more true than in the schools, as they are the psychological emergency rooms of our society. Consider this analogy. If the residents of a community decided to build a hospital, they would be sure to include a state-of-the-art emergency room. In addition to installing the latest technology, residents would want the hospital administration to hire the best-trained and most competent medical staff to do this most important work. When a patient presents at the emergency room, there are three essential tasks the staff must be prepared to perform. First, the team must stabilize the patient; that is, lower the risk of further trauma and bring vital signs to a level of reduced threat. Next, they must develop a diagnosis to determine what is causing the trauma. The third step is to make a decision as to whether the hospital has the resources to treat the patient, or whether the condition requires specialists at another site. The parallel with the task of the public school is strong. When a crisis breaks out at school, the staff need a skill set similar to that of the emergency room team. They need to know how to contain, stabilize, and de-escalate the student crisis; diagnose the factors behind how the crisis came to be; and determine in what setting the student can best be helped to manage the driving forces behind the crisis. LSCI provides these critical skills for adults who share the responsibility to support our at-risk young people. Regardless of the professional discipline, LSCI offers adults a way to turn a crisis around. It provides an opportunity to build strengths from weaknesses and relationships from alienation.

Schools and other child-serving systems are beginning to recognize the importance of early intervention for at-risk children and youth, and a number of sound approaches have been developed. LSCI is easily integrated into programs grounded in shared ethical values about human behavior. Here are a few examples:

• The Circle of Courage model (Brendtro, Brokenleg, & Van Bockern, 1992) is founded on creating positive and respectful learning environments based on universal needs for belonging, mastery, independence, and generosity. Schools using this strength-based approach have documented dramatic reductions in suspension and exclusion. (Visit the Web site at www.reclaiming.com).

• Developmental Therapy—Developmental Teaching (Wood, 1996) is an internationally recognized approach to working with troubled children. This results-based program provides a carefully constructed diagnostic and prescriptive system which considers four key life domains. Data from an assessment instrument determine where a child is functioning along a developmental continuum, and how to design learning activities which take the child to the next developmental stage. The nature of adult interactions from which the child can benefit changes as the child matures, and these roles are carefully monitored in Developmental Therapy—Developmental Teaching. For more information, visit the Web site at www.vga.edu/dttp.

• Re-ED (Re-Education of Emotionally Disturbed Children and Youth) (Cantrell, Cantrell, Valore, Jones, & Fecser, 1999), founded by Nicholas Hobbs (1982), is a wellness approach toward working with troubled and troubling children and youth. Re-ED is an ecological model based on several key concepts: (1) emotional disturbance is the manifestation of an imbalance in the arenas of home, school, and community, not solely a dysfunction within the child; (2) families are partners with professionals in the work of restoring balance to the ecology; (3) the frontline staff member in the treatment setting, knows as the "Teacher-Counselor" leads the treatment team and is informed by professionals from a wide variety fo disciplines. The Positive Education Program in Cleveland, Ohio, is a multiservice special education and mental health agency founded on the Re-ED principles. For more information, visit the Web site at www.pepcleve.org.

• Polly Nichols (1999) developed a program called *Clear Thinking* which is used by teachers and counseling professionals to help troubled children and adolescents. Using cognitive restructuring, Nichols's program takes students through a series of light and spirited activities which challenge old ways of thinking and build new ones.

Dark thoughts are whimsically personified through illustrations which add a tangible quality to the concepts. *Clear Thinking* uses a psychoeducational framework in which ideas are presented, real-life applications are investigated, new thoughts are practiced and repeated until they become automatic, and homework is assigned to assure that learning is generalized.

• The Resolving Conflict Creatively Program (RCCP) of Lantieri and Patti (1997) mobilizes students, staff, and families to develop peacemaking values and foster respect for diversity. RCCP is used in hundreds of schools nationwide and has reversed negative peer cultures in the most violent school environments. As with LSCI, conflict is seen as an occasion for growth rather than for punishment.

• Scandinavian school bully prevention research has led to comprehensive school interventions (Hoover, 1996). Bullies thrive if codes of silence give peer intimidation free reign. Thus, these programs transform the "silent majority" to create positive student cultures.

• The Positive Peer Culture model (Vorrath & Brendtro, 1985) was developed expressly to transform negative youth cultures into prosocial peer helping groups. Positive Peer Culture (PPC) has been shown to create safe environments in treatment programs serving highly troubled and violent youth (Gold & Osgood, 1992). Because time required for daily group meetings conflicts with curricular demands for most students, PPC has usually been targeted at special populations, such as students in alternative schools for youth at risk. The National Association of Peer Group Agencies provides certification in PPC.

• The EQUIP Program (Gibbs, Potter & Goldstein, 1995) also employs Positive Peer Culture groups, but adds training in thinking errors, moral development, and social skills. Like LSCI, this model uses problems as opportunities, although in peer-helping programs, students are trained to become the primary helping agents. Research on the EQUIP model documents sustained positive outcomes with antisocial youth in correctional settings.

The Building Safe and Reclaiming Schools model was developed by Long and Fecser (2001) as a school-wide competency based program for elementary schools to promote the physical and psychological safety of students and staff. Based on a pyramid concept, it provides three integrated levels of skills. All staff participate in 2 days of primary prevention skills and positive behavior management skills. Classroom teachers participate in 2 additional days of training to learn how to connect and respond to students with special needs and problems. Finally, two staff members participate in a 5-day advanced LSCI training program to learn skills needed to respond to student and school-wide crises in an effective and therapeutic way. A unique characteristic of this program is that the entire school staff must demonstrate these skills in order for the school to be certified and acknowledged as a Safe and Reclaiming School. For additional information, visit the Web site at www.lsci.org.

In recent years there has been a resurgence of interest in LSCI as a therapeutic strategy for working with troubled and troubling children and youth, and an accompanying interest in advanced training in LSCI. In response to that need, the LSCI Institute was founded in March of 1997. Using a multimodal format, trainees are guided to develop 26 essential competencies required for effective use of LSCI. Videotaped real-life sequences supplement readings and simulations in which trainees practice and develop skills. Certification in competency requires full participation in the five-day training program and the successful completion of both written and practical examinations. At this writing, over 5,000 professionals have completed the certification program. Approximately 38% of the certified professionals are clinicians, 43% are educators, and 19% are youth workers, juvenile justice staff, police, and security guards. Response to the training has been overwhelmingly positive. Advanced training in Life Space Crisis Intervention is available at over a dozen sites nationally, or through senior trainers across the country. For more information about the LSCI Institute and certification programs, visit the Web site at www.lsci.org.

A History of LSCI and Its Field Validation

As we enter the 21st century, we are able to look back with the clarity that time and distance bring to see the extensive growth and field validation that has occurred over the past 40 years with LSI/LSCI. It is evident that:

1. LSCI has been the only specific verbal intervention strategy to emerge for use by educators and others who work directly with students in crisis

2. Results of studies of a steadily expanding range and variety of field application for LSI/LSCI have been published over the past 40 years, primarily using qualitative research methodology.

3. Fundamental concepts and strategies have remained essentially intact since LSI was first developed in the 1950s, while variations for specific applications have been expanded considerably and reported in detail.

4. LSI/LSCI has been included as an intervention strategy in most college textbooks that discuss working with students who are socially, emotionally, or behaviorally disturbed, yet there has not been a textbook published, until this book, solely to teach LSCI.

In the early 1950s, Fritz Redl and David Wineman introduced the concept of the "marginal interview," later to be renamed "Life Space Interview" (Redl, 1959a, 1966), and now, "Life Space Crisis Intervention" (LSCI). Redl defined a student's *life space* as "direct life experience in connection with the issues that become the interview focus" (Redl, 1966, pp. 40–41). The term *life space* was used to imply greater proximity to a student's natural environment than is usual in more formal clinical settings. The term *marginal interview* had been used to distinguish the process from a formal psychiatric interview or clinical psychotherapy, which were, at that time, the only forms of intervention for troubled children and youth other than play therapy. Special education had not yet been developed for such students. There were few residential treatment programs; community mental health had not yet become a nationwide service concept as an alternative to mental hospitals where children and youth were typically housed on adult wards; and a juvenile justice system was just beginning.

The work of Redl and Wineman centered on the study of behavioral controls of aggressive, delinquent children and youth. They believed that behavioral control not only was the essential issue for the students they worked with but also was "the daily job of the most normal child in the pursuit of everyday life" (Redl & Wineman, 1952, p. 27). It was their contention that the problems of delinquent and aggressive students were magnified and intensified pictures of some of the troubles every child has to go through in learning self-control. They were convinced that the difference between the normal and the severely disturbed child was in the ability to handle the tasks of adverse circumstances by themselves if given adequate support, while disturbed students could not make use of genuine support from adults. It was their belief that strategies for effective teaching of behavior controls were an equally important pursuit for the parent and teacher of any child. LSI was one result of their extensive experimentation and study about ways to teach behavior controls while providing adequate support for personality development.

The roots of LSCI go back to the early 1900s in Europe, with the publication of a monumental book titled *Wayward Youth* by August Aichorn (1935), a Viennese educator and psychoanalyst who directed a school for delinquent boys. In his work Aichorn translated psychoanalytic concepts into operating principles that were useful in treating delinquents. This book had a major influence on the field of mental health and attracted international recognition by describing a psychodynamic approach to understanding and treating aggressive youths. The importance of the book is still recognized, and it is on the recommended reading list for all serious students in the field of mental health and delinquency.

One of Aichorn's most famous students, who also served as a teacher in his school, was Fritz Redl. Trained as a psychoanalyst by Anna Freud, Redl developed a commitment to treating delinquents. In 1936 he left Vienna and moved to New York City, and then, in 1940, to Detroit where he continued to expand his innovative approach with aggressive, delinquent, and disturbed youth in three major projects: The Detroit Group Project, The Detroit Project Group Summer Camp, and Pioneer House. The boys in these programs had generally poor controls over themselves and their aggressive impulses. They were frequently involved in personal and group crises, in which they either refused to participate or attempted to destroy group activity and cohesiveness. Redl's clinical research concerns were "to understand why children's controls break down, how some of them defend themselves so successfully against the adults in their lives, and what can be done to prevent and treat such childhood disorganization" (Redl & Wineman, 1957, p. 13).

To conduct these studies, Redl joined clinical insights and experience with David Wineman, a social worker from Wayne State University. Together Redl and Wineman planned, directed, and described in exacting detail the characteristics, conditions, and interventions developed during the life of these projects. They used carefully structured, descriptive, and anecdotal procedures to record the behavior of many hundreds of children with whom they worked in these settings. Their population was "literally thousands of behavioral incidents, comparable in nature, sampled on the basis of the involvedness of certain personality-parts, with the adult's clinical attitude kept relatively constant" (Redl & Wineman, 1957, p. 14).

The clinical attitudes Redl refers to are psychodynamic principles and the milieu concept around which the programs were organized (Redl, 1959b). The basic LSI was formulated here. Redl's three fundamental clinical premises continue to have considerable application today, as general program guides for those who work with troubled students in various settings:

1. Maintain an emotionally healthy environment. A therapeutic environment provides a psychological climate of support and protection from traumatic handling by any personnel, some interpersonal gratifications that are not contingent on behavior, and a degree of tolerance for deviancy and regression with safeguards to protect against escalation.

2. Plan program activities for psychological support. Provide for gratifying play free from goals associated with highly competitive games, arts and crafts, or other gadgets that require a level of performance that is difficult to achieve

3. Use LSI for therapeutic management of life events. Use LSI to highlight the implications of what the student's behavior is doing, what it means in value demands, and the consequences when "behavior spurts into the life scene with great velocity and intensity" (Redl & Wineman, 1957, p. 37).

As part of this research, detailed descriptions of behaviors of individual students and groups were compiled. The table at the end of this appendix summarizes the 22 major characteristics Redl and Wineman reported.

Redl and Wineman believed that adults who work directly with students during a crisis have the greatest opportunity to intervene in therapeutic ways and to make lasting changes. They emphasized the importance of the peer group, believing that the adults who work with youth frequently have to intervene immediately and therapeutically during a crisis. There is no time to wait until a caseworker or therapist can get to the scene. This conviction is made quite clear in two publications, *Children Who Hate* (Redl & Wineman, 1951) and *Controls from Within* (Redl & Wineman, 1952), later republished in a single volume, *The Aggressive Child*, in 1957. These writings provide the original field validation for LSI. LSI had become a major crisis intervention strategy; furthermore, it was a new way to take traditional clinical concepts of psychotherapy and apply them in action settings (Dittman & Kitchener, 1959).

The work of Redl and Wineman was radical and innovative for the times. It made a significant impact on the entire field of mental health, residential treatment, and special education for children and youth in crisis. It was the milestone contribution that expanded mental health concepts for those who work directly with troubled students in their natural settings on a daily basis. Redl also was convinced that while LSI was developed to help troubled children and youth, it could be used successfully with normal children who do not need therapy or special programs, but who are temporarily overwhelmed by intense, conflicting feelings like rage, fear, shame, anger, and guilt, or who are overwhelmed by unusual life events such as death, divorce, illness, accident, failure, or abuse. During these times, normal children behave more like emotionally disturbed children and need the intervention of a supportive and skilled adult trained in LSCI.

While Redl and Wineman were directing the Pioneer House Project, 60 miles northwest of Detroit, William Morse established the University of Michigan's Fresh Air Camp (FAC) for emotionally disturbed boys. LSI was adopted as a treatment strategy. Wineman had joined the staff in 1950, and Redl served as a major consultant. For the next several years, FAC became the mecca for milieu treatment, providing interdisciplinary training for psychiatry, social work, psychology, and special education (Morse & Wineman, 1957). Contemporary practices for using LSI in therapeutic camping also have their origins in this work (Morse & Small, 1959).

In 1953 Redl was appointed chief of the Child Research Branch of the National Institute of Mental Health (NIMH). During this time LSI was further refined and field-tested when Redl instituted another field validation of the Pioneer House Project. Nicholas J. Long, who had been trained by Morse, accepted an offer by Redl in 1956 to become director of this NIMH Residential Program. The project involved six of the most aggressive boys from the east coast of the United States. With ample clinical and research staff for this project, Redl continued his systematic study of various techniques and strategies of psychotherapy, program structure, group processes, LSI, and remedial education. This was an exciting and expansive time for those who worked in mental health for children and youth.

During the 1960s, major conceptual advances were made for providing therapeutic interventions other than traditional mental health services for emotionally disturbed and troubled youth. In this period LSI was extended beyond clinical settings into educational environments where it could be used by social workers, special educators, and principals (Long, Stoeffler, Krause, & Jung, 1961; Vernick, 1963). In 1961 Long and Newman published a monograph, *The Teacher's Handling of Children in Conflict*, which was one of the first attempts to translate many of Redl's principles, including LSI, into specific educational techniques for classroom teachers. Redl (1963) also edited a collection of reports about these applications of LSI for the *American Journal of Orthopsychiatry*, including a paper by Long (1963) reporting on issues in teaching LSI to graduate students. In 1963, Newman and Keith published a monograph entitled *The School-Centered Life Space Interview*. This publication included a series of expanded applications of LSI in school settings (Bernstein, 1963; Redl, 1963). In

1964 Morse, Cutler, and Fink published their national research findings on the first large-scale study of public school classes for the emotionally disturbed, highlighting the great variation of theories, strategies, and techniques developing in the field. From this study, it was clear that more structure and field validation of methods of intervention, including LSI, were needed.

Among the responses to this need for further field validation was a series of publications reporting on new uses for LSI (Faulk & Faulk, 1965; Morse, 1965). In 1965 Long published a monograph, *Direct Help to the Classroom Teacher*, emphasizing the role of the school psychologist as a consultant for crisis intervention and behavior management. That publication was followed by *Conflict in the Classroom* by Long, Morse, and Newman (1965), the first major textbook merging theory and practice from the fields of mental health and education. This textbook helped define the psychoeducational approach to special education and continued in use for two decades as a major resource for training teachers of emotionally and behaviorally disturbed students to use LSI as a psychoeducational strategy.

The significance of the social environment on the behavior of aggressive and disturbed students received increasing attention in the latter part of the 1960s. Redl expanded his previous work to reflect this new emphasis for LSI in a book entitled *When We Deal with Children* (1966). Newman (1967) continued expanding her applications of LSI in public school settings. Trieschman, Whittaker, and Brendtro (1969) published *The Other 23 Hours*, stressing the importance of controlling the milieu when designing and implementing an intervention program. They emphasized the necessity for structuring everything that happens to, with, and for pupils in that environment. LSI was among the procedures they advocated.

The 1970s brought several important refinements to the basics of the psychoeducational approach and to LSI as a major intervention strategy. In 1971 Morse published his concept of the Crisis Teacher and an operational outline for use of LSI by a Crisis Teacher. This work developed from Morse's consultation in the public schools and day treatment centers in the Ann Arbor, Michigan, area. These publications provided additional substance and structure to LSI as a specific intervention strategy and the specific skills needed by an adult to deal effectively with crisis intervention in the public schools.

The 1980s produced a series of studies and publications about LSI focusing on effective ways to use LSI for particular types of problems and adapting it to various age grous and program settings (DeMagistris & Imber, 1980). In 1981 Fagen produced an entire issue of *The Pointer* on LSI. This publication compiled the field-based experiences of many leaders in the field "methods" classes (e.g., Bloom, Dembinski, Fagen, Heuchert, Long, Merritt, Morgan, Morse, Sanders, Tompkins, and Werner). In this publication, Wood and Weller (1981) described how they adapted LSI to the developmental characteristics of students and emphasized the instructional objectives in the social-emotional-behavioral domains that can be achieved through LSI.

During this period, Mary M. Wood established the Rutland Psychoeducational Program in Georgia for seriously emotionally disturbed children and youth. This statewide network of services has reached 10,000 seriously disturbed students annually since 1975 (Swan, Wood, & Jordon, 1990). Wood and colleagues published the first therapeutic curriculum guide, *Developmental Therapy* (Wood, 1975, 1996), an applied synthesis of developmental theories. By expanding the psychoeducational approach within a developmental framework, Wood was able to combine mental health and education practices with existing theories about the development of learned behavior, personality, values, motivation, and anxiety. Wood's Developmental Therapy curriculum expanded the idea that LSCI can be used in a therapeutic intervention program to meet developmental objectives concerned with social communication and socialization in groups, as well as with behavioral, emotional, and cognitive development (Bachrach, Mosley, Swindle, & Wood, 1978; Developmental Therapy Institute, 1992; Williams & Wood, 1977; Wood, 1996).

Wood and associates conducted numerous field research studies and replications of the Developmental Therapy model. Their findings on the progress of students and on teachers' mastery of skills, including LSI, were submitted to the National Institute of Education Joint Dissemination Review Panel in 1975, 1981, and again in 1996, receiving validation three times as a data-based, field-validated program, which subsequently has been disseminated as an exemplary curriculum by the National Diffusion Network for over 25 years (Kaufman, Paget, & Wood, 1981; National Dissemination Study Group, 1985; Wood, Davis, & Swindle, 1996).

The work of Wood and associates through the Developmental Therapy Institute at the University of Georgia continued to include LSCI as a major verbal intervention strategy for teaching social communication and value-based problem solving, adapted to the particular developmental characteristics of students in various age groups—preschool, elementary and middle school, and high school. Their work also focused on teaching LSCI skills to both professionals and paraprofessionals (Wood, 1982, 1986; Wood, Combs, & Walters, 1986; Wood, Swan, & Newman, 1982).

In 1987 Naslund published a longitudinal, data-based study entitled "Life Space Interviewing: A Psychoeducational Interviewing Model for Teaching Pupil Insights and Measuring Program Effectiveness" (Naslund, 1985, 1987). She kept detailed records on 1,404 LSIs—every LSI conducted for an academic year with 28 severely disturbed students at Rose School in Washington, D.C. This school, established by Nicholas Long, was a community-based psychoeducational program combining mental health and special education services for severely emotionally and behaviorally disturbed students between ages 6 and 13. LSI was a major intervention strategy used in the program. Naslund's study examined changes that took place during an academic year while using LSI, looking specifically at (a) frequency with which a student is sent to the "crisis room" for LSI, (b) reasons for being sent, (c) frequency of use of physical restraint prior to LSI, and (d) types of LSI used.

Naslund's results revealed that students who were developmentally older, those who had been in the program longer, and those who had above average IQ showed the greatest decrease in their use of the crisis room for LSI, over time. Her results also showed that peer-related crisis was most frequent (364 incidents); while classroom work was the least used reason for referring a student (41 incidents). Other significant findings included an increase in classroom work, a decrease in loss of self-control, and an increase in self-initiated requests for follow-up LSIs, which suggests that students, by the end of the year, were utilizing LSI (talking about a problem with an adult) as a way to manage their own stresses.

Results of Naslund's study also provided valuable information about the extent to which physical intervention, preliminary to LSI, was needed. Four out of five students in her study could be managed on a verbal level without physical restraint during crisis intervention. She also reports, "One out of every 14 was severely out of control and required restraint for over 15 minutes" (Naslund, 1985, p. 108). The use of physical restraint declined significantly during the year.

Among the five types of LSI used during Naslund's study period, those designed to organize reality and correct distortions in perceptions ("Reality Rub-In") were used most frequently (170 times). However, over time, this type of LSI decreased while LSIs designed to teach new social skills ("New Tools Salesmanship") increased. This is consistent with the expectation that as students drop dysfunctional behavior and see social events and interpersonal interactions more realistically, they need additional LSCIs to learn more effective social skills for handling stress and crisis.

As we enter the new century, attention is drawn again to the concerns of 50 years ago—delinquent youth. The level of violence and alienation now is almost out of control. Students and the adults who work with them in educational settings, the juvenile justice system, alternative school programs, group homes, substance abuse programs, and detention centers are confronted with brutality, crisis, and aggression daily. Major institutions of business, industry, education, government, and religion are seeking ways to restore values in the regulation of behavior.

We have seen this need and believe that LSCI is a powerful tool for teaching responsibility for self-regulated behavior; we have drawn again on the benchmark work of others to enrich LSCI applications by going back to theory. The research and theories of Coles (1986), Kohlberg (1981, 1984), Lickona (1976, 1983), Selman (1980), Selman, Beardless, Schultz, Krupa, and Podorefsky (1986), and Turiel (1983) provide a wealth of new knowledge about values and moral development, the growth of interpersonal understanding, and social perspective-taking by children and youth. This new knowledge provides an added dimension to our understanding of how to make LSCI powerful and effective for students in crisis. The expanded LSCI puts emphasis on behavior regulated by insight and a value system. This is a big step for today's disturbed and alienated youth. But unless we make that step with them, it will not happen!

CHARACTERISTIC DISTURBANCES FOUND IN THE AGGRESSIVE, DELINQUENT BOYS FOR WHOM LSI WAS INITIALLY DEVELOPED

1. Low frustration tolerance

2. Reaction to insecurity, anxiety, or fear with rapid, extreme measures of panic, flight, or ferocious attacks and diffuse destruction

3. Low resistance to temptations to behave unacceptably from situations, gadgets, or the contagious behavior of others

4. Vulnerability to high levels of excitement stimulated by group excitement

5. Responsiveness to inner urges and impulses without restrictions or sublimation

6. Lack of capacity for "responsible care" of possessions, even those most valued

7. Resistance to change

8. Inability to prevent or deal with past emotional memories flooding the entire system and dominating a present life event

9. Fewer guilt feelings when the conscience should be working and inability to take corrective action to assuage their guilt

10. Inability to see their own contribution in a chain of events

11. Inability to switch to inner control when external controls on behavior are withdrawn

12. Exaggerated demanding and rejecting reactions to trusted adults who offer acceptance and relationship

13. Inability to recall and revive memories of previous satisfactions, achievements, or pleasures when a present life event proves unsatisfactory

14. Lack of realism about rules and regulations

15. Difficulty with concepts of time, postponement of an event, or future consequences

16. A paradoxical insensitivity to interpersonal reactions with a heightened sensitivity to peer group attitudes, principles, and expectations

17. Inability to learn from past experience about future situations, whether pleasant or unpleasant

18. Impaired ability to draw realistic inferences from what happens to others

19. Exaggerated reactions to failure, success, and mistakes

20. Impaired ability to react constructively to competitive challenges of sports and games

21. Difficulty adjusting to group roles that demand both sharing and restricting personal urges to control or dominate others

22. Failure to use rational problem solving in times of social crisis (Redl & Wineman, 1957, pp. 75–140)

Checklist for Rating Your LSCI Skills

Name of Staff Person _____

Name of Student _____

Start and End Time of LSCI _____

Date _____

Part One

Check the type of Reclaiming Intervention selected by the Interviewer:

☐ Reality Rub Reclaiming Intervention

☐ Red Flag Reclaiming Intervention

☐ New Tools Reclaiming Intervention

☐ Symptom Estrangement Reclaiming Intervention

☐ Massaging Numb Values Reclaiming Intervention

☐ Manipulation of Body Boundaries Reclaiming Intervention

Check the steps the Interviewer used during the LSCI:

☐ Drain off of emotional intensity

☐ Develop an accurate timeline

☐ Define the central issue and select the correct Reclaiming Intervention

☐ Assist the student in gaining insight into self-defeating behavior patterns

☐ Develop a plan and practice new behaviors

☐ Assist with transition to ongoing activity

Part Two

From the following list, rate the skills the Interviewer used effectively during the LSCI.

1 Almost never

2 Sometimes

3 Often

4 Most always

Nonverbal Body Language

Conveys support and alliance through body posture:	1	2	3	4
Uses eye contact or the opposite as needed to provide "space":	1	2	3	4
Varies voice quality and volume as needed:	1	2	3	4
Maintains physical proximity or distance as needed:	1	2	3	4

Relationship Skills

Engages in active listening:	1	2	3	4
Communicates respect for students:	1	2	3	4
Conveys confidence and optimism:	1	2	3	4
Avoids value judgements:	1	2	3	4
Avoids counteraggression:	1	2	3	4

Verbal Style

Uses concrete words for clarity:	1	2	3	4
Decodes and affirms accurately:	1	2	3	4
Uses imagery to motivate:	1	2	3	4
Maximizes student talk:	1	2	3	4
Uses a timeline to help students organize events:	1	2	3	4
Assists students in seeing cause-and-effect relationships:	1	2	3	4
Uses "I Messages" vs. "You Messages"	1	2	3	4

References

Aichorn, A. (1935). *Wayward youth*. New York: Viking.

Bachrach, A. W., Mosley, A. R., Swindle, F. L., & Wood, M. M. (1978). *Developmental therapy for young children with autistic characteristics*. Austin, TX: PRO-ED.

Beck, M. (1998). Today was his lucky day: A symptom estrangement problem. *Reclaiming Children and Youth, 7*, 113–117.

Bernstein, M. (1963). Lifespace interview in the school setting. In R. Newman & M. Keith (Eds.), *The school-centered life space interview* (pp. 35–44). Washington, DC: School Research Project, Washington School of Psychiatry.

Bloom, R. B. (1981). The reality rub-in interview with emotionally disturbed adolescents. *The Pointer, 25*, 9–25.

Brendtro, L. K., Brokenleg, M., & Van Bockern, S. (1992). *Reclaiming youth at risk: Our hope for the future*. Bloomington, IN: National Education Service.

Children's Defense Fund. (2000). The state of America's children yearbook. Washington, DC: Author. Retrieved September 26, 2000 from the World Wide Web: http://www.childrensdefense.org

Cholden, M. T., & Long N. J. (1998). A red flag reclaiming intervention with a talented but troubled high school student. *Reclaiming Children and Youth, 6*, 239–243.

Coles, R. (1967). *Children of crisis*. Boston: Little, Brown.

Coles, R. (1986). *The moral life of children*. Boston: Atlantic Monthly Press.

Dawson, C. (2000). Freeing an adolescent from negative peer influence: Manipulation of body boundary intervention. *Reclaiming Children and Youth, 8*, 233–238.

DeMagistris, R. J., & Imber, S. C. (1980). The effects of life space interviewing on academic and social performance of behaviorally disordered children. *Behavior Disorders, 6*, 12–25.

Developmental Therapy Institute. (1992). *The developmental teaching objectives for the DTORF–R: Assessment and teaching of social-emotional competence* (4th ed.). Athens, GA: Author.

Dittman, A., & Kitchener, R. (1959). Life space interviewing and individual play therapy: A comparison of techniques. *American Journal of Orthopsychiatry, 29*, 19–26.

Earls, F. (1986). Developmental perspective on psychosocial stress in childhood. In M. W. Yogman & T. B. Brazelton (Eds.), *In support of families* (pp. 29–41). Cambridge, MA: Harvard University Press.

Elder, G. H., Liker, J. K., & Cross, C. E. (1984). Parent–child behavior in the great depression: Lifecourse and intergenerational influences. In P. B. Baltes & O. Brim, Jr. (Eds.), *Life span development and behavior* (Vol. 6, pp. 109–158). New York: Academic Press.

Fagen, S. A. (1981). Conducting an LSI: A process model. *The Pointer, 25*, 9–11.

Faulk, U., & Faulk, G. (1965). Use of social worker and the life space interview with institutionalized children in the public school. *Child Study Center Bulletin, 1*, 27–31.

Fecser, F. A., & Long, N. J. (1997). Life space crises intervention: Using conflict as opportunity. *Beyond Behavior, 8*, 10–15.

Fecser, F. A., & Martin, J. (1995). A reality rub interview: Out for blood. *Journal of Emotional and Behavioral Problems, 4*, 45–51.

Garfinkel, L. (1998). Children with disabilities in the justice system. *Reclaiming Children and Youth, 6*,(2).

Gibbs, J., Potter G., & Goldstein, A. (1995). *The EQUIP program*. Champaign, IL: Research Press.

Gold, M., & Osgood, D. (1992). *Personality and peer influence in juvenile corrections*. Westport, CT: Greenwood Press.

Heuchert, C. M., & Long, N. J. (1981). A brief history of life space interviewing. *The Pointer, 25,* 5–8.

Hewitt, M. B., & Long, N. J. (1999). False alarm: A massaging numb value crisis intervention. *Reclaiming Children and Youth, 8,* 112–117.

Hill, J. W., & Long, N. J. (1999). Home for the holidays: A red flag carry-in reclaiming intervention. *Reclaiming Children and Youth, 8,* 39–44.

Hobbs, N. (1982). *The troubled and troubling child* (2nd Ed.). Cleveland, OH: American Re-Education Association.

Hoover, J. (1996). *The school bully-proofing handbook.* Bloomington, IN: National Education Service.

Kagan, J. (1986). Stress on and in the family. In M. W. Yogman & T. B. Brazelton (Eds.), *In support of families* (pp. 42–54). Cambridge, MA: Harvard University Press.

Kaufman, A. S., Paget, K. D., & Wood, M. M. (1981). Effectiveness of developmental therapy for severely emotionally disturbed children. In F. Wood (Ed.), *Perspectives for a new decade: Education's responsibility for seriously disturbed and behaviorally disordered children and youth* (pp. 176–188). Reston, VA: Council for Exceptional Children.

Koenig, D. A. (1997). I don't understand why the kids don't like me: New tools salesmanship for social survival. *Reclaiming Children and Youth, 6,* 48–52.

Koenig, D. A., & Long, N. J. (1999). I'm stupid. A carry-in, tap-in, reclaiming red flag crisis intervention. *Reclaiming Children and Youth, 7,* 236–242.

Kohlberg, L. (1981). *Essays on moral development: Vol. 1. The philosophy of moral development.* San Francisco: Harper & Row.

Kohlberg, L. (1984). *Essays on moral development: Vol. 2. The psychology of moral development.* San Francisco: Harper & Row.

Lantieri, L., & Patti, P. (1997). *Waging peace in our schools.* Boston: Beacon Press.

Lickona, T. (Ed.). (1976). *Moral development and behavior.* New York: Holt, Rinehart & Winston.

Lickona, T. (1983). *Raising good children.* New York: Bantam.

Long, N. J. (1963). Some problems teaching life space interviewing techniques to graduate students in education in a large class at Indiana University. *American Journal of Orthopsychiatry, 33,* 723–727.

Long, N. J. (1965). *Direct help to the classroom teacher.* Washington, DC: School Research Project, Washington School of Psychiatry.

Long, N. J. (1992). Looking beyond behavior and seeing my needs. *Journal of Emotional and Behavioral Problems, 1,* 35–38.

Long, N. J. (1993). I wish there was a law: Reality rub LSI. *Journal of Emotional and Behavioral Problems, 2,* 53–58.

Long, N. J., & Brendtro, L. K. (1996). A double struggle incident. *Reclaiming Children and Youth, 5,* 56–60.

Long, N. J., & Dorf, R. (1994). The tip of the iceberg: A red flag carry-in incident. *Journal of Emotional Behavior Problems, 2,* 30–34.

Long, N. J., & Fecser, F. A. (1996). *The life space crisis intervention video series* [Video]. Bethesda: NAK Production Associates.

Long, N. J., & Fecser, F. A. (2001). Building safe and reclaiming schools: A certification program of the LSCI institute. *Reclaiming Children and Youth, 9,* 229–233.

Long, N. J., & Gonsowski, R. (1994). A manipulation of body boundaries: The set up. *Journal of Emotional and Behavioral Problems, 3,* 30–35.

Long, N. J., & Kelly, E. F. (1994). The double struggle: The butler did it. *Journal of Emotional and Behavioral Problems, 3,* 49–56.

Long, N. J., Morse, W. C., & Newman, R. G. (Eds.). (1965). *Conflict in the classroom.* Belmont, CA: Wadsworth.

Long, N. J., & Newman, R. G. (1961). The teacher's handling of children in conflict. *Bulletin of the School of Education, Indiana University, 37*(4).

Long, N. J., & Pincione, D. (1992). The snowball blizzard incident: A reality rub life space interview. *Journal of Emotional and Behavioral Problems, 1,* 28–32.

Long, N. J., Stoeffler, V., Krause, K., & Jung, C. (1961). Life space management of behavioral crisis. *Social Work, 6,* 38–45.

Long, N. J., & Wilder, M. T. (1993). Massaging numb values LSI. *Journal of Emotional and Behavior Problems, 2,* 35–41.

McCarty, B. C. (1998). But I have to have a boyfriend. *Reclaiming Children and Youth, 7,* 49–55.

Merritt, C. A. (1981). Bandaids for the bumps. *The Pointer, 25,* 16–19.

Morgan, R. (1981). Group life space interviewing. *The Pointer, 25,* 37–41.

Morse, W. C. (1965). The mental hygiene viewpoint on school discipline. *The High School Journal, 48,* 396–401.

Morse, W. C. (1971). The crisis or helping teacher. In N. J. Long, W. C. Morse, & R. G. Newman (Eds.), *Conflict in the classroom* (pp. 485–490). Belmont, CA: Wadsworth.

Morse, W. C. (1981). LSI tomorrow. *The Pointer, 25,* 67–70.

Morse, W. C., Cutler, R. L., & Fink, A. H. (1964). *Public school classes for the emotionally handicapped.* Washington, DC: Council for Exceptional Children.

Morse, W. C., & Small, E. (1959). Group life space interviewing in a therapeutic camp. *American Journal of Orthopsychiatry, 29,* 27–44.

Morse, W. C., & Wineman, D. (1957). Group interviewing in a camp for disturbed boys. *Journal of Social Issues, 13,* 23–31.

Naslund, S. R. (1985). Lifespace interviewing: A descriptive analysis of crisis intervention with emotionally disturbed children in a special education school (Doctoral dissertation, American University, 1985). *Dissertation Abstracts International, 45/08A,* 2487. (DER 84-25243).

Naslund, S. R. (1987). Life space interviewing: A psychoeducational interviewing model for teaching pupil insights and measuring program effectiveness. *The Pointer, 31,* 12–15.

National Dissemination Study Group. (1985). *Educational programs that work* (11th ed.). Longment, CO: Sopris West.

Newman, R., & Keith, M. (Eds.). (1963). *The school-centered life space interview.* Washington, DC: School Research Program, Washington School of Psychiatry.

Newman, R. G. (1967). *Psychological consultation in the schools.* New York: Basic Books.

Nichols, P. (1999). *Clear thinking: Talking back to whispering shadows: A psycho-educational program for preteens, teens, and young adults* (Rev. ed.). Iowa City, IA: River Lights.

Petit, L. & Brooks, T. (1998). Abuse and delinquency: Two sides of the same coin. *Reclaiming Children and Youth, 6*(2).

Redl, F. (1959a). The concept of a therapeutic milieu. *American Journal of Orthopsychiatry, 29b,* 721–736.

Redl, F. (1959b). Strategy and techniques of the life space interview. *American Journal of Orthopsychiatry, 29a,* 1–18.

Redl, F. (1963). The life space interview in the school setting. *American Journal of Orthopsychiatry, 33,* 717–719.

Redl, F. (1966). *When we deal with children.* New York: The Free Press.

Redl, F., & Wineman, D. (1951). *Children who hate.* Glencoe, IL: The Free Press.

Redl, F., & Wineman, D. (1952). *Controls from within.* Glencoe, IL: The Free Press.

Redl, F., & Wineman, D. (1957). *The aggressive child.* Glencoe, IL: The Free Press.

Rogers, C. R. (1965). The interpersonal relationship: The core of guidance. In Mosier (Ed.), *Guidance: An examination.* New York: Harcourt Brace & World.

Ryan, E. (1997). The last call for help: A reality rub LSCI. *Reclaiming Children and Youth, 6,* 160–162.

Sanders, L. S. (1981). New tool salesmanship interview. *The Pointer, 25*, 32–33.

Selman, R. L. (1980). *The growth of interpersonal understanding.* New York: Academic Press.

Selman, R. L., Beardless, W., Schultz, L. H., Krupa, M., & Podorefsky, D. (1986). Assessing adolescent interpersonal negotiation strategies: Toward the integration of structural and functional models. *Developmental Psychology, 22*, 450–459.

Swan, W. W., Wood, M. M., & Jordon, J. (1990). Building a statewide program of mental health and special education services for children and youth. In G. K. Farley & S. G. Zimet (Eds.), *Day treatment for emotionally disturbed children* (Vol. 2, chap. 11). New York: Plenum.

Thomas, A., & Chess, S. (1984). Genesis and evaluation of behavior disorders: From infancy to early adult life. *American Journal of Psychiatry, 141*, 1–9.

Tompkins, J. R. (1981). Symptom estrangement interview. *The Pointer, 25*, 26–28.

Trieschman, A. E., Whittaker, J. K., & Brendtro, L. K. (1969). *The other 23 hours.* Chicago: Aldine.

Turiel, E. (1983). *The development of social knowledge.* Cambridge, England: Cambridge University Press.

Vernick, J. (1963). The use of the life space interview on a medical ward. *Social Casework, 44*, 465–469.

Vorrath, H., & Brendtro, L. (1985). *Positive peer culture* (2nd ed.). New York: Aldine de Gruyter.

Walker, B., Long, N. J., & Brendtro, L. K. (2000). I don't have to take that!: A taxonomy of the abuse of reality. *Reclaiming Children and Youth, 9*, 45–51.

Warnock, G. J. (1971). *The object of morality.* London: Methuen.

Werner, A. (1981). Massaging numb values interview. *The Pointer, 25*, 29–31.

Williams, G. H., & Wood, M. M. (1977). *Developmental art therapy.* Austin, TX: PRO-ED.

Wood, M. M. (1975). *Developmental therapy.* Baltimore: University Park Press.

Wood, M. M. (1982). Developmental therapy: A model for therapeutic intervention in the schools. In T. B. Gutkin & C. R. Reynolds (Eds.), *A handbook for school psychology* (pp. 609–629). New York: Wiley.

Wood, M. M. (1986). *Developmental therapy in the classroom.* Austin, TX: PRO-ED.

Wood, M. M. (1996). *Developmental therapy—developmental teaching: Fostering social–emotional competence in troubled children and youth* (3rd ed.). Austin, TX: PRO-ED.

Wood, M. M., Combs, M. C., & Walters, L. H. (1986). Use of staff development by teachers and aides with emotionally disturbed and behavior disordered students. *Teacher Education and Special Education, 9*, 104–112.

Wood, M. M., Davis, K. R., & Swindle, K. (1996). Talking into the air: LSI. *Journal of Emotional and Behavioral Problems, 2*, 45-52.

Wood, M. M., Swan, W. W., & Newman, V. (1982). Developmental therapy for the severely emotionally disturbed and autistic. In R. L. McDowell, G. W. Adamson, & F. H. Wood (Eds.), *Teaching emotionally disturbed children* (pp. 264–299). New York: Little, Brown.

Wood, M. M., & Weller, D. (1981). How come it's different with some children? A developmental approach to life space interviewing. *The Pointer, 25*, 61–66.

Wylie, M. S. (1998, May/June). Public enemies. *Family Therapy Networker Magazine*, 24–28.

Further Reading

Apter, S. J., & Conoley, J. C. (1984). *Child behavior disorders and emotional disturbance*. Englewood Cliffs, NJ: Prentice Hall.

Bettelheim, B. (1977). *The uses of enchantment*. New York: Vintage.

Bommarito, J. W. (1977). *Prevention and clinical management of troubled children*. Washington, DC: University Press of America.

Brendtro, L. K., & Long, N. J. (1996). A crisis of conscience. *Reclaiming Children and Youth, 5,* 129–135.

Brendtro, L., & Van Bockern, S. (1998). *The Developmental Audit of Delinquency*. Sioux Falls, SD: W. K. Kellogg Foundation, Augustana College.

Broderick, D., & Long, N. J. (1996). An intervention in classroom gender abuse. *Reclaiming Children and Youth, 5*(2), 110–114.

Brown, G., McDowell, R. L., & Smith, J. (1981). *Educating adolescents with behavior disorders*. Columbus, OH: Merrill.

Cantrell, M. L., Cantrell, R. P., Valore, T. G., Jones, J. A., & Fecser, F. A. (1999). A revisitation of the ecological perspectives on emotional/behavioral disorders. In L. M. Bullock & R. A. Gable (Eds.), *Third CCBD Mini-Library Series*. Reston, VA: Council for Exceptional Children.

Dembinski, R. J. (1981). The opening gambit: How students avoid the LSI. *The Pointer, 25,* 12–15.

Fecser, F. A., Seiman, S. A. & Long, N. (1992). The double sucker punch. *Journal of Emotional and Behavioral Problems, 1,* 38–41.

Heuchert, C. M. (1983). Can teachers change behavior? Try interviews. *Academic Therapy, 18,* 321–328.

Hewitt, M. B. (1995). Countering the creative misbehavior of staff splitting. *Journal of Emotional and Behavioral Problems, 4,* 48–53.

Kaufmann, J., & Lewis, C. (1974). *Teaching children with behavior disorders*. Columbus, OH: Merrill.

Kerr, M. M., & Nelson, C. M. (1989). *Strategies for managing behavior problems in the classroom* (2nd ed.). Columbus, OH: Merrill.

Knoblock, P. (1983). *Teaching emotionally disturbed children*. Boston: Houghton Mifflin.

Long, N. J. (1995a). He was making fun of me: A red flag carry-over crisis. *Journal of Emotional and Behavioral Problems, 3,* 46–51.

Long, N. J. (1995b). Prosocial signs and sayings. *Journal of Emotional and Behavioral Problems, 4,* 42–48.

Long, N. J. (1996). Reflecting on parental aggression in our lives. *Reclaiming Children and Youth, 4,* 18–22.

Long, N. J. (1997). The therapeutic power of kindness. *Reclaiming Children and Youth, 5,* 242–247.

Long, N. J., & Brendtro, L. K. (2000). New ways of seeing for a new millennium. *Reclaiming Children and Youth, 8,* 194–197.

Long, N. J., & Daniels, D. (1993). Christmas at the mall. *Journal of Emotional and Behavioral Problems, 1,* 41–44.

McDowell, R. L., Adamson, G. W., & Wood, F. H. (Eds.). (1981). *Emotional disturbance*. New York: Little, Brown.

Morse, W. C. (1985). *The education and treatment of socioemotionally impaired children and youth*. Syracuse, NY: Syracuse University Press.

Newcomer, P. L. (1980). *Understanding and teaching emotionally disturbed children*. Boston: Allyn & Bacon.

Parese, S. B. (1999). Understanding the impact of personal crisis on school performance in troubled youth. *Reclaiming Children and Youth, 8,* 181–187.

Paul, J. L., & Epanchin, B. C. (1982). *Emotional disturbance in children.* Columbus, OH: Merrill.

Reinert, H. R. (1980). *Children in conflict* (2nd ed.). St. Louis: Mosby.

Rich, H. L. (1982). *Disturbed students: Characteristics and educational strategies.* Austin, TX: PRO- ED.

Rogers, C. R. (1967). The therapeutic relationship: Recent theory and research. In C. H. Patterson (Ed.), *The counselor in the school: Selected readings* (pp. 228–240). New York: McGraw-Hill.

Shea, T., & Bauer, A. M. (1987). *Teaching children and youth with behavior disorders* (2nd ed.). Englewood Cliffs, NJ: Prentice Hall.

Swanson, H. L., & Reinert, H. R. (1979). *Teaching strategies for children in conflict.* St. Louis: Mosby.

Wood, M. M. (Ed.). (1979). *The developmental therapy objectives* (3rd ed.). Austin, TX: PRO-ED.

Wood, M. M. (Ed.). (1981a). *Developmental therapy sourcebooks: Vol. 1. Music, movement, and physical skills.* Austin, TX: PRO-ED.

Wood, M. M. (Ed.). (1981b). *Developmental therapy sourcebooks: Vol. 2: Fantasy and make-believe.* Austin, TX: PRO-ED.

Wood, M. M. (1986). Developmental therapy. In C. R. Reynolds & L. Mann (Eds.), *Encyclopedia of special education* (Vol. 3, pp. 499–500). New York: Wiley.

Wood, M. M., Brendtro, L. K., Fecser, F. A., & Nichols, P. (1999). Psychoeducation: An idea whose time has come. In L. M. Bullock & R. A. Gable (Eds.), *Third CCBD Mini-Library Series.* Reston, VA: Council for Exceptional Children.

Author Index

Subject Index